AFRICAN ISSUES

Sudan
Looks East

T0313526

AFRICAN ISSUES

Sudan Looks East

Edited by
DANIEL LARGE
& LUKE A. PATEY

China, India
& the Politics
of Asian Alternatives

JC JAMES CURREY

James Currey
in an imprint of
Boydell & Brewer Ltd
PO Box 9, Woodbridge
Suffolk IP12 3DF
and of
Boydell & Brewer Inc.
668 Mt Hope Avenue
Rochester, NY 14620, USA
www.boydellandbrewer.com
www.jamescurrey.com

1 2 3 4 5 15 14 13 12 11

British Library Cataloguing in Publication Data
Sudan looks east : China, India and the politics of Asian
alternatives. — (African issues)
1. Sudan—Foreign relations—Asia. 2. Asia—Foreign
relations—Sudan. 3. Sudan—Foreign relations—20th
century. 4. Sudan—Foreign relations—21st century.
5. Investments, Asian—Sudan.
I. Series II. Large, Daniel. III. Patey, Luke A.
327.6'24'05-dc23

ISBN 978-1-84701-037-7 (James Currey paper)

Papers used by Boydell & Brewer are natural, recyclable products
made from wood grown in sustainable forests.

Typeset by Long House, Cumbria, UK
Printed in Great Britain
by CPI Group (UK) Ltd, Croydon, CR0 4YY

CONTENTS

LIST OF FIGURES

NOTES ON CONTRIBUTORS

Alexandra Cosima Budabin received her PhD in Political Science at the New School for Social Research, New York. She is a Visiting Assistant Professor of Human Rights in the Department of Political Science, University of Dayton.

Laura James is a Middle East analyst specialising in the interface between political and economic issues. She has worked as an advisor on Sudan's economy for the Assessment and Evaluation Commission monitoring Sudan's Comprehensive Peace Agreement, the UK's Department for International Development and the Economist Intelligence Unit. She completed her doctorate at the University of Oxford, where she was also a College Lecturer, and is the author of *Nasser at War: Arab Images of the Enemy* (Basingstoke: Palgrave 2006).

Daniel Large is research director of the Africa Asia Centre, Royal African Society at the School of Oriental and African Studies, London, and research associate with the South African Institute of International Affairs. He also directs the Rift Valley Institute's Sudan Open Archive (www.sudanarchive.net). His publications include *China Returns to Africa: A Rising Power and a Continent Embrace* (London: Hurst, 2008), co-edited with Chris Alden and Ricardo Soares de Oliveira.

Roland Marchal is Senior Research Fellow at the Centre National de Recherche Scientifique (CNRS), based at the Centre d'Etudes et de Recherches Internationales, (CERI), Paris. His publications include *Afrique Asie, une autre mondialisation* (Paris: Presses de Sciences-Po, 2007).

Leben Nelson Moro is Acting Director, Directorate of Scientific and Cultural External Relations, and Assistant Professor at the Center for Peace and Development, at the University of Juba. He received his D.Phil. in Development Studies from the University of Oxford in 2008. His principal areas of research are development-induced displacement and resettlement, focusing on oil-induced displacement in Sudan, and forced migration.

Luke A. Patey is a research fellow at the Danish Institute for International Studies. His research focuses on the influence of oil on civil war and the peace process in Sudan and the rise of Asian national oil companies from China, India, and Malaysia. His work has been published in *African Affairs*, *The Journal of Modern African Studies*, and *Third World Quarterly*.

Harry Verhoeven is a doctoral researcher at the Department of Politics and International Relations, University of Oxford (St Cross College). His research focuses on the political economy of the Al-Ingaz Regime: he specialises in conflict, development and the politics of water and agriculture in Sudan. He is the convenor of the Oxford University China-Africa Network and the Oxford Central Africa Forum.

Peter Woodward is Professor Emeritus at the School of Politics and International Relations, University of Reading. He was a Lecturer in Political Science at the University of Khartoum until 1971, when he joined the University of Reading. His books include *Condominium and Sudanese Nationalism* (London: Rex Collings, 1979), *Sudan 1898–1989: The Unstable State* (Boulder: Lynne Rienner, 1989), and *US Foreign Policy and the Horn of Africa* (Aldershot: Ashgate, 2006).

ACKNOWLEDGEMENTS

We owe our greatest thanks to the contributing authors whose hard work and insights made this volume a reality. Their patience to adapt to fast moving events in Sudan leading up to the historical separation of South Sudan allowed us to also reflect on what the future might hold for Asia's role in the two Sudans.

The volume grew with momentum during a set of international conferences arranged by the Danish Institute of International Studies in collaboration with Sudanese, Chinese and Indian researchers. We thank Safwat Fanous and Atta al-Battahani at the University of Khartoum, Gulshan Dietl and Ajay Dubey at Jawaharlal Nehru University and Ruchita Beri at the Institute for Defence Studies and Analysis in New Delhi, as well as Suolao Wang at Peking University. They each provided tremendous support and inspiration to our work. Additional thanks are due to Douglas Johnson and Lynn Taylor at James Currey, Gill Lusk, John Ryle, Christopher Kidner, Laura Barber, Chris Alden, Richard Dowden, Edward Thomas, Mathew Arnold, Thorsten Benner and especially Ricardo Soares de Oliveira. Responsibility for any errors remains ours.

ACRONYMS

ABIM	Islamic Youth of Malaysia (*Angkatan Belia Islam Malaysia*)
AU	African Union
AMIS	African Union Mission in Sudan
BJP	Bharatiya Janata Party
Bpd	barrels per day
CAR	Central African Republic
CBoS	Central Bank of Sudan
CPA	Comprehensive Peace Agreement
CPC	Communist Party of China
CNPC	China National Petroleum Corporation
COMESA	Common Market for Eastern and Southern Africa
DDF	Darfur Development Front
DLF	Darfur Liberation Front
DOP	Declaration of Principles
DPA	Darfur Peace Agreement
DRC	Democratic Republic of Congo
DUP	Democratic Unionist Party
ECOS	European Coalition on Oil in Sudan
ESPA	Eastern Sudan Peace Agreement
FDI	Foreign direct investment
GDP	Gross Domestic Product
GNPOC	Greater Nile Petroleum Operating Company
GoNU	Government of National Unity
GOS	Government of Sudan
GoSS	Government of Southern Sudan
HCENR	Higher Council for the Environment and Natural Resoures
ICC	International Criminal Court
ICF	Islamic Charter Front
ICID	International Commission of Inquiry on Darfur
IGAD	Inter-Governmental Authority on Development (formerly IGADD, Inter-Governmental Authority on Drought and Desertification)

IMF	International Monetary Fund
IOC	International Olympic Committee
JEM	Justice and Equality Movement
LoC	Line of Credit
MEM	Ministry of Energy and Mining
NCP	National Congress party
NDA	National Democratic Alliance
NIF	National Islamic Front
NPC	National Petroleum Commission
OECD	Organisation for Economic Co-operation and Development
OIC	Organisation of the Islamic Conference
OLS	Operation Lifeline Sudan
ONGC	Oil and Natural Gas Corporation
OVL	Oil and Natural Gas Corporation Videsh Limited
PAS	Pan-Malaysian Islamic Party
PCP	Popular Congress Party
PDF	Popular Defence Forces
PDOC	Petrodar Operating Company
PIAC	Popular Islamic and Arabic Conference
RMB	Renminbi
Rs	Rupees
SAF	Sudan Armed Forces
SDC	Save Darfur Coalition
SCP	Sudan Communist Party
SDTF	Sudan Divestment Task Force
SLA	Sudan Liberation Army
SPLM/A	Sudan People's Liberation Movement/Army
SSDF	South Sudan Defence Forces
SSLA	South Sudan Legislative Assembly
SSU	Sudan Socialist Union
UN	United Nations
UNAMID	African Union/United Nations Hybrid Mission in Darfur
UNMIS	UN Mission in Sudan
UMNO	United Malays' National Organisation
UP	Umma Party
US	United States (of America)
WFP	World Food Programme
WNPOC	White Nile Petroleum Operating Company

Sudan
Looks East

Introduction

DANIEL LARGE
& LUKE A. PATEY

Anyone visiting the 2010 Shanghai World Expo witnessed a rather different image of Sudan from that commonly portrayed in international headlines. This was a vision of Sudan enjoying peace, prosperity and flourishing development. Proudly on display were the provisions of the 2005 Comprehensive Peace Agreement (CPA) between the government of Sudan in Khartoum and the Sudan People's Liberation Movement/Army (SPLM/A). The 22-year-long civil war between the two sides left over two million Sudanese dead and uprooted millions more. Despite the achievements of this historic agreement, the message in Shanghai seemed far away from the situation in Sudan at the time. Not only was the country still mired in conflict in its western region of Darfur, but southern Sudanese were looking ahead to voting in a referendum on seceding from a united Sudan.[1] Such inconsistencies were not uncommon regarding Sudan. Although it may not have been apparent to the mainly Chinese visitors to the Shanghai version of Sudan, there are also strikingly different views on China's role there, depending on whether one is standing in the United States, China or Sudan.

In the United States, China's relations with Sudan only began to receive mainstream attention in the past decade, becoming a media story after war in Darfur became a global issue in 2004. Darfur gave meaning to China's role in Sudan. American activists tightly linked China to the civil war and accusations spread that Beijing was bankrolling a genocide undertaken by Sudan's government through billions of dollars in oil investments. China's relations with Sudan fitted nicely into the formula of Beijing's close ties with other troublesome African governments and rogue states at large; Beijing went where there was oil, no matter what the consequences. China has been seen to be neglecting grievous human rights abuses in Sudan and blocking further international sanctions. Overall, Beijing was the most coveted international ally of a criminal government in Khartoum. But travel to China, and the story on Sudan sounds quite different.

[1] For describing Sudan, geographical areas (like northern, western or eastern Sudan) are distinguished from political units, like Southern Sudan, which was a formal entity between 1972 and 1983, and 2005 and 2011.

1

When following Sino-Sudan relations in China what is often first heard is how current ties have a deep history. The past is steeped in shared colonial experience and the post-colonial affinity of South-South relations. Today, China is seen as responsible for tremendous economic achievements in Sudan, pulling the country away from misery by investing in its oil industry. Whereas Western media typically portray Sudan as a failed state on the verge of complete collapse under civil war and poverty, China more often regards Sudan as a land of opportunity. Sudan is a beacon of China's successful engagement in Africa, bursting with examples of people-to-people friendship and mutually beneficial commerce. A similar tune can be heard in New Delhi or Kuala Lumpur: Sudan has provided an outstanding chance for India and Malaysia to engage in practical South-South cooperation while bolstering their presence in the international oil industry.

The final viewpoints come from Sudan. In Khartoum, China is seen as having come to Sudan's aid when everyone else had abandoned it, pleasing in particular the National Islamic Front (NIF) Al-Ingaz, or Salvation, regime which seized power in June 1989 and later became the National Congress party (NCP). For this reason, China's role had an altogether different meaning in southern Sudan. Like Darfur rebel groups later on, China was a sworn enemy of the SPLM/A during the North-South civil war. But after the CPA, former enemies slowly became new friends. The former rebels-turned-government in southern Sudan began to warm up to the idea of what an economic and political partnership with China and Asia could provide. In the struggle over defining China and Asia's role in Sudan, local perspectives across the country are often lost in the flurry of international debate. Beyond elite politics, common Sudanese attitudes towards China are much more diverse. Altogether, the wide spectrum of perspectives on Sudan's relations with China and Asia battle for space, with some old understandings dying hard and others rapidly being overturned as new relationships are fostered.

This book explores Sudan's dynamic relations with China, India and its other Asian partners, notably Malaysia, over the past two decades.[2] Sudan's relations with China have been internationalised in more visible ways since 2004 when, more than anything, Darfur brought China's engagement in Sudan to a wider, more global audience, influencing coverage and perceptions of China's expanding role in Africa in the process. But for all China's salience in Sudan's recent external relations, the actual nature and significance of the Chinese role in Sudan, which long-predated the Darfur controversy, have been paradoxically neglected. Attention to China, furthermore, has overshadowed the role of India, Malaysia and other Asian engagements in Sudan. This points to the need for a deeper, more empirical grounding of these respective engagements,

[2] The term 'Asia' is problematic in so far as it bundles together a diverse range of actors from East Asia, South Asia, and Southeast Asia. Nonetheless, some utility can be ascribed to the expression as shorthand.

examining what they are, rather than what they are supposed to be or do, and locating these appropriately within the Sudanese context.

To begin with, current ties between Sudan and its Asian partners should be contextualised in terms of their relations with the central state in Khartoum and a prior-existing political economy of unbalanced development. What might be thought of as a new chapter in Sudanese politics defined by the Chinese role in reality follows on from a longer history of political and economic dominance by ruling elites in Sudan's central riverain Nile Valley. Anglo-Egyptian colonial rule (1899-1956) bequeathed a political legacy in the form of an authoritarian central state, whose political authority has been contested by its outlying, peripheral regions.[3] The entrenched political and economic marginalisation of southern Sudan, as with Darfur and eastern Sudan, has been a rallying call for a series of armed rebellions. A further colonial legacy was Sudan's economic geography and the central state's orientation toward income-generating economic schemes benefiting the ruling centre.[4] Southern Sudan was particularly neglected and, as a result, unprepared at the time of Sudan's independence in 1956.[5]

At first predominantly extractive, and later more commercial, the Asian engagements were in effect inserted into, compounded and would be affected by Sudan's historically-produced political economy. The impact of Asian investment, most evident in the oil sector, has largely conformed to the historical pattern of Sudanese politics, more than substantially altering it, with external investment being especially subject to conditioning by Sudan's politics of the central state and relations with its peripheries. Yet Sudan's present relations with Asian states demonstrate that other important historical shifts have been under way over the past two decades. Oil has replaced cotton as Sudan's dominant single export commodity[6] and, accompanying this shift, China has become northern Sudan's most important external partner. The composition of Sudan's external trade partners has also changed.[7] The advent of Sudan's oil

---

[3] See Alex de Waal, 'Sudan: The Turbulent State', in Alex de Waal ed., *War in Darfur and the Search for Peace* (London: Justice Africa, 2007), pp. 1-38; Justin Willis, 'The Ambitions of the State', in John Ryle, et al eds., *The Sudan Handbook* (Oxford: James Currey, 2011), pp. 54-62.

[4] G.N. Sanderson, 'The Ghost of Adam Smith: Ideology, Bureaucracy, and the Frustration of Economic Development in the Sudan, 1934-1940', in M. W. Daly ed., *Modernization in the Sudan: Essays in Honor of Richard Hill* (New York: Lillian Barber Press, 1985).

[5] Douglas H. Johnson, *The Root Causes of Sudan's Civil Wars* (Oxford: James Currey, 2003).

[6] Anglo-Egyptian Sudan had concentrated export markets, due largely to the dominance of cotton.

[7] Britain was Sudan's most important export destination and source of imports before the Second World War, and remained 'Sudan's number one customer and supplier' at independence. *[Sudan] Economic Survey, 1957* (Khartoum: Economic Section, Ministry of Finance and Economics), pp. 14-15. Between 1933 and 1939, on average Britain bought around 51% of Sudan's exports (Egypt taking 12%, India 10.4%, France 5.3%, and the USA 4.2%). Britain and India bought 82% of the Sudan's cotton in 1939. Britain was also Sudan's leading supplier of imports, accounting for an average of 27.5% of mostly manufactured imports between 1933 and 1939 (Egypt supplying 19.4%, Japan 17.9%, and India 5.8%). M. W. Daly, *Imperial Sudan: The Anglo-Egyptian Condominium, 1934-1956* (Cambridge: Cambridge University Press, 1991), pp. 103-104.

economy, concurrent with international sanctions, has driven a structural reorientation of northern Sudan's external trade towards new Asian markets, alongside the continuation of economic links with the Middle East. Sudan's imports are now conditioned by sanctions, and trade with China and other industrial exporters like Japan or South Korea. Such macro shifts are set against historic new political developments within Sudan brought about by the January 2011 vote for southern secession.

This introduction provides a thematic guide to the context and nature of Sudan's 'Look East' relations. Like the book as a whole, it devotes particular attention to Sudan's relations with China and India. It begins by considering the consequences that historical interactions have held for relations since 1989. Second, it argues that the importance of the NIF/NCP period in power after 1989 is fundamental. Its mode of rule, civil war and confrontation with regional and international powers coupled with its 'Look East' policy squarely directed Sudan's economic and political engagement towards Beijing, Kuala Lumpur and New Delhi. Third, the economic ties that came out of the NIF's engagement with China and other Asian countries were fostered in large part thanks to Sudan's budding oil sector, but would progress beyond oil. Fourth, Sudan's political relations with China, India and other Asian partners are outlined. Here, it is again best to look beyond the robust formal state-to-state bilateral links to garner a more comprehensive understanding of how Sudan's Asian partners have engaged with and adapted to its political changes. The creation of the Government of Southern Sudan (GoSS) following the CPA opened the door for political and economic engagement directly with the South. Finally, regional and international dimensions of relations are reflected upon. If China has become an important factor in Khartoum's international relations, then Sudan became an unexpectedly prominent factor in China's African and international politics.

The Endorsement of History: Old Friends, New Actors

History is important, beyond merely providing incidental background to current links: as interpreted and mobilised in political practice, the past plays out in the present.[8] Because history is appropriated for political ends, and understood and experienced in different ways between and within myriad contexts, there are multiple possible ways to approach this subject. Mainstream Western media coverage tends to focus on recent and current relations. Official northern Sudanese and Chinese media and government statements, by contrast, accentuate historical ties to justify and legitimate contemporary relations. Elsewhere, the Indian government,

[8] See Julia C. Strauss, 'The Past in the Present: Historical and Rhetorical Lineages in China's Relations with Africa', *China Quarterly*, Vol. 199 (2009), pp. 777-795; Chris Alden and Ana Cristina Alves, 'History and Identity in the Construction of China's Africa Policy', *Review of African Political Economy*, Vol. 35, No. 115 (2008), pp. 43-58.

while generally less vocal in public on Sudan, also employs history to promote and defend its relations with Khartoum. Malaysian political rhetoric on Sudan tends to invoke Islamic connections. As a common platform, however, a stylised form of South-South cooperation founded on a common colonial history has been an important alternative point of reference for Khartoum.

Sudan's historical relations with China have been defined by the shared experience of hardship and resistance against outside interference in internal affairs, beginning with nineteenth-century British imperialism. More recently, this has manifested itself in Chinese economic engagement countering the influence of US sanctions against Sudan. China and Sudan formally celebrated their official Golden Jubilee fiftieth anniversary of diplomatic relations with a series of events from February 2009. Marking the official commencement of post-colonial relations, this, and Sudan's support for China's bid to assume its position at the UN, the establishment of relations in 1959 followed a longer history of indirect ancient trade ties and colonial links (featuring a minor but symbolic Sudanese history in China). The most prominent historical connection linking Sudan with China is that of the British imperial figure, Charles Gordon.

The legend of 'Chinese Gordon', as he became known, began in China and was confirmed by his death in Sudan.[9] Successive generations of post-independence Sudanese and Chinese statesmen have used Gordon as a shared symbol of both violent imperialism and heroic resistance. When Premier Zhou Enlai visited Khartoum in 1964, the fact that the Sudanese people had 'finally punished' Gordon was a rare case of a genuine common colonial experience between China and Africa.[10] Chinese accounts tend to view Gordon in the same unambiguous terms.[11] Gordon has been a feature not just in official relations but also for visiting Chinese friendship delegations and tourism.[12] The shared experience of European colonialism was later fed by other forms of outside influence on Sudan's affairs.

From 1969 to 1985, Khartoum's relations with Beijing under the military rule of President Jaafar Nimairi improved to the point of being

---

[9] Appointed General by the Qing dynasty, Gordon commanded the Ever-Victorious Army militia against the Taiping rebels from March 1863. After serving as Governor General of Egyptian-governed Sudan, Gordon was killed in Khartoum after victorious Mahdist rebel forces captured the city in 1885.

[10] W. A. C. Adie, 'Chou En-lai on Safari', *The China Quarterly*, No. 18 (1964), p. 192.

[11] See, for example, Zhang Guobin, 'Where the Two Niles Meet', *ChinaAfrica* 20, No. 2 (February 1996), p. 51.

[12] In June 2002, for instance, the leader of a Chinese military delegation to Sudan was quoted as saying: 'Like the Chinese people, the heroic Sudanese people were also once repressed by the British Colonist Gordon, thus the people of both China and Sudan are comrades in arms from the same battle.' 'Sudanese Defense Minister, Chief of General Staff Meet with Visiting Chinese Military Delegation', *Xinhua*, 4 June 2002. During a Sudanese Council of Friendship visit to China in June 2000, it was duly noted that 'the brave Sudanese people' had killed Gordon, 'a British butcher stained with the blood of officers and men of the Taiping Uprising, and avenged the Chinese people'. Gao Xuesong, 'Delegation of the Sudanese Council of Friendship with the Peoples Visits China', *Voice of Friendship*, Vol. 21, No. 5 (2000), p. 8.

described as 'excellent'.[13] Following Sudan's brief foreign policy shift towards the Soviet Union, relations with China took off following Beijing's support for Nimairi in 1971 over the attempted Communist coup against him. Beijing's decisive loyalty and support for Nimairi's defeat of the plotters and violent crackdown on the Sudan Communist Party out-manoeuvred Moscow. Nonetheless, China was not an especially impor-tant foreign partner of or domestic actor within Sudan, though a number of Chinese aid projects were mounted, symbolised by Friendship Hall in Khartoum.[14] The 1980s were a relatively quiet period of relations but nonetheless influential for what came later. Sudan's civil war spread after 1983. China's relations with Africa, under Deng Xiaoping, underwent transition as modernisation at home was prioritised. But China still undertook a number of projects and trade continued on a limited basis. The Communist Party of China (CPC) and Nimairi's Sudan Socialist Union party signed a friendship and cooperation protocol early in 1983. Attempts were made to expand economic links, including after Nimairi's fall from power in 1985, and to establish other political connections between Khartoum and Beijing. Following the 1989 NIF military coup, however, with Sudan becoming increasingly isolated and Chinese national oil companies looking for international opportunities, the histor-ical bond between the two countries found new meaning. In a similar manner, a shared colonial experience has also marked current relations between Sudan and India.

Along with China, Sudan's relations with India have re-emerged rather than begun. During the Sudan-India commemoration of 50 years of diplo-matic relations in 2006, Sudanese President Omar al-Bashir praised cen-turies-old ties between the two countries.[15] The civilizations of the Nile Valley and the Indus Valley had been in contact for thousands of years. Indian traders from Gujarat had come to Sudan in the late 1800s and still operate in the markets of Omdurman today.[16] India's political leaders during the colonial period often stopped by Sudan on the way to visit Britain in the drive for independence. Mahatma Gandhi, for example, visited the Indian community in Port Sudan on his way to London in 1935. Jawaharlal Nehru made a similar stopover with his daughter Indira in 1938, continuing to London to argue that if England was to face down fascism in Europe it must also correct its own imperialism in India.[17]

[13] Dunstan M. Wai, 'The Sudan: Domestic Politics and Foreign Relations under Nimiery', *African Affairs*, Vol. 78, No. 312 (1979), p. 317.

[14] See Ali Abdalla Ali, *The Sudanese-Chinese Relations Before and After Oil* (Khartoum: Sudan Currency Printing Press, 2006).

[15] Omar al-Bashir, 'President's Forward, Golden Jubilee of Sudan-India Ties', in Harun Riaz ed., *Sudan in Focus* (New Delhi: Embassy of Sudan, 2006), p. 6.

[16] Some 2,500 Indian settlers and expatriate workers are reported to live in Sudan (Omdurman, Kasala and Port Sudan); 'Indians in Sudan: Of potluck and cultural bonding', *The Hindustan Times*, 5 February 2005.

[17] The Omdurman Indian School established in 1944 would similarly become a must stop for visiting Indian dignitaries in the future.

India's founding fathers had an impact on Sudan. Sudan's Graduates' Congress, which led the struggle for independence, modelled itself on the Indian National Congress.[18] During World War II, Indian forces played a critical role in the liberation of parts of Sudan during the East Africa campaign, prompting Sudan to later fund the 'Sudan Block' of India's National Defence Academy in Pune in honour of their sacrifice. A shared colonial experience stretched over to common international outlooks during the Cold War.

In the run-up to Sudan's independence from Anglo-Egyptian rule, India provided the chief election Commissioner, Sukumar Sen, for its first multi-party election in 1953. A year earlier, Sen had tackled the enormous task of overseeing India's first ever general election. He spent nine months in Sudan, utilising the same system of balloting in identifying parties by different symbols and colours as he had devised in India, both populations being predominantly illiterate. Political relations were fostered early on following the independence of India and later Sudan. India opened a Liaison Office in Khartoum in April 1955, before Sudan's official independence on 1 January 1956. Sudan's interim Prime Minster, Ismail al-Azhari, had visited India on his way to attend the 1955 Asian-African conference in Bandung. At the conference, Prime Minister Nehru is said to have written 'Sudan' on his handkerchief to create an improvised flag for the country, thus welcoming Sudan into the international community before its formal independence.[19] Both countries saw their relations as a model of South-South cooperation, supporting the restructuring of the United Nations and the Non-Aligned Movement.

The same tune was struck in Sudan's relationship with Malaysia. Dr. Mahathir Mohamad, the former Malaysian Prime Minister, had long been an advocate of building Afro-Asian relations. In 1964, before becoming Malaysia's leader, Dr. Mahathir was elected chairman of the Afro-Asian People's Solidarity Organisation's committee for Malaysia. Other committee members dubbed Mahathir 'Osagyefo', evoking the title of Kwame Nkrumah, the first leader of independent Ghana and influential pan-Africanist.[20] Mahathir would remain a steadfast supporter of South-South cooperation during his long tenure as Malaysian Prime Minister. Thus, rather than materialising over the past two decades, it was during the colonial period and thereafter that the political and economic engage-

---

[18] 'Sudan India's Relations', Embassy of the Republic of the Sudan, New Delhi, India, <www.sudanembassyindia.org/sudan_india_relations.html> (accessed: 10 May 2010); 'India and Sudan Partners in Development', Embassy of India in Khartoum, <www.indembsdn.com/eng/india_sdn_partners.html>, (accessed: 12 May 2010).

[19] Daniel Large, 'Sudan's Foreign Relations with Asia: China and the Politics of 'Looking East', ISS Occasional Paper 158 (Pretoria: Institute for Security Studies, 2008), n.4. Nehru visited Sudan in July 1957 with el-Azhari repaying the favour in the same year. High-level visits continued, with President Ibrahim Abboud travelling to India in 1964 and later President Jaafar Nimairi in 1974.

[20] Barry Wain, *Malaysian Maverick: Mahathir Mohamad in Turbulent Times* (New York: Palgrave Macmillan, 2009), p.23.

ment with non-Western countries formed as an alternative focus for Sudan's foreign relations.

The active integration of history into formal political processes can be seen in the prominent use of historical rhetoric by Sudan, China and other Asian states in their current relations. Longstanding 'traditional' connections are regularly referred to as complementing today's 'modern' relations. Government meetings, for example, routinely cite historical links as a means of demonstrating shared connections. India's statement at the 65th session of the UN General Assembly in September 2010, for example, cited Nehru's successful efforts to enable Sudan's participation at Bandung in 1955 and 'age old ties' in the process of being 'cemented in modern times with people to people contacts, trade and commerce, investments and a broad commonality of outlook on global issues'.[21] But the use of historical rhetoric can convey a misleading sense of the importance and continuity of relations over time.

Despite a long history of Chinese ties with Sudan, especially the north, China had never played an important domestic role there until comparatively recently. The same can be said of India and Malaysia. The use of historical rhetoric as a substitute for substantive history has not always comfortably accommodated the nature of more recent consequential and controversial relations. Sudan is also playing a role in the latest phase of China and India's invigorated, globalising world history. In similar ways, both countries have made their own history in Sudan. It represents an outpost for overseas expansion and is bound up in broader processes of rising global influence. And mobilising a shared history and common identity with Sudan has been one method utilised by Asian governments to ascribe legitimacy to current relations and defend these against criticism. The historical context found strong meaning after Sudan's 1989 military coup.

Breaking the Siege: the NIF Turns East

The June 1989 NIF coup and its subsequent mode of rule were instrumental in forging the relations Sudan developed with China and other Asian countries. The NIF regime followed prior contacts between Sudan and China, but would develop relations in qualitatively new ways. The circumstances of NIF-governed Sudan – civil wars, political Islam and adversarial foreign relations – combined to make Khartoum turn to Beijing. Prior to the NIF coup, Sudan had passed through a phase of political instability and economic crises. The shifting pattern of its foreign relations, mounting inherited debt and internal fiscal crises spurred Khartoum to explore different options for external assistance. The

---

[21] Statement by S.M Krishna, External Affairs Minster at the High Level Meeting on Sudan [read out by Ambassador Harsh V Shringla, Joint Secretary] at the 65th session of the UN General Assembly, 24 September 2010.

support by Hassan al-Turabi, the regime's key Islamist ideologue and power broker, for Saddam Hussein's Iraq in the first Gulf War produced a regional and international political backlash, triggering a marked reduction in international aid and reinforcing the NIF's need to turn elsewhere for external support.

Besieged and all but broke, the NIF regime was desperate for barter trade and commodities from the Middle East. The army was discontented and demanding resources. After Libyan support, Khartoum turned to Tehran in an alliance that enabled debt cancellation, access to subsidised Iranian oil, and loans for a weapons buying spree from China in 1991. Bashir had visited Beijing in November 1990, and was received by President Jiang Zemin. Besides harbouring uncertainty about the nature of Sudan's new regime, the Chinese government had domestic priorities.[22] Attempts were made to expand business relations after the coup. While not in anything like the same league as subsequent oil investments, these resumed prior contacts and entailed working relations between the NIF and Beijing.

China's relations with the NIF should be located in relation to the political trajectory of the 1989 Islamic revolution and the politics of an internally divided regime. As Woodward explains here (see Chapter 1), there was little distinction between Turabi's domestic Islamist project and that to be exported to the world. Sudan became a centre for a host of Islamist terrorist groups. The decisive act of foreign policy overstretch by more radical elements in the NIF was the June 1995 assassination attempt on the Egyptian President Mubarak in Addis Ababa. This triggered international condemnation, catalysed efforts by regional powers against the more radical elements in Sudan, and added impetus to Washington's support for regime change by proxy 'front-line' African states.[23] In seeking to pursue a less destabilising foreign policy, President Bashir's reaction in part represented an attempt to balance the regime by the head of its more conservative military core, against Turabi and Khartoum's other ambitious Islamist ideologues. This would reach a head in the power struggle of 1999.

From the Chinese government's perspective, a less Islamist Sudan appeared to be more palatable. President Bashir's next visit to Beijing came in the aftermath of the Mubarak assassination attempt and before the UN Security Council actions in response in 1996.[24] It was pivotal in the conversion and upgrading of Sudan's China relations from 'tradi-

---

[22] Uncertainty about the NIF's Islamic agenda was also mixed with Beijing's concern about its restive northwestern province, the Xinjiang Uyghur Autonomous Region, in which Islam was important. See S. Frederick Starr ed., *Xinjiang: China's Muslim Borderland* (Armonk: M.E. Sharpe, 2004).

[23] See Alex de Waal, 'The Politics of Destabilisation in the Horn, 1989-2001', in Alex de Waal ed., *Islamism and its Enemies in the Horn of Africa* (Hurst: London, 2004), pp. 182-230.

[24] China's position during the UN Security Council negotiations is worth noting. Besides condemning terrorism, it expressed opposition to Chapter VII sanctions. See UN Security Council 16 Press Release, SC/6214 3660th Meeting (PM) 26 April 1996. China abstained from

tional' to 'strategic', to use the official description, principally through 'energy cooperation' and the entry of the China National Petroleum Corporation (CNPC) into Sudan. The NIF approached the Chinese government for help in a context of protracted civil wars, a US policy of containment and other international sanctions against Khartoum.[25] Khartoum's need for alternative sources of economic and political support also increased as its relations with Iran and other Middle Eastern states became more difficult. China, however, 'broke the siege' of Western pressure. Relations were produced more by circumstances than by any political affinity: the government of Sudan debated the merits of turning to China; then, as now, the ruling NIF/NCP has held mixed views on its China policy. However, the Chinese government's principle of non-interference in internal affairs, and opposition to the political condemnation and pressure mobilised against the NIF regime, was welcomed by Khartoum, as was China's offer to construct an oil refinery.[26] The CNPC was able to provide similar commercial terms to those of the American oil major Chevron, which exited Sudan in 1992, and promised the rapid completion of an export pipeline some 1,600 kilometres long. But the promise of an oil refinery won the Chinese a leading role in Sudan's oil sector.[27] China, in its own strategic terms, successfully exploited an opportunity shaped by Sudan's political circumstances, in the process benefiting from the unintended consequences of Western policy on Sudan.

Not under the control of major Western oil companies, Sudan represented a strong opportunity for China and played a significant early role in China's strategic energy expansion abroad. Sudan was targeted as a long-term overseas oil supply base, which could also assist the growth of emergent Chinese companies with global ambitions and enable access to neighbouring African and Middle Eastern regional markets. Regarded as a friendly state with high resource potential,[28] Sudan was thus both an overseas raw material supply base and an arena to support the global development of Chinese corporations.[29] For China, Sudan became a model engagement in Africa: an outpost demonstrating the technical accomplishments of Chinese oil companies, China's first overseas refinery

[24 (cont.)] the subsequent UNSC resolution 1054 (1996), which demanded that Sudan extradite three suspects wanted in connection with the assassination attempt and that Sudan desist from supporting terrorism.

[25] The US designated Sudan a state sponsor of terrorism on 12 August 1993. UN sanctions in 1996 were followed by US sanctions in 1997, and an American missile attack on a pharmaceutical factory in Khartoum North in 1998.

[26] Awad al-Jaz, 'The Oil of Sudan: Challenges and Achievements,' in Peter Gwynvay Hopkins ed., *The Kenana Handbook of Sudan* (London: Kegan Paul, 2007), p. 673.

[27] Luke A. Patey, 'State rules: oil companies and armed conflict in Sudan', *Third World Quarterly*, Vol. 28, No. 5 (2007), pp. 1009-10.

[28] '*Zhongguo gongren zoujin Sudan*' ('Chinese workers enter Sudan'), *Shijie Zhishi (World Knowledge)* No. 9 (2004), pp. 42-43.

[29] Yun Zongguo, '*Sudan shiyou kaifa xiangmu qianjing guangkuo*' ('Prospects for Sudan oil development project broad'), *Guoji Jingji Hezuo (International Economic Cooperation)*, No. 5 (1997), pp. 22-23.

and China's largest overseas dam construction project at Merowe. Sudan was an important and, from China's perspective, successful case of directed investment: in 'Chinese oil investments overseas, CNPC's Sudan operation represents the single most outstanding success'.[30] The militarisation of oil development in the 1990s, however, meant that such notions were incongruent with the experiences of civilian populations in Sudan's southern oil-bearing regions. Moreover, as Moro details in this book (Chapter 3), oil-related problems continued for local populations after the CPA. Underpinned by economic diplomacy, the NIF's 'Look East' foreign policy was also instrumental in bringing Sudan closer to other Asian countries.

Sudan's relations with Malaysia after 1989 have also been important. On 7 June 1991, Omar al-Bashir, then Chairman of Sudan's Revolutionary Command Council, was greeted by Prime Minister Dr. Mahathir at the Kuala Lumpur International Airport to begin a three-day official state visit to Malaysia. A number of economic, scientific and technical agreements were signed during the state visit, amidst hopes of ramping up what were then rather meagre economic ties between the two countries.[31] At a state banquet in honour of Bashir's visit, Malaysia's Sultan Azlan Shah called on the Islamic community to rebuild solidarity after the Persian Gulf War, for developing countries to 'work together and speak with one voice'.[32] He hoped that Bashir's visit would spark mutual beneficial economic relations with Sudan, and it did.

Led by Bashir, the visiting Sudanese delegation emphasised their intentions to liberalise Sudan's economy and the incentives they were prepared to offer investors. In particular, they were eager to attract Malaysian investment in their rather dormant oil sector at the time. The circumstances suited Petronas, Malaysia's national oil company, quite well. It was just beginning to make investments in the international oil industry and by the late 1990s became a key player in Sudan behind CNPC, its Chinese counterpart. With US sanctions coming into place at the time, Petronas was seen to be feasting on 'forbidden fruit'.[33] As a result, international human rights organisations, such as Amnesty International, called on it and other oil companies to leave Sudan on account of oil's detrimental influence on the North-South civil war. One Malaysian view was that such calls ignored the 'humanitarian aspect of the oil endeavour', that oil could actually benefit Sudan's development, infrastructure and the suffering of its population.[34] This was not a novel stance. Western oil companies, including Canada's Talisman, publicly

[30] Linda Jakobson and Zha Daojing, 'China and the worldwide search for oil security', *Asia-Pacific Review*, Vol. 13, No. 2 (2006), p. 67.

[31] 'Malaysia and Sudan sign two pacts', *New Straits Times*, 7 June 1991.

[32] 'King: Act to rebuild Islamic Solidarity now', *New Straits Times*, 7 June 1991.

[33] Paddy Bowie, *A Vision Realised: The Transformation of a National Oil Corporation* (Kuala Lumpur, Orillia Corporation: 2001), pp. 275-277.

[34] *Ibid.*, p. 281.

defended their operations in Sudan with similar rebuttals. But unlike Petronas and other Asian national oil companies, pressure from human rights activists and the US government led to the withdrawal of Talisman in March 2003. The combination of US containment and economic opportunity in Sudan's oil sector was again encouraging for and conducive to further Asian engagement, in this case India's national oil company, ONGC Videsh.

The exit of Talisman, and shortly after those of Swedish and Austrian oil companies, brought India into the fold of a now almost entirely Asian-dominated oil sector in Sudan. Former Indian President APJ Abdul Kalam visited Khartoum in October 2003, the first Indian President to visit Sudan in over 28 years.[35] While he spoke fondly of the centuries-old cultural bond between India and Sudan, the Indian President was mainly in Khartoum for business. Oil had reacquainted long-lost friends and would reignite economic ties that had decades earlier been dominated by cotton.[36] Kalam signed a bilateral agreement on investment with Sudan during his visit to place a political stamp on growing economic ties between the two countries.

India's entry in these circumstances occurred after Khartoum's apparent foreign policy shift towards China and the NIF's internal power struggle. President Bashir, in particular, needed economic and political alternatives, a necessity which had been heightened after he prevailed over Turabi in the power struggle of 1999. Sudan's accelerated transformation into a petro-state, a state dominated by its oil income enabling new material and patronage capabilities, was also part of the NIF's transformation from revolutionary to more self-interested politics in which elite interests and regime perpetuation were primary objectives. The petro-state logic in Sudan can be compared to other contexts in Africa.[37] Sudan stands out, however, as a case where the primary agents at first delivering and then operating its oil industry have not been the established oil majors that dominate the international industry but comparative new-comers connected to the foreign policy interests of Beijing, Kuala Lumpur and New Delhi. Sudan's isolation from Western countries in the 1990s on account of NIF rule altered the nature of investors in its budding oil sector. Yet while oil is at the foreground of Sudan's 'Look East' economic foreign policy, relations with China and other Asian countries quite quickly expanded into other sectors thereby further expanding business relations that had predated oil investments whilst also developing new ones.

---

[35] Ministry of External Affairs, 'India – Sudan, Joint Statement', Press Release, Ministry of External Affairs (India), New Delhi, 22 October 2003.

[36] Priya Mutalik-Desai, 'Bilateral Trade Agreements: The Indo-Sudan Experience', *Economic and Political Weekly* Vol. 8, No. 19 (12 May 1973), pp. 880-884.

[37] See Ricardo Soares de Oliveira, *Oil and Politics in the Gulf of Guinea* (London: Hurst, 2007).

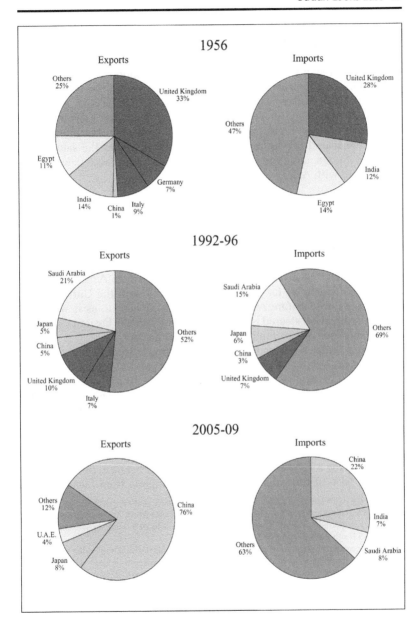

Figure 1 Sudan's trading partners
Source: Department of Statistics of Sudan's Ministry of Social Affairs; Central Bank of Sudan

Commerce in Command

China and oil stand out in Sudan's foreign economic relations. Despite early interest on the part of China in business opportunities in the 1980s and after 1989, Sudan was open to Chinese oil business in large part because it was legally closed to American business. Despite some European trade and investment, reputational costs and divestment pressures have scared off the majority of other business. At the same time, however, Sudan continues to develop a more multifaceted economic engagement with Asia.

Overall trade
China and other Asian countries have come to dominate Sudan's external trade. After 1956, this gradually shifted away from West European and North American trading partners, and then, after the NIF took power, underwent a dramatic alignment towards Asia after the start of oil exports (see Figure 1).[38] This underlines that the NIF's turn to Asia was just as much one dictated by its deteriorating relations with the United States and Europe, even before American sanctions kicked in, as it was by a change in direction steered by oil towards Asia. Middle Eastern countries throughout have represented constant trading partners.

China is Sudan's top trade partner. According to Bank of Sudan statistics, China accounted for 76% of Sudan's exports and 22% of imports from 2005 to 2009. Sudan has been China's third largest overall trade partner in Africa, behind Angola and South Africa.[39] Total trade reached US$8.2 billion in 2008 before dropping to around US$6.4 billion in 2009.[40] Crude oil comprehensively dwarfs all other Sudanese exports, representing around 90% of Sudan's total export value.[41] China has nominally been the main consumer, taking 82% of Sudan's oil exports, with Japan also accounting for a significant share (see Figure 2).[42] From 1999-2009, oil made up 98% of the value of China's total imports from Sudan.[43] As a

---

[38] On average, between 1992 and 1996 and 2005 and 2009, Sudan's exports to Asia rose from 20% to 88%, falling from 36% to 3% for Western Europe and North America respectively. In the same two periods, imports from Asia rose from 22% to 42%, and those from Western Europe and North America dropped from 35% to 23%.

[39] Strictly speaking, Nigeria now competes with Sudan for this position and Sudan was China's eighth largest export market in Africa in 2008, having been seventh in 2006 and 2007. For a summary, see Mark George, 'China-Africa Two-Way Trade: Recent Developments' (London: DFID, January 2009).

[40] *China's Customs Statistics Yearbooks* (General Administration of Customs); *China Statistical Yearbooks* (China Statistics Press).

[41] IMF, 'Sudan, Country Report No. 08/174', (IMF, 2008); IMF. 'Sudan, Country Report No. 09/218' (IMF, 2009).

[42] Energy Information Administration, 'Country Analysis Briefs: Sudan', November 2010, <http://www.eia.doe.gov/emeu/cabs/Sudan/Oil.html>, (accessed: 30 November 2010).

[43] *China's Customs Statistics Yearbooks* (General Administration of Customs); United Nations Statistical Division, Commodity Trade Statistics Database, <http://comtrade.un.org/db/>, (accessed: 27 November 2010).

Figure 2 (*left*) Sudan's oil export partners (2005–9)
Source: Central Bank of Sudan

Figure 3 (*below*) China's oil imports
Source: China Customs Statistical Yearbooks (General Administration of Customs); UN comtrade

Figure 4 (*bottom*) China's trade with Sudan
Source: China Statistical Yearbooks (China Statistical Press)

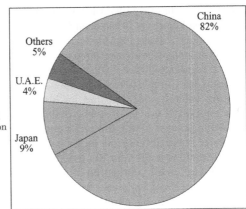

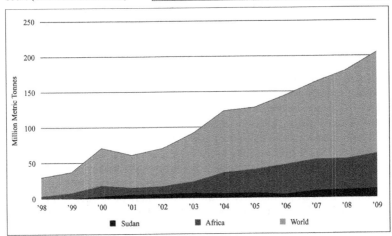

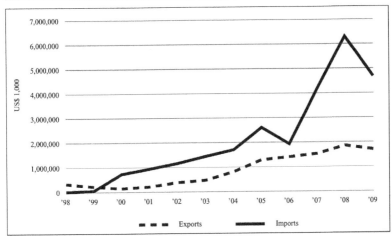

result, Sudan has provided China with 5.6% of its total oil imports in that period (see Figure 3). It has been China's sixth largest oil supplier behind Saudi Arabia, Angola, Iran, Oman, and Russia respectively (Angola being by far China's largest African source of oil imports at close to 14%). There is some disagreement in statistical sources on how much Sudanese crude oil accounts for China's total oil imports. Ultimately, however, Sudanese oil imports generally only account for less than 1% of total Chinese energy consumption. It is a small source of energy for China in a range from coal and oil to nuclear power and wind power.[44] Therefore, although a notable source of total Chinese oil imports, Sudan first and foremost is a key investment destination for the national oil company CNPC. For instance, CNPC's equity oil production in Sudan was significantly higher than China's imports of Sudanese crude in 2006, suggesting that the company sold much of its oil allowance from Sudan on international markets, which was corroborated by a spike in Japan's Sudanese oil intake that year.[45] The commercial rewards of oil investment stand out rather than Sudan acting merely as a direct source for China to satisfy its burgeoning oil import needs. Another developing dimension of China's economic relations with Sudan has seen increased Chinese exports in recent years.

Rising overall trade volumes also reflect growing Chinese exports to Sudan. Sudan's imports from China have risen sharply by over 640% since oil exports began in 1999, averaging over US$900 million a year to 2009. This is still a fraction of Sudan's exports, measuring on average US$2.3 billion a year in the same period. The trade balance clearly favours Sudan (at US$1.4 billion; see Figure 4). Still, one effect of the creation of an oil export sector amidst international sanctions was an increase in the business opportunities for Chinese products, amongst others, in the Sudanese market, particularly in the north. There have been appreciable increases in Chinese imports since 2000 of such items as garments, textiles, furniture, electronic goods, cars, or construction materials like steels or cement. Sudan has thus grown as an export destination for man-ufactured Chinese goods,[46] which also involves Sudanese and other African entrepreneurs importing Chinese products to sell within Sudan. The broad China-Sudan trade pattern is consistent with China's wider Africa trade profile. On average, the percentage increase of Sudan in China's total Africa trade closely matched the increase in Africa as part of China's total world trade over the past two decades.[47] It is similarly

[44] International Crisis Group, 'China's Thirst for Oil', Crisis Group Asia Report, No. 153 (9 June 2008), p. 24.

[45] Erica S. Downs, 'The Fact and Fiction of Sino-African Energy Relations', *China Security*, Vol. 3, No. 3, 2007, pp. 46-7.

[46] UN Statistical Division, Commodity Trade Statistics Database, <http://comtrade.un.org/db/>, (accessed: 27 November 2010).

[47] On average, in the eleven years before Sudan began exporting oil from 1988-1998 its share in China's total Africa trade was 4.12%. After oil exports started in 1999, to 2009, it was 8.47%. During the same two periods, Africa went from 1.4% to 2.77% of China's total world trade. *China's Customs Statistics Yearbooks* (General Administration of Customs); *China Statistical Yearbooks* (China Statistics Press).

characterised by the export of primary commodities to China (crude oil, cotton, timber or copper) and the import of manufactured Chinese products.

While not engaged in Sudan to the same extent as China, India is representative of a larger mixed group of Asian countries, including Malaysia, Japan and South Korea, which have also offered the NCP important economic partnerships. Since 2005, trade between India and Sudan has increased nearly three-fold to over US$900 million in 2009-10.[48] Similar to China, it was oil that led to the expansion of economic ties.

Oil

Oil has been and remains at the heart of relations, dominating Sudan's economic ties with China, India and Malaysia. The industry has had a significant influence on Sudan's economy but faces a number of challenges, as James considers here (see Chapter 2). Beginning in September 1995, CNPC bought a concession, Block 6, formerly operated by Chevron in Southern Kordofan. Just over a year later CNPC won a leading stake in the Greater Nile Petroleum Operating Company (GNPOC) along with Petronas, accessing what have until recently been Sudan's highest yielding oil concessions, Blocks 1, 2 and 4, lying mainly in Unity State (see Figure 5). The location of key oilfields in these concessions, such as Heglig, was heavily disputed between the NCP and SPLM during the CPA's interim period. In 2000, CNPC won a commanding share (41%) in the Petrodar Operating Company in Blocks 3 and 7 in Upper Nile State, which began to produce significant exports in 2006. The venture was again undertaken with Petronas but also later included SINOPEC, another of China's leading national oil companies. In 2005, CNPC won a further majority holding in Block 15 on the Red Sea, adding the adjacent Block 13 to its Sudan portfolio two years later. CNPC's investment in Sudan was critical for the international expansion of Chinese oil service companies, such as China Petroleum Material and Equipment Corporation and the Great Wall Drilling Company. In 2002, GNPOC president Zhou Jiping said that the influx of Chinese exports into Sudan were valued at 1.35 times more than CNPC's initial investment, with over 6,000 Chinese petroleum workers active in the country.[49] Indeed, the services provided by CNPC's subsidiaries can at times be more profitable than the company's actual oil production.[50] China's widespread engagement in Sudan's oil sector has been followed up by Malaysia.

Malaysian oil investment has been important since the 1990s. Only CNPC is more widely involved in Sudan's oil sector than Petronas. In addition to its exploration and production activities in the GNPOC and Petrodar consortiums, Petronas is in the retail business through service

---

[48] Department of Commerce, Government of India, 'Export-Import Data Bank', <http://commerce. nic.in/>, 17 August 2010, (accessed: 21 September 2010).

[49] Bo Kong, *China's International Petroleum Policy* (Santa Barbara: ABC-CLIO, 2010), pp. 88-89.

[50] Interview with oil service company representative, Khartoum, 14 October 2010.

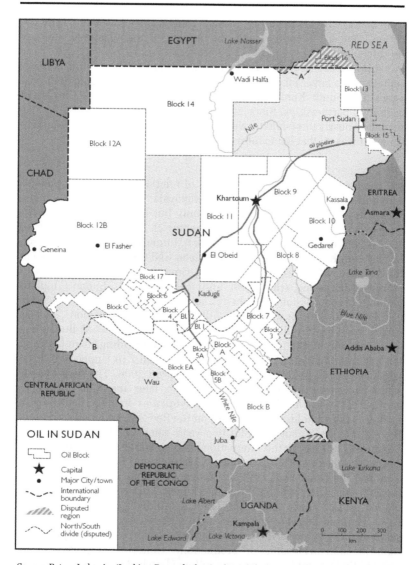

Source: Patey, Luke A., 'Lurking Beneath the Surface: Oil, Environmental Degradation, and Armed Conflict in Sudan', in Päivi Lujala and Rustad, Siri Aas (eds), *High Value Natural Resources and Post-Conflict Peacebuilding*, London: Earthscan, 2011.

Designed by Allan Lind Jørgensen for the Danish Institute of International Studies

Figure 5 Sudan oil concession map

stations and oil depots.[51] Despite the threats of civil war and difficulties of operating in a harsh climate, Sudan represented the largest contingent of Petronas staff outside Malaysia at 300 members, often including the families of workers.[52] When visiting Khartoum in 1998, Prime Minister Dr. Mahathir said at a dinner hosted by the Sudanese Joint Chamber of Commerce that Malaysia needed to trade more with countries such as Sudan in order to rebuild its economy after the Asian financial crisis.[53] During that visit, he opened Petronas' Sudan headquarters, and Malaysian involvement in the oil sector grew in the years that followed. Although not nearly at the same level as Chinese firms, oil sub-contracting is a particularly noteworthy area of Malaysian business; a substantial proportion of the contracts awarded by the Petrodar consortium, for example, have gone to Malaysian companies. PECD secured a $68 million contract to build the new GNPOC head office in Khartoum in October 2006.[54] After Malaysia, India represents the third major player in Sudan's oil sector.

The ruling NCP tactfully brought India into Sudan's oil sector in an effort not just to broaden its Asian economic partners against Western isolation but also to balance Chinese interests from over-dominating. In late 2002, both CNPC and Petronas were keen to acquire Talisman's abandoned quarter stake in the lucrative GNPOC. The NCP, however, orchestrated a lobbying mission to Beijing and Kuala Lumpur to persuade the companies and their governments to yield their contractual rights to the abandoned shares.[55] Soon after, India's ONGC Videsh joined its Chinese and Malaysian counterparts in GNPOC. Khartoum did not want either CNPC or Petronas to own a majority share in its main oil venture, but rather to balance its Asian partners. By August 2003 the Indian company also bought stakes in Blocks 5A and 5B in southern Sudan (relinquishing the latter in 2009 after three unsuccessful exploration wells were drilled).[56] The oil sector also boosted Indian exports to Sudan with, for example, the pipe maker PSL Ltd winning a US$190 million contract to supply 785 kilometres of pipeline for the Melut Basin Oil Development Project. The opportunity ONGC Videsh found in Sudan, however, would also be increasingly accompanied by challenge, as Patey examines in this book (see Chapter 4).

Despite the continual centrality of oil in the Chinese and other Asian

[51] Through Petronas Carigali Nile Ltd., a subsidiary of Petronas.

[52] Bowie, *A Vision Realised, op. cit.*, pp. 307-308.

[53] 'PM: Barter trading a solution to currency, shares depreciation', *New Straits Times*, 14 May 1998.

[54] 'Malaysia's PECD Secures $68.5 Mln Contract in Sudan', *Bernama*, 12 October 2005.

[55] 'Petronas to hit ONGC's overseas investment plan', *The Times of India*, 18 December 2002; Chris Varcoe, 'Sudan sale to close in March', *The Calgary Herald*, 1 February 2003; Scott Haggett, 'Out of Africa: Talisman closes the book on Sudan', *The Calgary Herald*, 13 March 2003; Sanjay Dutta, 'Diplomatic arm-twisting clears Sudan oil deal', *The Times of India*, 14 March 2003.

[56] 'OVL to quit in Sudan', *Times of India*, 27 April 2009.

economic engagements in Sudan, relations have progressively gone beyond oil and into mining, infrastructure, agriculture, and the service sector. Indeed, after serving as a bridgehead for wider Chinese, Malaysian and Indian business expansion in Sudan, oil is considered a pillar industry for the country's economic growth. Altogether, the Asian national oil companies held stakes in Sudan's various oil consortiums amounting to 90% of total oil production in 2009, China with 46%, Malaysia 34% and India 10%.[57] This domination of the oil sector has stood out in Asia's economic relations with Sudan over the past two decades. However, the Asian engagement in Sudan's economy has gone well beyond oil.

Sudan as a market

Northern Sudan has grown as a comparatively developed, profitable market for those companies and entrepreneurial traders able to do business there without legal risk from US sanctions. Chinese brands like Haier or Hisense have established themselves and compete with other Japanese, South Korean or Indian products. The recent appreciable growth of non-oil business reflects a trend that has seen the concentration of Chinese investment in energy change amidst a diversifying range of business operations, including interest in northern Sudan-based manufacturing opportunities.[58] From a predominantly state-backed process involving key national oil companies, the profile of Chinese business engagement has evolved to feature a greater variety of businesses, ranging from the larger state-owned enterprises (SOEs) to small and medium enterprises and independent entrepreneurs. Not all efforts to enhance China's links with Sudan have gone to plan. Direct Beijing-Khartoum air links, for example, did not take off.[59] The Chinese role in Sudan's economy, furthermore, is contentious at different levels, from local complaints concerning the quality of Chinese goods to debates about the impact of Chinese competition on Sudan's industry. However, there has been a recent upswing of new projects suggestive of an enhanced investment drive and continued Chinese business expansion in Sudan.

Transport and energy infrastructure construction is prominent in the Chinese economic role, closely related to credit lines from China's policy banks. The Chinese imprint on the construction of roads, bridges and even railways is striking (not to mention Khartoum's new airport project). Chinese finance and companies have played a notable role in constructing

---

[57] Sudanese Petroleum Corporation, 'Statistics for Crude Oil and Productions', <http://www.spc.sd/en/statics_crude.php>, (accessed: 19 November 2010).
[58] Jing Sangchu, '*Sudan zhanhou touzi he chengbao shichang*' [Investment and the Market of Contracted Projects in post-war Sudan], *Guoji Shichang* [*International Market*], 4 (2004), pp. 43-45.
[59] Following four test flights until in late 2009, Hainan Airlines reportedly decided, on the grounds of economic viability, to change its planned direct Beijing-Khartoum flight and transit through Dubai instead. 'Airliner cancels direct flights between Sudan, China', *Al-Ra'y al-Amm* (Khartoum, in Arabic), 2 January 2010 (via BBC Monitoring).

power stations and electricity networks.[60] Dam construction stands out as a notable area of Chinese involvement, a sector that in 2010 alone saw the completion of one major project, the start of another and continuation of work on other dams. President Bashir inaugurated the final electricity unit at the Merowe hydroelectric power station in April 2010, finishing construction of the Merowe dam complex at a time when Sudan's elections dominated the political landscape. Merowe was used to symbolise Bashir's success in advancing economic progress, but has been a particularly controversial Chinese-led project, linked to environmental concerns, the forced displacement of affected populations and continuing resistance.[61] Not long afterwards, President Bashir also attended the signing of a new contract with two Chinese companies to undertake the Upper Atbara Dams Complex Project in eastern Sudan. As Verhoeven explores here (see Chapter 6), China's role in the NCP's 'hydro-agricultural mission' has been vital in the NCP's efforts to advance a 'Sino-Sudanese model of development' and has been fundamental to the regime's efforts to reorientate its political role whilst looking ahead to northern Sudan's post-oil economic future. Indian companies have also gone beyond oil, investing in Sudan's energy and transport infrastructure.

Indian Tata buses, Maruti cars, and Bajaj auto-rickshaws are part of Khartoum's expanding traffic.[62] In August 2006, at a business fair in Sudan's capital, 75 Indian companies explored business opportunities in the oil sector but also in power, infrastructure, textiles and agriculture under the slogan 'Indian enterprise, Sudan advantage'.[63] Multiple lines of credit from the Export-Import Bank of India totalling almost US$625 million have been provided to foster Indian investment in Sudan. Mostly state-owned Indian companies in power and transport infrastructure have taken part.[64] Indian Railway Technical and Economic Services provided three locomotives to the Sudan Railway Corporation to replace

[60] Sudan inaugurated a new 405-megawatt, US$680 million power plant in March 2010. The Finance Ministry signed an agreement with China's Export-Import Bank for a US$274 million loan to fund the construction of a 630 km transmission network. The network will supply electricity from the new Al Fola power plant, in Northern Kordofan State, to both Northern and Southern Kordofan and Darfur. 'Sudan to Open USD680 Million Power Plant on March 24, SUNA Says', *Bloomberg*, 21 March 2010.

[61] See, for example, Ali Askouri, 'China's Investment in Sudan: displacing villages and destroying communities', in Firoze Manji and Stephen Marks eds., *African Perspectives on China in Africa* (Oxford: Fahamu, 2007), pp. 71-86.

[62] 'India makes strategic moves in distant Sudan', *Sudan Tribune*, 26 December 2003.

[63] '75 Indian Companies organize mega trade show in Sudan', *Sudan Tribune*, 14 August 2006.

[64] 'Exim Bank Extends US$25 MN LOC to Government of Sudan', *Engineering Export Info-Bulletin*, Vol. 11, No. 9, 2 March 2009; a US$50 million US line of credit in January 2004 to finance exports of machinery and locomotives and other goods from India to Sudan; a US$350 million Line of Credit (LoC) to Bharat Heavy Electricals Ltd. in January 2006 to construct the Kosti Combined Cycle Power Plant; a US$41.9 million LoC to Sudan (completed by Indian firm Angelique International) to finance the Singa-Gadaref transmission and sub-station project also in January 2006; a US$48 million LoC to Sudan for agriculture, education and infrastructure projects in February 2007; and, finally, a US$52 million LoC in July 2007 for infrastructure and livestock projects.

an aging fleet that had not been able to secure an upgrade due to long-standing sanctions.[65] Through Sudan's National Electrical Corporation, Bharat Heavy Electricals Ltd is investing US$457 million in a 500 MW combined cycle power plant in Kosti that was set to be completed by early 2011.[66] Agriculture is another area where the government of Sudan has sought to cultivate relations with Asia.

Contemplating finite oil reserves in Sudan, the Sudanese, Chinese and Indian governments have lauded agriculture as representing the future of economic relations. Sudan remains a predominantly agricultural economy. Because oil production is already declining in the GNPOC blocks, and is expected to stagnate and decline further over the next two decades, it is understandable why so much hope is once again being invested in Sudan's agricultural sector. For Sudan and China, a partnership around agriculture presents the possibility of sharing their respective strengths: Khartoum looks to China for technology and technical assistance, and Beijing looks to Sudan as a country of unfulfilled agricultural potential. The Sudanese and Chinese Ministers of Agriculture signed an agricultural cooperation protocol in Beijing in June 2008. Chinese enterprises have worked on agricultural development cooperation projects, including an Agricultural Technology Demonstration Centre, and established a small number of farms. Such links have thus far been largely at the experimental stage but are increasing.[67] Besides interest from a number of Middle Eastern states, agriculture is also prominent in Sudan's relations with India.

The Indian Prime Minister Manmohan Singh called on India and Africa to increase agriculture investments in the quest for food security at the April 2008 India-Africa Forum Summit in New Delhi. He said that Sudan had the potential not only to feed the whole of Africa, but also the rest of the world.[68] India has provided several lines of credit to support agriculture and livestock investments in Sudan. The Punjab Chief Minister Parkash Singh Badal met a high-level Sudanese delegation from Khartoum State in early 2010 to assess the initiation of joint ventures in agriculture and other sectors.[69] China and India are not alone in seeking to expand agriculture and other sectors of Sudan's economy. Malaysia and South Korea stand out as other Asian business partners for Sudan.

[65] 'Indian RITES dispatches three locomotives to Sudan Railway', *Sudan Tribune*, 21 October 2005.

[66] Sudan later asked BHEL to construct a 1,000 MW plant at Port Sudan paid for in oil in a potential agreement with ONGC Videsh. Utpal Bhaskar, 'Sudan offers payment in oil for power project', *LiveMint*, <http://www.livemint.com/2010/05/02211540/Sudan-offers-payment-in-oil-fo.html>, (accessed: 22 September 2010).

[67] In June 2009, the Chinese company ZTE signed two memoranda of understanding with the Sudan government for agricultural projects in northern and eastern Sudan. In mid-March 2010, the Ministry of Agriculture allocated ZTE approximately 10,000 hectares of land, a deal presented as occurring within China and Sudan's agricultural cooperation framework.

[68] Ministry of External Affairs, India, 'Joint Press Conference following the conclusion of first India-Africa Forum Summit 9th April 2008, Vigyan Bhavan, New Delhi', Speech 13808, <http://meaindia.nic.in/speech/2008/03/09ia02.htm>, (accessed: 20 September 2010).

Malaysian business is active outside the oil sector and has been urged forward by the Malaysian and Sudanese governments. The former Malaysian Prime Minister, Abdullah Ahmad Badawi, promoted Sudan as an investment opportunity to Malaysian business during his 2007 visit to Sudan, identifying agriculture and food as sectors having particular potential, and noting that Sudan could provide access to the Common Market for Eastern and Southern Africa (COMESA) and the Greater Arab Free Trade Area for Malaysian business.[70] He also argued that Malaysia and Sudan had much to contribute to bilateral trade expansion as well as within the Organisation of the Islamic Conference (OIC). Sudan also operates business relations with South Korea. Following on from a longer post-colonial history, and links after 1989,[71] South Korean business more recently has sought to enhance economic relations with Sudan, partly due to the identified opportunities of the oil-boom era. The Korea Business Center opened in Khartoum in November 2009, aiming 'to give aggressive support for Korean corporations to enter the oil development industry to increase resources for Korea'.[72] It has also sought to develop agricultural operations and acquire land in northern and southern Sudan, though how much substance there is thus far is unclear.[73] Fronted by Khartoum's shiny Samsung stores and the ubiquitous Made-in-Sudan Korean cars produced by Hyundai's manufacturing partnership with GIAD, South Korean business in Sudan today is conspicuous.[74]

[69] 'India: Punjab to start joint ventures with Sudan Government', 25 January 2010, <www.punjabnewsline.com>, (accessed: 10 May 2010).

[70] 'Sudan offers opportunities to Malaysian investors', *Sudan Tribune*, 14 April 2007.

[71] The founder and chairman of Daewoo, Kim Woo-choong, established a Sudan branch in 1976, apparently regarding the country as a model for Africa. Daewoo developed a large business group operating in Sudan, with four main corporations: ITMD (tire maker), SKCCC (construction), GMC (pharmaceutical) and BNB (banking). As part of a debt-equity swap arrangement, Daewoo bought into the Gezira Tannery (taking a 60% stake when it was privatised in March 1993) and the Friendship Palace Hotel (taking a 60% stake when it was privatised in March 1993).

[72] According to it's director, Kim Dal-heon, as quoted in Arirang Sudan Special Series, 'Spring of Sudan, Dark continent', PART 3: Korean Corporations Bring Hope to Sudan', 25 March 2010; accessed via Youtube.

[73] In May 2009, a summit meeting between President Bashir and President Lee Myung-bak in Seoul agreed on agricultural cooperation, especially farmland for Korea in Sudan. The first phase of the programme was due to be a wheat cultivation 'pilot program' in an area of 840 million square meters, designated as a joint venture among Korean, Sudanese and Arab companies. One report quoted the Sudanese Ambassador to Korea to the effect that 4.2 billion square meters of land in northern Sudan and 2.7 billion square meters in central Sudan had 'been prepared for Korea.' (Kim Se-jeong, 'Korea Will Grow Wheat in Sudan end of this year', *Korea Times*, 16 June 2008) but uncertainty surrounds this arrangement.

[74] Daewoo International partnered with Shinpoong Pharm and a Sudanese drug manufacturer to expand production at the General Medicine Company in Khartoum. Hyundai licenses the Accent passenger car to be assembled by Sudan's GIAD company. LG Company reportedly shifted its regional office from Nairobi to Khartoum, a reflection of the volume of distribution of its products in Sudan. Daedong Industrial Machinery Co. Ltd. has successfully established itself, undertaking diesel power plant overhaul and maintenance work in such places as Port Sudan, Dongolla, Karima, Faw, Kassala, Atbara, Fashir and Khartoum. It lists GNPOC and WNPOC as its international partners <http://www.edimco.com/eng/03/0301_02.php>.

Finally, Asian companies have been active in Sudan's service sector. Chinese service businesses have expanded as part of a more established Chinese community in northern Sudan, seen most obviously in the form of hotels, restaurants, medical clinics and stores, or travel companies. The growth of Chinese small businesses in Sudan, however, has rubbed up against Sudanese competition. It has been regionally differentiated. Since the CPA, for example, a small Chinese and Indian business community has grown in the South, most obviously in Juba, its capital from 2005. This marks a further trend in Asian business engagement in Sudan, namely, the emergence of a new economic frontier in southern Sudan, a development supported by a political thrust from both China and India.

The Politics behind Business

Political relations between Sudan and its key Asian partners have been critical to the negotiation, management and development of business partnerships and to Khartoum's foreign relations. What are often presented and thought of as essentially economic relationships are deeply, inherently political, something not always sufficiently appreciated by attention to formal institutional interaction. Until recently, Sudan-China or Sudan-India relations effectively meant links between the governments in Khartoum, Beijing or New Delhi, which continue to operate predominantly bilateral relations. An additional element of major significance was added following the CPA, namely, the development of links with Juba. The CPA established two governing entities as part of a six-year interim period: a Khartoum-based Government of National Unity (GoNU) operating on a power-sharing basis between the NCP and the SPLM, and the semi-autonomous GoSS based in Juba under SPLM control. The Chinese, Indian and Malaysian governments have followed a dual-track process in continuing relations with the NCP and developing new links with the SPLM.

The governments of Sudan and China have established close political relations. In foregrounding political equality, state sovereignty, non-interference, and mutual benefit, these relations have been managed on the basis of a different set of principles from those deployed by Sudan's more established international partners. Political relations between Beijing and Khartoum remain firmly bilateral.[75] These extend to forms of cooperative interaction in regional organisations like the Forum on China-Africa Cooperation or the China-Arab Cooperation Forum, and international organisations like the UN or the G77. Despite Chinese participation in Sudan's two major peacekeeping operations, the UN Mission in Sudan (UNMIS), created to support the CPA, and the African

[75] Interview with senior Chinese official, Khartoum, January 2011.

Union/UN Hybrid Mission in Darfur (UNAMID),[76] China has not been integrated into other multilateral bodies. It became more active in these in recent years, notably over Darfur and in Juba, but bilateralism reigns in Beijing's relations with Khartoum. Four aspects of this are worth noting. First, government relations are structured into official cooperation channels, notably the Joint Sudanese-Chinese Ministerial Committee. Key NCP leaders have been involved in managing China relations.[77] Similarly, China's relations with Sudan have been directed by senior leaders and supported by different government branches, passing since 1989 from early relations under President Jiang Zemin to the deepening of ties under President Hu Jintao since 2003. Other top Chinese politicians, notably Zhou Yongkang, a powerful member of China's Politburo and former General Manager and Party Secretary of CNPC, have also been instrumental in advancing Sudan ties. Second, political relations are multi-tiered. Not confined to interactions between central government ministries, these feature other levels of government, including at state level. A third area is political party cooperation between the CPC and the NCP, which is especially significant, given the power and role of both ruling parties. This has involved rituals of rhetorical solidarity and expressions of support by the CPC for the NCP.[78] The NCP reciprocates, supporting Beijing's One China policy and offering occasional gestures of practical assistance to the CPC.[79] This strand of political relations also testifies to the significance of non-material links, and NCP interest in China's political experience. Finally, Chinese SOEs, the NCP and Sudan's central state ministries conduct their own relations, a form of corporate-state interaction that is particularly important in China's 'energy diplomacy' with Sudan.[80] These, in effect, are bilateral relations but proceed within wider political ties between Khartoum and its different Asian partner states, and since 2005, the GoSS.

---

[76] See *Lanjui xia de Zhongguo miankong* [*Blue Helmets from China*] (Beijing: Waijiao Chubanshi, 2010), for an official account featuring the Chinese peacekeeping role in UNMIS and UNAMID.

[77] These, unsurprisingly, represent key members of the NIF, from President Bashir to the long-term Energy Minister and then Minister of Finance, Awad Ahmed al-Jaz.

[78] Seen, for example, in the CPC's message of congratulation and 'admiration' to the NCP's general conference in November 2005. Political support for the NCP was notably expressed on 22 March 2009 when Vice Minister Li Jinjun, of the International Department of the CPC's Central Committee, spoke of the CPC's rejection of the ICC and its ongoing support for Sudan. 'Chinese delegation in Sudan for golden jubilee gala', *Sudanese Media Centre*, Khartoum, 22 March 2009.

[79] During a visit by an NCP delegation to Beijing in July 2008, the senior NCP politician, Mustafa Osman Ismail, donated US$100,000 to the CPC to aid China's response to the Sichuan earthquake. 'CPC To Promote Cooperation With Sudan's National Congress', *Xinhua*, 9 July 2008.

[80] For example, Sudan's former Minister of Energy and Mining, Al-Zubayr Ahmad al-Hasan, visited China in August 2008 at the invitation of CNPC. 'Minister of Energy and Mining Visits China', *Suna* (Khartoum), 12 August 2008.

Military relations are a less documented but nonetheless significant area of China's state and business links with Khartoum.[81] Military links and arms supplies between China and Sudan have a long history; if the US was once Khartoum's leading military backer under Nimairi, then more recently China has emerged as an important military ally. Chinese technical assistance with the development of northern Sudan's military-industrial complex in the 1990s has been documented. The exact nature and extent of this is unknown, but the indications are that it involved supervision of arms assembly processes and help with the construction of three weapons factories near Khartoum.[82] Links between China's People's Liberation Army (PLA) and the Sudan Armed Forces (SAF) appear to have been re-energised following a trip to Beijing by the SAF Chief of Staff, Abbas Arabi Abdalla, in March 2002 and fully-fledged meetings featuring Abdalla, Sudan's then Defence Minister Lt. Gen. Bakri Hassan Salih and a senior Chinese military delegation. This was the beginning of a series of high-level meetings in Beijing and Khartoum between SAF, the PLA and China's Central Military Commission. In addition to indirectly helping to finance Khartoum's acquisition of weapons on the international market through increased oil sales, China has also been a significant arms supplier to northern Sudan, though not by any means the only one.[83] For instance, the UN Panel of Experts established by UN Security Council Resolution 1591 (2005) documented the 'prominence of Chinese manufactured arms and ammunition' in Darfur, citing the role of companies such as China North Industries Corporation.[84]

China's aid programme forms a final strand of political relations, though it has close, overlapping connections to economic relations in a very different context from the older Chinese aid programme.[85] An important dynamic related to this is China's development finance in Sudan, which assumes various forms but primarily entails funding mechanisms

---

[81] On 7 January 2002, Sudan's government reportedly paraded the hardware produced in its military complex to the public in Khartoum's Green Square. See Daniel Large, 'Arms, oil and Darfur: The evolution of relations between China and Sudan', Small Arms Survey Issue Brief No. 7, August 2007.

[82] These include the Military Manufacturing Complex on the Khartoum-Medani highway in northern Sudan, which reportedly specialises in light weapons, machine guns, and ammunition. The second main complex, GIAD, was opened by President Bashir in October 1999. See, for example, Christian Aid, *The Scorched Earth: Oil and War in Sudan* (London: Christian Aid, 2001), p. 19.

[83] Chinese arms sales to Sudan occurred during the government of Sadiq al-Mahdi (1986-1989). In 1991, China delivered on an Iranian-funded contract worth an estimated USD 300 million by supplying two helicopters, one hundred 1,000-pound high-altitude bombs and a large cache of ammunition. A Chinese team was also sent at the time to instruct Sudanese pilots and aircrews in high altitude bombing. *Sudan Update* (2000).

[84] 'Report of the Panel of Experts established pursuant to resolution 1591 (2005) concerning the Sudan' (2009), p. 83.

[85] For this new context, see Wang Meng, '*Cong Sudan Gean Kan Zhongguo Waijiao Zhi Cheng Zhang*' ('The Maturing of China's Arabian Diplomacy: A Case of Sudan', *Alabo Shijie* (*The Arabian World*), No. 2 (March 2010, pp. 19-26).

underpinning Chinese investment.[86] As well as being a significant source of credit for Sudan, China has also written off debt.[87] Following a longer post-colonial history, today, if narrowly defined, China's aid remains limited in the context of overall economic relations. It features the continuation of established aid links, including medical, as well as more recent newer forms including a humanitarian aid programme to Darfur.[88] Chinese assistance has more recently supported 'development projects' in Darfur and east Sudan implemented by Chinese companies, including in water and road construction. This is presented as a tangible contribution towards economic development, regarded as having the greatest efficacy in overcoming the causes of conflict.[89] Such programmes acquired disproportionate importance in China's wider African and international diplomacy on Darfur, and could also be used to respond to criticism and communicate positive messages to a domestic Chinese audience. Following the CPA, and in tandem with its outreach to Juba, China has developed an aid programme for the South.

South Sudan's political relations with China and other Asian states are of recent origin and thus much less developed. The 'one Sudan, two systems' framework created by the CPA in principle allowed other powers to recognise and engage both the central GoNU and the GoSS. The SPLM's post-war external relations were premised on constructive engagement and attracting external investment. After devastating conflicts, and a history of chronic underdevelopment, the south's need for investment was

[86] For more details and analysis, see Samai Satti Osman Mohamed Nour, 'Assessment of Effectiveness of China Aid in Financing Development in Sudan', UNU-MERIT Working Paper, January 2011. More generally, see Deborah Bräutigam, *The Dragons Gift: the real story of China in Africa* (Oxford: Oxford University Press, 2009).

[87] Underlining its 'serious concern' for Sudan's debt burden, the IMF estimated public and publicly-guaranteed debt to total some $35.7 billion for the end of 2009. This mainly reflected an increase in accumulated interest arrears, but also included new debt from Arab multilateral and bilateral creditors, as well as from China and India. The Chinese government has previously written off debt to Sudan (for example, President Hu Jintao announced the cancellation of debt worth some $70 million during his February 2007 visit to Khartoum). Details about this combination of writing off debt and contracting new loans are difficult to ascertain, but Sudan's China debt has increased in recent years. One calculation holds that the share of China in Sudan's total debt increased from 0.9% in 1999 to 13.45% in 2007 (Samai Satti Osman Mohamed Nour, 'Assessment of Effectiveness', *op cit.*, pp. 14-15). The amount is proportionally not very large but still represents a part of Sudan's wider debt burden. In 2009, debt related to infrastructure development projects and financing peace agreement commitments 'amounted to $693 million, mainly from China.' The IMF noted that 'These loans, which are earmarked for infrastructure projects such as roads and power transmission grids, have a long maturity and appear to have a grant element due to their generally moderate interest rate.' See 'Sudan: Article IV Consultation—Staff Report; Debt Sustainability Analysis; Staff Statement; Public Information Notice on the Executive Board Discussion; Statement by the Executive Director', IMF Country Report No. 10/256, June 2010, at para. 21.

[88] See Jago Salmon and Daniel Large, 'Darfur case study', in Adele Harmer and Ellen Martin eds., *Diversity in Donorship: field lessons* HPG Report 30 (London: Overseas Development Institute, 2010), pp. 49-58.

[89] See, for example, Zhai Jun, *'Zhongguo jiji tuidong jiejue Daerfuer wenti'* ['China actively pushed the resolving of the Darfur problem'], *Qiushi Zazhi* 11 (2007), pp. 61-63.

considerable. The CPA also enshrined the right of self-determination to be exercised via a referendum on whether the south would secede from or remain within a united Sudan. Recognition of the south's independence aspirations, coupled with the geography of the main oil fields in southern Sudan, drove Beijing's need to respond to the new political reality in Juba. The drivers of this process of courtship have featured a combination of pragmatism, mutual need and the prospect of mutual benefit.

In engaging the GoSS, Beijing responded to political imperatives flowing from investment protection concerns, as Large examines here (see Chapter 8). The GoSS sought China's support for political reasons. Beijing's relations with the GoSS developed late, being importantly expanded following the creation of China's Juba consulate in 2008. Its evolving engagement moved from hedging its bets on the question of Southern secession towards more actively preparing for this likelihood. The CNPC also intends to open up an office in Juba, having made social investments there after a company representative frequently shuttled back and forth between Khartoum and Juba in the lead up to South Sudan's independence.[90] China's engagement aims to support Juba and promote China's position in the south. Efforts to improve political relations continue, including through nascent CPC-SPLM party cooperation. China has not been alone in expanding relations in Sudan from the central government in Khartoum to reaching out to the GoSS in Juba.

Khartoum has long maintained political ties with the Malaysian government, but more recently Malaysia has also cultivated relations with the GoSS. Awad Ahmed al-Jaz, the influential former Sudanese oil minister, described Malaysians as 'friends of yesterday, today and tomorrow who came to Sudan during difficult circumstances.'[91] This has involved notable connections between Islamist movements in both countries, as Roland Marchal explores in this book (see Chapter 5). Islam has played a leading role in promoting economic relations between the two countries, but the business logic of oil investment and commerce has also been important. This can be seen in the recent development of relations with the south, which follows on from previous links. During his three-day visit to Khartoum in 1998, Malaysia's former Prime Minister Dr. Mahathir met the then Assistant to the President of Sudan, Riak Machar, who became the influential Vice-President of Southern Sudan after 2005. The on-again, off-again southern rebel commander had split from John Garang's SPLA in 1991 and signed the Khartoum Peace Agreement with the government in 1997. The meeting between Machar and Mahathir was presented as demonstrating to Malaysia Sudan's steps towards peace. Machar, however, was keen on southern separation at the time, which became a reality in 2011.[92] This political

---

[90] Interview with political analyst, Khartoum, 11 October 2010.
[91] Quoted in 'Sudan and Malaysia sign billion-dollar oil refinery deal', *AFP*, 29 August 2005.
[92] 'New constitution edges Sudan on to democratic road', *New Straits Times*, 13 July 1998.

transition places Malaysian oil interests in Sudan closely tied to the south. Earlier on after the CPA, Petronas established a retail presence in Juba. Its main oil stakes, as a partner in GNPOC and Petrodar, mostly lie both in the south, as well as the only concession in which Petronas has a leading stake, the White Nile Petroleum Operating Company (WNPOC) in southern Unity State. Following the January 2011 referendum, Petronas became the first-mover among the Asian national oil corporations by signing a Memorandum of Understanding on energy cooperation with the soon-to-be independent South Sudan.[93] The agreement came just a few months after Petronas realised that its relations in Sudan, one of its most crucial international investments, were largely with the northern government and not the SPLM/GoSS.[94] Recognising the changing political cal winds, the national company moved to bolster its standing with the GoSS before independence. The political transformation of the SPLM into the ruling party of the GoSS after the CPA has also altered India's relations with the south.

Since the successful entry of India's national oil company, and the subsequent visit of former Indian President Kalam to Khartoum in October 2003, India has maintained close political ties with the NCP. Awad Ahmed al-Jaz and Bakri Hassan Salih visited India in 2003.[95] India's activities in the South began shortly after the signing of the CPA. In 2005, the Indian Minister of State for External Affairs, Shri E. Ahamed, who had represented India at the signing of the CPA, later in the same year led an 18-member business delegation to meet the GoSS leadership in Juba.[96] India opened a Consulate General in Juba in October 2007 and in early 2008 brought 15 officials from the GoSS to the Foreign Service Institute in New Delhi for diplomatic training. As the southern referendum approached, India called for a 'timely, credible, and transparent' vote in which the 'popular will' of southerners would be respected.[97] The establishment of the GoSS laid the roots for growing relations between India and a fully independent South Sudan.

Sudan's other Asian partners have also displayed an increased presence in the south since 2005. There has been interest in assessing further investments and development projects in different parts of southern Sudan from a number of Asian states.[98] These include South

---

[93] 'Petronas first to deal with Juba', *Africa Energy Intelligence*, No. 648, 23 March 2011.

[94] Leslie Lopez, 'Sudan Referendum Poses Dilemma for Malaysia's Petronas', *The Straits Times*, 14 January 2011.

[95] Ministry of External Affairs, Government of India, *Annual Report 2003-2004* (New Delhi: Ministry of External Affairs, 2004), p. 60.

[96] Ministry of External Affairs, Government of India, *Annual Report 2005-2006* (New Delhi: Ministry of External Affairs, 2006), p. 56.

[97] Interview, senior Indian official, Khartoum, 12 October 2010.

[98] In January 2010, for example, the Indian, South Korean and Indonesian ambassadors visited Lakes State where they were escorted around by State government officials. Manyang Mayom, 'Indian, Korean, Indonesian ambassadors on investment trip to S. Sudan', *Sudan Tribune*, 16 January 2010.

Korea, which has also long operated political relations with Khartoum and an aid programme focused on the North.[99] Overall, the move from dealing exclusively with the central government in Khartoum to increasingly engaging the GoSS demonstrates an adaptation by Sudan's Asian partners to the politics surrounding South Sudan's independence in 2011. Another major process that has marked the political relationship between Sudan's Asian partners, China almost entirely, has been conflict in Darfur. This made the regional and international politics of Sudan's Asian foreign relations more apparent.

Solidarity under Strain?

China's salience in relation to Darfur introduced new geopolitical dimensions into Sudan's foreign relations. China was not alone in facing pressure over Darfur as a result of its relations with Khartoum, but it dominated external coverage, upstaging India in the process. Sudan came to exercise unusual influence in China's world diplomacy. What had been a comparatively uncomplicated bilateral relationship exemplifying mutual benefit for both governments evolved into the defining case of China's African involvement, with consequences for China's wider international relations far exceeding previous expectations. If China initially benefited from the NIF's adversarial foreign relations, and resulting Western policy on Sudan, Khartoum's destructive military efforts in Darfur created a serious foreign policy conundrum for Beijing.

The Chinese government's more engaged role over Darfur was discernible before the 'genocide Olympics' campaign led by activist groups in the US.[100] The conflict in Darfur, which led to the deaths of hundreds of thousands of civilians and displaced millions more, enhanced the self-interested dynamic for China to promote a political resolution. Changes in its regional relations, notably Chad's switch from Taipei to Beijing in 2006, also altered its strategic calculus in the context of the greater Darfur regional conflict and links between conflict in Chad and Sudan. Darfur rebel groups targeted oil facilities, increasing pressure from within. International factors also were an important influence on Chinese diplomacy. The Chinese government was in an exposed position as the government of Sudan's primary international patron. Discussion in government circles and more generally in China about its role in Sudan demonstrated

---

[99] A Korean business delegation toured Juba in 2010 where they reportedly expressed interest in investing. Interview with GOSS official, Juba, September 2010.

[100] See Sharath Srinivasan, 'A Marriage Less Convenient: China, Sudan and Darfur', in Kweku Ampiah and Sanusah Naidu eds., *Crouching Tiger, Hidden Dragon: Africa and China* (Durban: University of Kwazulu-Natal Press, 2008), pp. 55- 85. See also Liu Hongwu and Li Xinfeng, *Quanqiu Shiye xia de Daerfuer Wenti Yanjiu* (Darfur Issue under the Global Perspective) (Beijing: World Affairs Press, 2008).

contested argument about China's international image and Sudan policy.[101] China's exposure to criticism over Darfur brought sustained international scrutiny and condemnation. This 'China campaign' and its impact are examined by Budabin here (see Chapter 7). The campaign and the possibility of a boycott of the 2008 Beijing Olympic Games, which would have been a major political embarrassment, appears to have briefly energised Beijing's response. Chinese diplomacy became more publicly active, vocal and engaged.

While addressing international concerns, however, Beijing continued practical support for President Bashir's government. Chinese diplomacy pursued the challenging balancing act of trying to appease different, conflicting constituencies: attempting to be seen as a progressive force by supporting moves to establish UNAMID and the political process aimed at a negotiated solution in Darfur, while continuing to support the NCP. China's diplomacy became more involved in Sudanese politics through its efforts to exercise 'influence without interference' over the NCP's leaders on Darfur (though conspicuously not, it seems, on the volatile question of Abyei, bound up more within North-South relations and the CPA).[102] China's role in the transition from the African Union to a UN peacekeeping mission prior to UN Security Council Resolution 1769 (31 July 2007) that authorised this, involved 'active persuasion'. By seeking Sudanese government consent to admitting UN blue helmets, despite staunch opposition led by President Bashir, the Chinese government was negotiating the boundaries of its non-interference principle.

Khartoum also sought China's support, and that of other Asian allies, against the International Criminal Court (ICC). The UN Security Council Resolution 1593 (31 March 2005) made a Chapter VII referral of Darfur to the ICC. China abstained, much to the NCP's disappointment, but subsequently expressed strong reservations and called for a suspension of the ICC process.[103] The ICC's arrest warrants over Darfur were issued on 4 March 2009, notably for President Bashir, who was accused of crimes against humanity and war crimes. The following day, Khartoum ordered the expulsion of 16 NGOs from Darfur, Abyei, Blue Nile, and Southern

---

[101] For one interesting take, noting, for instance, the problems with China's 'silent approach' in the Darfur crisis and the need for greater protection of overseas interests, see Liu Hui, '*Zoujin Feizhou Zhongguo liyi zaoshou de tiaozhan: yi Sudan weili*' ['Walking into Africa China's benefits of being challenged: the case study of Sudan'], *Xue Shu Luntan* [*Academic Forum*] 2008 No.3 pp. 55-58.

[102] Li Anshan, 'China and Africa: Policy and Challenges', *China Security* Vol. 3, No. 3 (2007), p.77.

[103] On 31 July 2008, for example, after the UN Security Council voted to extend UNAMID's mandate, Ambassador Wang Guangya branded the ICC's indictment 'an inappropriate decision made at an inappropriate time'. See UN Security Council press release SC/9412 (5947th meeting), 'Security Council decides to extend mandate of African Union-United Nations Hybrid Operation in Darfur by 14 votes in favour, 1 abstention', 31 July 2008. China, like Sudan, the US and India, is not a signatory to the Rome Statute that established the ICC in July 1998.

Kordofan for alleged cooperation with the ICC. The UN Security Council failed to agree on a response; a French motion shortly afterwards condemning Sudan and urging a reversal of the expulsions was blocked by China and Libya, the then President of the Security Council. Both favoured inserting reference to an Article 16 deferral that could suspend the prosecution for a year with the possibility of an indefinite, unconditional suspension thereafter. Beijing's support for such a move appeared relatively clear-cut in principle, but its willingness to lead such a process was far less obvious. Beijing instead preferred to anchor its position in the opposition of the AU and the Arab League. Just as China has stretched the plausible meaning of non-interference in Sudan, it has also shied away from fully blocking Western initiatives to hold Sudan's leader to account, a position not lost on the NCP. Though not nearly at the same level as China, Sudan's other Asian partners have also responded to the rise of Darfur on the international agenda and the ICC arrest warrant for President Bashir.

In 2008, after the ICC prosecution charged President Bashir in July, Awad Ahmed al-Jaz led a delegation to New Delhi to meet Indian ministers of External Affairs, Finance, Railways and Petroleum and Natural Gas.[104] The Sudanese were drumming up further economic engagement from India while at the same time calling on New Delhi for political support against the ICC. Al-Jaz handed over a letter to the then Indian Minister of External Affairs, Pranab Mukherjee, stating that Bashir was innocent of the charges and that the western powers were conspiring against him. The delegation was keen to depict the crisis in Darfur as Sudan's equivalent to Kashmir in the hope of winning Indian political backing in international forums against outside interference in domestic affairs. The *chargé d'affaires* at the Sudanese embassy in New Delhi compared the struggles of Nehru and Gandhi to those of Bashir with the ICC.[105] Albeit representing a stance established long before its oil engagement, India has persistently opposed sanctions against Sudan over the Darfur conflict and maintained a political line that underlined 'Sudan's territorial integrity and sovereignty' against outside interference.[106] Nonetheless, Khartoum did not receive the support it had hoped for from India against the ICC warrant.[107] An Indian statement following the Sudanese delegation's visit in 2008 said that India was neither a signatory to nor had it ratified the instrument establishing the ICC. Yet it avoided taking a strong position on the matter of Bashir's indictment. Malaysia and South Korea have taken slightly more open positions on the ICC indictment.

---

[104] Vijay Simha, 'Carte Blanche', *Tehelka Magazine*, Vol. 5, Iss. 45 (15 November 2008).
[105] 'Sudan seeks India's help against ICC 'targeting its president', *Indo Asian News Service*, 6 March 2009.
[106] Ministry of External Affairs, Government of India, *Annual Report 1999-2000* (New Delhi: Ministry of External Affairs, 2000), p. 45.
[107] Simha, 'Carte Blanche', *op cit.*

Malaysia has supported Sudan on the international stage. Its former Prime Minster Badawi, for example, argued against the imposition of sanctions on Sudan during his state visit to Khartoum in April 2007. Malaysia's position as the then Chair of the OIC, which Sudan had joined in 1969, meant that this statement attracted wider attention to an organisation that Sudan had looked to for international support.[108] His predecessor, Dr. Mahathir, had previously lashed out against the US government after its August 1998 targeted bombing against Khartoum, calling America a 'bully' and wondering ostentatiously if Malaysia might also experience a US strike in the name of self-defence.[109]

South Korea may have tried to be seen to engage positively on Darfur but has enhanced relations with the government of Sudan.[110] Its then Minister of Foreign Affairs, Ban Ki-moon, visited Sudan in March 2006, returning in September 2007 as UN Secretary-General. This was followed by a number of visits to Seoul by Sudanese leaders, motivated by political interests and interest in attracting South Korean investment.[111] Ban Ki-moon, in his new UN role, made an official visit to South Korea in July 2008 and reportedly asked Seoul to become more active on Darfur,[112] but South Korea has not otherwise played a particularly important role. International attention towards Sudan's Asian partners on the Darfur issue has squarely fallen on China.

Conclusion: Towards the New Sudans

China's importance to Sudan today, and in different ways that of India, Malaysia and other non-Western investors, demonstrates the very different meaning that the notion of 'looking East' came to assume after 1989, compared with that Khartoum briefly imported during the Cold War. Against a backdrop of independent Sudan's previous attempts at non-alignment, and changes in Middle Eastern politics, 'looking East' had meant engaging with the socialist alternative that was Soviet Moscow. Khartoum's brief experiment under Soviet tutelage occurred in the midst

---

[108] President al-Bashir, for example, after meeting Badawi in 2007, called on the OIC to help Sudan 'confront western pressure to accept international forces in Darfur.' *AFP*, 'Malaysia urges against Sudan sanctions', 17 April 2007.

[109] 'Outraged Yeltsin denounces `indecent' US behaviour', *The Independent*, 22 August 1998; 'Malaysia regrets US air strikes in Afghanistan, Sudan', *Xinhua*, 21 August 1998.

[110] South Korea and Sudan manage political relations through a Foreign Minister-level mechanism: the first Sudan-Korea Joint Committee session was held in Seoul in August 1991; the second in Khartoum in April 1996; the third came in Seoul in October 2003, when both Ministry's of Foreign Affairs signed a cooperation Memorandum of Understanding.

[111] President Bashir visited South Korea in May 2008; Awad Ahmed al-Jaz visited in July 2008; Former Minister of Energy and Mining Al-Zubeir Ahmed al-Hassan visited in October 2008, and in September 2009 the Chairman of Sudapet, Salah Wabi, visited South Korea.

[112] 'Outcome of the meeting Between Minister and the UN Secretary', MOFAT press release, 9 July 2008.

of a bipolar world system offering an ideological choice between competing political and economic alternatives. The markedly different context of Sudan's position in the world today is defined not simply by Western containment but also by its experience of the role of China, India and Malaysia during the past two decades. This has proceeded within the broader contours of economic globalisation driven by the increasingly powerful Chinese economy, now the world's second largest. Instead of the former socialist Peoples China, modern China in Sudan is defined by competitive capitalism with Chinese characteristics.

Led by China, Sudan's 'Look East' engagement appears at first sight to introduce 'new' dynamics – political, economic, developmental, and cultural – that in recent years have widely come to be considered as alternatives to the West. Closer examination of the politics of these, however, reveals that the differences in the terms of such engagements are accompanied by important continuities brought about by the context and conditioning within Sudan, notably the central state's governing methods and use of external resources for domestic political purposes. As the book's Conclusion explores, this raises questions about their ultimate distinctiveness as alternatives to Sudan's more established partners.

The image of peace, prosperity and development portrayed of Sudan at the 2010 Shanghai Expo was even further removed from events in Sudan following the 2011 January referendum and in the troubled end of the CPA's interim period before South Sudan's expected declaration of independence on 9 July 2011. International attention and engagement had shifted towards Darfur from 2004 and away from the CPA and Sudan's North-South politics. Darfur became a defining aspect of Sudan's international relations, but concern about the CPA returned in the build-up to the Southern referendum and then independence. The prospect of two new Sudans meant that China, India and Malaysia were faced with continuing established relations with partners in Khartoum, whilst developing new relations with the GoSS. The nature and meaning of 'Look East' was set to be redefined.

1
Sudan's Foreign Relations since Independence

PETER WOODWARD

Sudan's foreign relations have reflected a number of domestic and international factors. The long history of indigenous state formation on the middle reaches of the Nile had always involved relations with neighbouring areas, and sometimes wider international relations as well. Nubian and Meroitic civilisation in Sudan's far north is now seen as being more distinct from Pharoanic Egypt than in the past, including clashes between the two. The Coptic Christian states that succeeded Meroe also maintained changing relations with both Egypt to the north and Abyssinia (Ethiopia) to the south-east. Following the decline of those states and the emergence of the Islamic Funj kingdom based upon Sennar, relations with Abyssinia in particular remained a source of periodic conflict; and the Funj also had to come to terms with the rising independent state of Darfur to the west. However, rather than reflecting further chapters in indigenous state formation, the modern territory of Sudan was largely carved out of north-east Africa by other powers: Egypt's invasion of the region in the nineteenth century (from 1820/21) largely created Sudan's modern boundaries as well as setting up its modern state structures; while after the period of Mahdist rule, at the end of the century and following the Anglo-Egyptian conquest of 1898, British imperialism dominated Egypt and Sudan, before both the latter gained their independence.

Independence for Sudan in 1956 brought continuing external pressures on the country's foreign relations. Egypt, in particular, had major concerns. One aspect was the Nile and Egypt's need to control and develop its water supply flowing for much of its length through Sudan from its sources in East Africa and Ethiopia. Another was the part that Egypt played in Sudan's domestic politics and international relations because of the 'special relationship' the two countries had long had, sometimes producing cooperation and at other periods significant strain. At the same time, wider international interest in Sudan's foreign relations continued, even after the era of the imperialism of the Great Powers of Europe was replaced following World War Two by the rivalry of the superpowers: the United States and the Soviet Union. The immediate concern for the superpowers was Sudan's strategic position on the Nile, the Red Sea, and the western flank of the main oil-producing areas in the

Middle East. The end of Cold War rivalry reduced Sudan's strategic importance internationally, in that this factor was less contested, but it did not end it.

While external factors have influenced Sudan's foreign relations, domestic factors have also been extremely important. The length and depth of conflict in Sudan, and the record of governmental instability, reflect the fact that Sudan has long been a comparatively weak state endeavouring to govern in a country with multiple economic, religious, racial and ethnic cleavages. The wars in southern Sudan in 1962–72 and 1983–2002 may have been the most notable products of these divisions, but they are by no means the only ones. Sudan's divisions and conflicts have all, in different ways and at various times, been linked to its external environment. A major factor in Sudan's foreign relations has therefore been the management of the international dimensions of the country's domestic problems.

The above international and domestic factors make Sudan's foreign relations appear largely reactive, and for most of the time since independence that has been the case. When more ideologically motivated regimes have been in power, however, there has been an understandable temptation to link a domestic drive for radical change with a more assertive foreign relations stance. Equally understandably, there have also been international responses to such attempts at assertiveness, which have indicated the limits of such ideological ventures in the light of Sudan's international and domestic situation. Presenting a condensed chronological and thematic analysis of Sudan's changing foreign relations across time since independence, this chapter seeks to contextualise and better understand Sudan's more recent foreign relations, including with China, India and other external partners. China, in particular, had a history of engagement with Sudan since independence, in part because of its rivalry with the Soviet Union in Africa and elsewhere; India's connection, however, was comparatively low before the 1990s.

Post-Colonial Sudan, 1956–69

One of the first academic articles on Sudan's foreign relations appeared in 1969 and remarked that 'For most of the Sudan's independence the main feature of its foreign policy has been the lack of one.'[1] Nevertheless, even then there were domestic factors that gave rise to foreign relations with elements of tension in them.

The two major political parties in the liberal democratic periods of independent Sudan's governance (1956–58, 1965–69 and 1986–89) both had historic external links. The National (later Democratic) Unionist Party had links with Egypt, which had fostered its emergence in Sudan's nationalist period before 1956; the Khatmiyya *tariqa* (or Sufi order),

---

[1] John Howell and Mohamed Beshir Hamid, 'Sudan and the outside world, 1954–1968, *African Affairs*, Vol. 68, No. 273 (1969), p. 299.

around which the party was centred, had close historic connections with Egypt, while some Unionist merchants had commercial ties as well. However, the Unionists were far from Nasserite in their outlook. The Umma Party, meanwhile, had close political and commercial links with Britain and, as it had done before independence, generally looked to the West to help to ward off Egyptian pressures. The Umma Party was under the patronage of the Mahdi family, the descendants of Muhammad Ahmed al-Mahdi who led the successful revolt against Egypt's rule in Sudan in the late nineteenth century, and who continued to view Egypt with suspicion thereafter.

It was a foreign relations issue – whether or not to accept a proffered American aid package - that unexpectedly triggered the political crisis in Parliament of 1958, which resulted in Umma Party encouragement for the military coup led by General Abboud. Once in power in November 1958, Abboud duly accepted the US aid package; he also went on to negotiate a new Nile Waters agreement with Egypt the following year. With those relations resolved for the moment, Abboud became increasingly embroiled in domestic affairs, especially as conflict developed with the opening of the first civil war in the south.

The first experience of an attempt to take a more assertive stance in international relations came under the interim government of 1964-65 following the popular overthrow of Abboud's regime, known as the October Revolution. Sudan's interim civilian leaders sought to take a radical stance on a number of issues: declaring in favour of the Nasserists in Yemen's civil war; encouraging the Eritrean secessionists on Sudan's eastern border; and backing the Congolese Simba revolutionaries to the south. They also hoped to negotiate an end to the civil war in the South, which had indeed sparked the uprising against Abboud. The stances on Eritrea and the Congo, however, only produced a backlash as the Ethiopian and Congolese governments predictably aided the Southern Anyanya guerrillas, which in turn made an end to Sudan's civil war harder to achieve.

The failure of Sudan's short-lived radical foreign policy contributed to the restoration of the dominance of the old parties following the country's 1965 elections. Under the new Prime Minister, Mohamed Ahmed Mahjoub, the war in southern Sudan was pursued more vigorously and accompanied by an unsuccessful diplomatic offensive to repair relations with Sudan's African neighbours and reduce support for the Southern guerrillas. Mahjoub was also diplomatically active in the Arab world, where he tried to pitch Sudan as an arbiter in the increasingly bitter rivalries of the radical and conservative camps in the Middle East. The high point of his political career came with the Khartoum summit to repair inter-Arab relations in the wake of the devastating defeat in the June 1967 war.[2] For the remaining two years of Mahjoub's premiership, however, there was less of a role for him in Arab affairs, while the worsening war in

---

[2] Muhamed Ahmed Mahjoub, *Democracy on Trial* (London: Michael Joseph, 1973).

the south (now involving increasing Israeli support for the Anyanya guer-rillas to tie down Sudan's army) continued to strain Sudan's relations with its African neighbours.

While the first years of independence had been dominated by domestic issues that had exposed the difficulties inherent in the state from the outset, highlighted by the opening of civil war in the south, it was also clear that Sudan's international relations would face problems as well. Relations with Britain, the former imperial power, were damaged by the Suez invasion of 1956 and the 1967 Six-Day War. The Cold War saw reluctant acceptance of US aid by the government of Sudan, but dif-ferences with it over Arab-Israeli issues, though there was an avoidance of significant contact with any communist powers. Northern Sudan's general Arab and Islamic orientation, which partly accounted for its sympathy with Eritrean separatists as well as its approach to the civil war in the south, brought hostility from Ethiopia and East Africa including their support for southern rebels.

Under Nimairi, 1969–85

The failure of Sudan's second period of parliamentary government to address the country's worsening problems led predictably to another military coup. The years from Jaafar Nimairi's coup in 1969 until his overthrow in 1985 were marked by his dominance in foreign policy-making, tempered by the exigencies of the domestic political environ-ment. He began with one of the outbursts of radicalism. Sudan's earlier 'brief fit of radicalism' in 1964 had leftist inclinations, and Nimairi's main ally in his 1969 coup was the Sudan Communist Party, which naturally looked to the Soviet Union.[3] With its continuing links to Egypt, Moscow needed little encouragement to extend its activities southwards into Sudan, and military aid in particular was soon arriving in some quantity. Yet Nimairi himself was always more of a pan-Arabist than a Marxist, and was soon also pursuing a new union with Egypt and Libya, where Colonel Qaddafi had taken power in 1969. The strands of communism and Pan-Arabism in foreign policy could have been compatible and the new Sudanese regime stood firm as, with Libyan and Egyptian help, a Mahdist uprising was bloodily crushed in 1970. However, internally a split devel-oped between Nimairi and Sudan's communist leadership that led in 1971 to a coup and counter-coup in which Libya and Egypt helped Nimairi to re-gain power. The Soviet Union was associated with the failed attempt and relations with Moscow were broken. Beijing's relations with Khartoum, however, were enhanced by the Chinese government's steadfast support for Nimairi (and opposition to the Soviet Union).[4]

[3] Howell and Hamid, 'Sudan and the outside world', *op cit*, p. 301.
[4] S. Cronje, M. Ling and G. Cronje, *LONRHO: Portrait of a Multinational* (Harmondsworth: Penguin, 1976), pp.178-183.

Regime security was now once more the top priority of Sudan's foreign policy, but not through the proposed new union, since relations with Egypt and Libya quickly cooled. The death of the Egyptian leader Nasser in 1970 had taken much of the impetus out of the proposed union. Egypt remained linked to the Soviet Union until late 1972, while the Addis Ababa peace agreement with Southern Sudan in 1972 necessarily involved playing down any Egyptian connection, because of Southern Sudanese susceptibilities. Instead, it was to the West that Nimairi started to turn, especially as the latter appreciated the strategic blow dealt to the Soviet Union by its links to the losers in the coup and counter-coup of 1971.

Sudan's relations with the West, and especially the United States, were consolidated steadily. Having been broken with the June 1967 war, relations were restored and soon American companies were arriving in Sudan, most notably Chevron, which by the end of the decade was planning to develop a significant oil field in Southern Sudan near Bentiu. Once Soviet military aid started flowing into Ethiopia from 1978, the US did likewise in Sudan (and Somalia, where the Soviets had been ejected, because of their opposition to the 1977 invasion of Ethiopia). However, Nimairi's reconciliation with the Muslim Brotherhood in 1978, followed by his adoption of Islamic law in 1983 and the subsequent renewal of civil war in Southern Sudan, brought a rapid loss of confidence towards him in Washington, which did nothing to protect him at the time of his overthrow in 1985.

Throughout the 1970s Sudan's relations with Egypt improved, especially as both countries were now firmly in the Western camp. In 1974 long-term plans for the integration of the two states were announced, and in 1976 Egypt helped Nimairi survive another serious coup attempt, this time one backed by Libya, which had turned from friend to foe after Nasser's death, with regard to its two eastern neighbours.[5] Sudan's attachment to Egypt even survived the latter's peace treaty with Israel in 1979, though later there was disillusionment in Egypt, especially when the renewal of war in Southern Sudan in 1983 brought an end to the joint Egyptian-Sudanese project to build the Jonglei Canal that was intended to increase the flow of water to the north.

Sudan had also been courting other new friends in the 1970s: the newly oil-rich Arab states across the Red Sea. For their part, these were seeking investment opportunities for agricultural development. Sudan's huge land area seemed an outstanding opportunity. Capital flowed in from Arab states, in tandem with technical cooperation from Western countries, but by the end of the decade it was clear that there had also been substantial waste and corruption. There was, however, one major outcome of this activity in the form of the giant Kenana sugar project. At the same time, Sudan's new Arab friends were less than enamoured with

Sudan's support for Egypt's 1978 Camp David peace deal with Israel, even though it was somewhat reluctantly given.

The 1972 peace agreement in Southern Sudan had, however, improved relations with Sudan's African neighbours, at least for a while. Uganda, in particular, welcomed the peace, which saw a period when both northern Uganda (with President Idi Amin, a northerner, in power) and Southern Sudan posed no significant cross-border threat to one another.[6] Ethiopia had helped make the Addis Ababa peace agreement in 1972 and hoped for Sudan's help with regard to the Eritrean war, but subsequently the 1974 Ethiopian revolution and the intensification of civil wars in the north of the country ensured Ethiopia's support for the Sudan People's Liberation Army (SPLA) when war returned to Southern Sudan from 1983.[7]

Nimairi's pursuit of a radical Arab socialist foreign policy in his early years had fallen apart over his widening split with the communists in his military government. It forced him back into an increasingly personal leadership in both domestic and international politics. Domestically he developed shifting patterns of patron-client relationships, first with Southern Sudan but later under challenges from within northern Sudan with others there, especially after 1977 with the growing Muslim Brotherhood. That pro-Islamist swing, however, contributed to the alienation of Southern Sudan and the eventual return of civil war. Foreign policy largely mirrored these developments, with Nimairi, as the client of more powerful international actors, trying to involve patrons to help his domestic agenda. Egypt's swing to the US under President Sadat in the early 1970s helped Nimairi become the client of both. It even seemed for a time that with his 'breadbasket' strategy gaining Gulf Arab support, Nimairi might be able to embark on economic development based on oil and agriculture that could transform the country. However, repeated serious attempts in the North to overthrow him forced Nimairi into a path of reconciliation with the growing Islamist movement that not only contributed to renewed civil war in the south but also resulted in rebel attacks that shut down both the prospect of oil exports and expanded water supplies for agricultural development in the north via the Jonglei Canal. A popular uprising in April 1985 brought the downfall of his regime, just as it had done Abboud's in 1964.

Democratic Sudan, 1985-89

Sudan's foreign relations in the post-Nimairi era were largely concerned with trying to handle his legacy, first under the Transitional Military

[6] Peter Woodward, 'Uganda and southern Sudan: peripheral politics and neighbour relations', in H Hölger Bernt Hansen and Michael Twaddle eds., *Uganda Now: Between Development and Decay* (Athens: Ohio University Press, 1988).

[7] Dunstan Wai, 'The Sudan: domestic politics and foreign affairs under Nimeiri', *African Affairs*, Vol. 78, No. 312 (1979), pp. 297-317.

Council led by Siwar al-Dhahab, and then the elected coalition governments of Prime Minister Sadiq al-Mahdi from 1986. At the top of the agenda was the re-opened civil war, and the external influences that could be brought to bear upon it. The SPLA had received initial support from Ethiopia, now firmly aligned with the Soviet Union, which was keen to see Sudan embroiled in civil war at a time when Nimairi was still supported by the US. In an effort to address the situation, al-Dhahab met the Ethiopian leader Mengistu in 1986, but it was difficult for the two governments to come to a mutual accommodation with regard to their respective internal wars. Ethiopia, while supporting the SPLA, did, however, facilitate contacts between it and various Sudanese political groups in the years that followed. Libya proved more straightforward. Colonel Qaddafi had supported the SPLA because of his strong hostility towards Nimairi. Once the latter was gone, he was quick to revert to his then more normal pan-Arab position and back the new governments in Khartoum, including lending military aircraft for the war in southern Sudan.

The renewal of civil war also contributed to the continuing decline of Sudan's economy, a matter which affected its foreign relations as well. The IMF and World Bank, under the influence of the US, had been very generous in dealing with Sudan in the later Nimairi years, but his downfall, and improved relations between Sudan and Libya (at that time depicted by the US as a dangerous enemy), worsened relations with America and in 1986 Sudan was declared ineligible for further IMF credits. The situation was made worse by the famines of the 1980s in Sudan's eastern and western regions, which were revealing not only climatic and environmental problems but also the effects of war on Sudan. The famines brought not only an invasion of international NGOs into the country, but growing international criticism of internal developments, especially the failure to end the debilitating war in such dire circumstances, and in spite of the country having returned to liberal democracy. Internal political and economic problems clearly were driving Sudan's foreign policy, but with the domestic political turmoil as coalition governments came and went, it was hardly surprising that there was very little coherence in policy-making. Indeed the factions and parties in Sudanese politics were in part, at least, making their own foreign policies as a dimension of their rivalry for power.[8]

Yet international as well as domestic pressure was growing for a settlement of the Sudanese civil war, and it was believed in late 1988 and early 1989 that progress was being made. It was alleged that it was partly from fear of a settlement between Sudan's then coalition government and the SPLA, which was expected to require the lifting of Nimairi's Islamic laws, that the National Islamic Front (NIF) – formerly the Muslim Brotherhood – coup of 30 June 1989 took place.

[8] Peter Woodward, 'External relations after Nimeiri,' in Peter Woodward ed., *Sudan After Nimeiri* (London: Routledge, 1991).

In the brief interlude between Nimairi's downfall and the NIF coup Sudan's foreign policy was once more largely reactive. As Prime Minister, Sadiq al-Mahdi had ambitions to be a significant regional player, but continuing civil war in the south, famine in parts of eastern, western and later Southern Sudan, as well as a debt-ridden weak economy, severely restricted him. The main change was his improvement in relations with Libya, which went from cooperation back to opposition to Nimairi in the 1970s, but the price was growing suspicion from the US. His government was clearly struggling at home and abroad before finally falling in 1989.

The National Islamic Front, 1989-2000

Sudan's foreign relations have, as already mentioned, largely been reactive, reflecting its domestic instability. The 1989 coup, however, brought another radical regime to power that was determined to push forward a more assertive foreign policy. It was the first time that a radical Islamic group had taken power in the Arab and Sunni Muslim world. Aiming to make Sudan a beacon of change for the region and the wider Muslim community, its agenda was international as much as it was domestic.

In the view of the NIF's leading ideologue, Hassan al-Turabi, the building of an Islamic State in Sudan was intimately related to foreign policy. Muslims, he announced, should aspire to build a Muslim Commonwealth. European imperialism had bequeathed the model of the nation-state to the Muslim world, but it had proved to be a 'resounding failure'.[9] Nationalism and other secular ideologies had also been a part of that failure. Though the Organisation of the Islamic Conference (OIC) had been established under Saudi Arabia's leadership in the 1960s, it was the work of countries that collaborated closely with the West and was thus 'politically impotent and totally unrepresentative of the true spirit of the community that animates the Muslim people'. Instead, a new beginning was needed and 'once a single fully-fledged Islamic state is established, the model would radiate throughout the Muslim world.'[10] The aim should be that, thus inspired and reformed, self-managing countries would become parts of the restored Muslim caliphate. The potential of Muslims to combine to achieve a major international impact had been shown in Afghanistan during the 1980s, and had not only driven the Soviet Union out of that country but had contributed to its collapse. The need to maintain the radical Islamist impetus was heightened by the 1990-91 Gulf War, which showed the resurgence of the power of the West in the Middle East aided by the collaboration of many Arab regimes. In contrast, Sudan sided with Iraq (which had also been supplying

---

[9] Turabi's address to the Royal Society of Arts, London, 27 April 1992.
[10] *Ibid.*

Khartoum with arms), thus ensuring further unpopularity in the international community, including most of the Arab world, which generally backed the liberation of Kuwait.

In addition to proclaiming the ideology that would inspire Sudan's new foreign policy, Turabi was also installed as the secretary-general of the new Popular Islamic and Arabic Conference (PIAC) established in 1991. It soon came into confrontation with the OIC, which cancelled a conference scheduled for Khartoum in 1992, though relations were improved partially when Sudan rejoined the OIC in 1994. Turabi, in addition, tried to promote religious dialogue – rather than confrontation – with Christians around the world. In particular, he sought and established diplomatic relations with the Vatican, which was concerned about southern Sudanese Catholics. Similar relations were attempted with the Church of England; other church representatives were invited to interfaith conferences in Khartoum.

If these contacts were intended to help in political as well as spiritual relations, then they were largely a failure. Sudan soon became regarded as a home for Islamic militants of all kinds, often perceived abroad as terrorists seeking to destabilise various states. Referred to officially by Sudan as 'brothers in Islam', these included Iranians, Afghan veterans from different countries (including Osama bin Laden with his al-Qaeda followers), Islamic Jihad from Egypt, Hizbollah from Lebanon and both Hamas and the Palestinian Liberation Organisation from Palestine. As a result, in 1993 the US added Sudan to its list of countries supporting international terrorism.[11] As well as giving some help with training the various Sudanese security units, these 'brothers in Islam' were accused of a variety of international activities from Algeria to Iran and down into the Horn of Africa. The latter was an area regarded as a particular concern to Sudan, especially with the large Muslim populations in Ethiopia, Eritrea and Somalia; indeed, Turabi was widely quoted as saying that he foresaw a future of Islamic countries stretching from North Africa to the Indian Ocean. However, the thought that the downfall of Mengistu in Ethiopia and the independence of Eritrea might result in good relations with Sudan (since the latter had been a past refuge for their new rulers) was soon replaced with worsening relations and accusations that Sudan was backing militant Islamic groups in both countries. Claims that Sudan was supporting a group called Jihad Eritrea led to Eritrea laying a formal complaint with the UN, and then in 1994 breaking off relations with Sudan and giving more help to the growing Sudanese opposition movement. Ethiopia was less vocal in opposing Sudan, but there was mounting concern at possible Sudanese support amongst the Muslim Oromo and Somalis of western Ethiopia. Meanwhile, in Somalia itself, both Sudan and Iran were working to encourage local Islamist groups.[12]

---

[11] Peter Woodward, *US Foreign Policy and the Horn of Africa* (Aldershot: Ashgate, 2006), Ch.3.
[12] Peter Woodward, *The Horn of Africa: politics and international relations* (London: I.B. Tauris, 1996), Ch.6.

Another alleged target for Sudan was Egypt, where militant Islamic groups appeared to be increasingly active in the early 1990s, for which the Egyptians blamed Sudan. In response, Egypt re-activated the long-dormant issue of the disputed Halayeb area on the border between the two countries. In mounting anger with its southern neighbour, Egyptian troops occupied the area, and in response Sudan could do little more than protest. East African states were less obvious targets for Islamic activities, but nevertheless were relevant to Sudan's foreign policy. This was especially the case with Ethiopia, where the overthrow of President Mengistu in 1991 had been a blow to the SPLA fighting in southern Sudan. Khartoum welcomed the SPLA's setback and believed that military victory could be pursued. An important part of the SPLA's recovery lay in the expansion of its links with Uganda, which now became the main conduit for its external support. In response to Uganda's help to the SPLA, Sudan government forces in the south gave assistance to a bizarre northern Ugandan armed movement known as the Lord's Resistance Army (LRA) led by William Kony, a former Roman Catholic catechist.[13] Instead of an alliance with Uganda's Muslim minority, Khartoum was thus helping a quasi-Christian movement seeking to prey upon northern Uganda, especially through child abduction.

Kenya was less directly involved with Sudan, but there was an awareness of the political potential of the country's Muslim minority, and moves were undertaken to block it. The Islamic Party of Kenya was banned and described as 'Arab fundamentalists'; in 1993 its leader, Sheikh Khalid Halala, was arrested for incitement when he called for a jihad. Awareness of an Islamic threat was maintained by the 1998 bombing of the US embassy in Nairobi, after which America launched a missile attack on an alleged Sudanese chemical weapons facility, the Shifa factory in Khartoum North.

Sudan's foreign policy has also had a Zaire (later Democratic Republic of Congo, DRC) dimension unrelated to Islam. With its long-running hostility to Uganda, it was unsurprising that Sudan generally opposed the former with regard to developments in Zaire/DRC. Indeed, Uganda claimed that Sudanese troops made use of Zaire/DRC territory in their efforts to fight the SPLA and destabilise Uganda.

With regard to Sudan's western neighbours, Chad and the Central African Republic (CAR), the situation was different again. Deby, who also took power in 1989 (launching his assault on the capital from Darfur), was seen as a fellow Muslim and a useful ally for Sudan; however, as with the CAR, Sudan was comparatively cautious, recognising the influence of France in both countries. Turabi was partly educated in France and regarded France as the most pro-Sudan of European states, partly because of its perceived desire to extend its influence in Sudan where 'the Anglo-Saxons' (the US and Britain) were largely adopting a policy of isolation.

[13] R. Doom and K. Vlassenroot, 'Kony's message: a new *koine*? The Lord's Resistance Movement in Northern Uganda', *African Affairs*, Vol. 98, No. 390 (1999), pp. 5-36.

Sudan's attempt to be a beacon of Islamism for the region came to a head in 1995 when it was accused of complicity in the attempted assassination of Egypt's President Mubarak in Addis Ababa. Following that incident, UN sanctions were imposed on Sudan as a result of its failure to hand over three of the would-be assassins, who had escaped from Addis Ababa and taken shelter in the country. Sudan soon realised how isolated it had become, and the extent to which it had been labelled a 'pariah state'.[14] Through its interventionist policies, it had made itself a host of enemies: the majority of its neighbour states, the US (then indubitably the world's one remaining superpower), and much of Europe as well. Isolation was having an economic as well as a political impact, with foreign aid drastically cut back and worsening relations with the IMF, which all contributed to the country's accelerating downward economic spiral.

Nor had Sudan's policies won significant countervailing friends. It had been close to Iraq, but following the latter's overwhelming defeat in the Gulf War it could do little to assist Sudan. Iran was another new ally which did help significantly with obtaining arms in the early 1990s, but by the middle of the decade Tehran was discouraged by Sudan's continuing domestic problems, while Iran itself was then moving towards renewed participation in the international community.

With far more enemies than friends, Islamist Sudan was beginning to pay the price of its earlier aggressive assertiveness. This was particularly revealed as the Sudanese opposition in the National Democratic Alliance (NDA) began to unite more and escalate the civil war, not only in southern but now also in eastern Sudan. The new offensive had the support of neighbouring states, especially Uganda, Ethiopia and Eritrea; and the US also seemed ever more belligerent with Secretary of State Madeleine Albright appearing to call for the overthrow of the Sudan government, while on a visit to Uganda in 1997.

As the all-round pressure on Sudan mounted, the government saw the need to retreat from its isolation and began instead a carefully targeted 'charm offensive'. This was accompanied by shifts in the NIF leadership. The influence of the NIF's *eminence grise,* Hassan al-Turabi, was waning. The PIAC was shut down. In 1999 a major split developed which saw Turabi ousted from power following the failure of a challenge he mounted against President Bashir. However, unlike Sudan's previous military ruler, Nimairi, Bashir was essentially the army's commander with much of policy-making being handled by a secretive clique surrounding him. With regard to foreign policy, the Foreign Minister, Mustafa Osman, was very much the face of the regime (and known as 'Mr Smiley' for his efforts), but other civilians such as Mohammad Osman Taha and Salah al-Din Atabani were also active. Europe looked promising, in parts at least, especially as Sudan's oil prospects began to develop, attracting new commercial interest in the country. As seen, France had

[14] Tim Niblock, *'Pariah States' and Sanctions in the Middle East: Iraq, Libya, Sudan* (Boulder: Lynne Rienner, 2001).

always been quite promising, and relations had been closer since Sudan had arrested the wanted terrorist 'Carlos the Jackal' and handed him over to France.[15] In Germany and Italy as well, there was some response to Sudan's overtures, though Britain remained distant, having chosen to support the American missile attack of 1998.

There were also attempts to improve relations with those African states supporting the NDA. This was particularly important with regard to the repeated negotiations between the Sudan government and the SPLA, which since 1994 had taken place under the auspices of the Inter-Governmental Authority for Development (IGAD), comprising a number of regional states (including Sudan) and backed by Western friends – later partners – of IGAD. In 1999, after years of largely unsuccessful and desultory negotiations, IGAD established a permanent secretariat in Nairobi (headed by a Kenyan diplomat), with the aim of intensifying efforts towards a settlement of Sudan's civil war.

Sudan was greatly helped in its attempt to improve relations with its neighbours by the unexpected outbreak of war between Eritrea and Ethiopia in 1998. Both countries were now preoccupied with their own conflict, and ready for improved relations with their western neighbour. It did not result in their total abandonment of the NDA, but it did mean that there was less enthusiasm in either country for supporting it. Relations with Egypt also improved. Egypt was particularly concerned that the IGAD process would result in the division of Sudan, which it expected would have the effect of complicating future negotiations on the question of the Nile waters. In consequence, Egypt sought to win the backing of all sections of the NDA. Egypt also tried to launch its own initiative with regard to Sudan's peace negotiations, with the support of Libya, which was, by now, keen to project itself as an important actor in Africa. At the same time, Egypt had also sought to divide President Bashir, with whom it thought it could work, from Hassan al-Turabi (perceived as the arch-Islamist and responsible for the assassination attempt on Mubarak), and rejoiced when this occurred in 1999.

While these issues of international politics appeared so clearly in Sudan's public image, there was a new economic foreign policy at work. The hopes of oil development during the Nimairi years were to be re-kindled through alliances with major Asian countries, especially China, Malaysia and later India. Though the SPLA had not been defeated, it proved possible to clear the oilfields near the North-South border with the support of sufficiently ruthless partners, and in 1999 Sudan became an oil exporter.[16] Although the relationship with the new Asian friends was primarily economic, it inevitably had international political implica-

---

[15] Gérard Prunier wrote that Illich Ramirez Sanchez (alias 'Carlos the Jackal') 'Was sold by the Sudanese government to the French Interior Minister Charles Pasqa.' G.Prunier, *The Rwanda Crisis, 1959-1994: A History of a Genocide* (London: Hurst, 1995), p. 219.

[16] Leben Moro, 'Oil development induced displacement in the Sudan', *Luce Fellowship Paper No. 10*, Durham, 2009.

tions especially with regard to China, a permanent member of the UN
Security Council.

Foreign policy and the Comprehensive Peace Agreement

The Comprehensive Peace Agreement (CPA) of 2005 was the result of a
conjunction of interests within Sudan and internationally. On the
domestic front, the two parties to the agreement, effectively the National
Congress Party (NCP, formerly the NIF) and the SPLM/A, both saw advantages in peace; while internationally there was wide support and no significant spoilers. Domestically the NCP had come to realise that there was
little chance of military victory in the South, while peace could stabilise
access to oil and potentially open further oil fields. The SPLA recognised
that it could not stop the existing oil flows, though they were intermit-
tently interrupted, and that the NCP was being strengthened by oil
revenues on which it was entirely missing out. The unsuccessful peace
talks since 1994 had also gone a considerable way to creating an agenda
for negotiation, especially on the thorny issue of Islam. Building on
IGAD's 1994 Declaration of Principles, the Machakos Protocol of 2002,
which preceded the negotiation of the full CPA, stated that there would
be Islamic law in the north of Sudan and a secular south, with the latter
holding a referendum on separation; meantime, both parties would
endeavour to make unity attractive.

The immediate international support for the CPA came from Sudan's
neighbours and three outside countries with particular interest in its
politics. IGAD was the responsible regional organisation, in which Kenya
played a leading part as well as hosting the various rounds of negotiations. Other IGAD members were less involved, but none had an interest
in seeking to disrupt the talks. Kenya looked not only for kudos but also
economic links with Southern Sudan, as did Uganda. Ethiopia was
developing economic links with Northern Sudan, especially on oil; while
Eritrea wished to retain links with Sudan rather than provoke it while the
Eritrea-Ethiopia dispute remained unresolved. (Egypt and Libya had
sought a peace initiative of their own but had been discouraged by the
US, which they had no wish to offend.) For its own part, the Clinton
Administration had begun sharing intelligence on Islamism with Sudan
in 2000, following attacks in East Africa and Yemen, while the incoming
Bush administration was backed by the Christian right, which had a par-
ticular concern for Southern Sudan. Norway had a similar concern, while
Britain, as the former imperial power, felt a residual responsibility. The
US, Norway and Britain together formed what was known as the Troika,
and played a major role in furthering the negotiations. Sudan's new
economic partners in Asia and the Gulf were supportive, seeing stability
and eventual unity as benefiting their own interests in the country.

The CPA also, however, contained elements that led to new domestic conflict that was to have international repercussions. From the outset there had been criticism that the CPA was an exclusive agreement involving only the NCP and the SPLM/A. The lesson that some drew was that this demonstrated that the way to emerge a winner from a peace process in Sudan was to fight. This was the lesson drawn by some of the leading groups which launched attacks on government forces in Darfur in April 2003, within months of the Machakos Protocol. The government's response was to arm local militias known as *janjawid,* of the kind that both sides had used repeatedly in Sudan's conflicts for decades. There were hopes for a new peace process for Darfur in Abuja in 2006, but the negotiations essentially came to naught, with only one faction out of three signing the Darfur Peace Agreement in 2006, beyond contributing to deepening divisions amongst the Darfur opposition groups.

Sudan was hopeful that Darfur would not prove to be a major international problem, beyond relations with Chad that proved a complicating factor. However, the popular concerns, especially in the US, with the conflict raging in Darfur led to accusations of 'genocide' in 2004, exactly ten years after the Rwanda genocide in which the UN was seen to have stood aside during the butchery. Now the UN showed great concern, even holding a special Security Council session in Nairobi to consider Sudan and especially Darfur. It was also decided that the AU, rather than IGAD, should take the lead in this new conflict, and for the first time an AU monitoring force (African Union Mission in Sudan, or AMIS) was put into the region. But, in spite of supposed ceasefires, there was no peace to monitor, and the small inadequate force could do little beyond observing the ongoing conflict. In an effort to stiffen AMIS, a UN component was later added (the AU/UN Hybrid Mission in Darfur), but to little more effect.

The disarray in Sudan after the signing of the CPA was matched by disarray in the international community. The US spoke of genocide and maintained sanctions on Sudan in spite of the CPA. The European powers were softer but knew their publics were hostile to the Sudan government. Arab and African states were concerned, with Chad also becoming a major factor. Sudan's new Asian friends remained largely uncritical in public, though China appointed an envoy and engaged in quiet diplomacy. The major dividing issue internationally turned out to be the International Criminal Court (ICC), which had been established by the UN Security Council. Following the Security Council's referral of Darfur to the ICC, three Sudanese were indicted on war crimes and charges of crimes against humanity, including President Bashir. The ICC had been contentious from the outset, and the international community was now divided over the issue of arresting Bashir, with his Asian friends amongst the reluctant. By 2010 the disarray in Sudan and internationally was combining to threaten the CPA process itself.

The independence of South Sudan changes foreign relations for both states substantially. They will have to treat each other as separate states, with much still to be decided between them including crucial issues such as border relations, the separation of financial arrangements including responsibility for Sudan's large foreign debt and the rent to be charged by North Sudan on the pipelines carrying what will now be South Sudan's oil. Without direct access to most of the oil revenues, North Sudan will see a major drop in government revenues and will cultivate relations with Saudi Arabia and the Gulf states to partially offset this loss. The South will develop relations with its African neighbours, especially Kenya and Uganda as well as South Africa. Both countries will seek to develop relations with the US, while continuing their growing ties with China and neighbouring Ethiopia.

Conclusion

The premise of this chapter has been that Sudan's internal problems have largely accounted for the fact that for most of the years since independence its foreign relations have been mainly reactive: making moves in response to the changing international situation that would endeavour to limit the impact on successive governments of domestic instability, especially the wars in southern Sudan. This has resulted in relations not only with neighbouring states, especially African neighbours most directly connected to Sudan's civil wars in various ways, but also Sudan's position in the Cold War. After a brief flirtation with the Soviet Union, it was to the US that Nimairi turned, not only as a foreign-policy move, but also in the hope that it would be politically and economically useful in domestic politics as well. But for Nimairi, as for all other Sudanese leaders, it was to be domestic politics that brought downfall, for its intensity is such that in the end it generally counts for more in regime stability than the support that has been given by foreign patrons.

At the same time, it was also mentioned that there have been occasional attempts to play a more assertive, and even interventionist, role in foreign policy. The attempts of the leftist radicals in the 1960s were short-lived and soon collapsed for both internal and external reasons. The foreign policy pursued in the name of the Islamist movement from 1989 was far more ambitious and sustained. Yet, to be successful, it had to succeed on at least one of two counts. It had to be capable of igniting the kind of developments amongst Muslim communities in neighbouring states that it was claimed the regime was achieving in Sudan: and/or Sudan had to be capable of projecting threatening force, most probably indirectly by support for armed groups in neighbouring states. As it was, Sudan proved incapable of doing either. There was no large-scale sustained Islamic upsurge lit by the beacon of the 1989 coup, nor could armed groups undermine neighbouring regimes. Instead, as opposition to the regime mounted amongst the Sudanese, neighbouring states and others gave it increased backing.

In the end the regime was forced to retreat and try to adopt a more 'orthodox' foreign policy, repairing relations with many countries from whom it had earlier been estranged. By the end of the 1990s, a new factor had emerged that added to this reconciliation from both sides: oil. The development of oil and Sudan's emergence by the end of the century as a modest oil exporter, but possibly with large potential, naturally influenced foreign relations. Like all regimes in Sudan (and many elsewhere), the connections between political power and economic opportunity are strong. Those associated with the NIF had strengthened their financial positions as its influence grew before 1989 and they expanded it rapidly thereafter, in spite of overall continued economic deterioration nationally. Oil development was a powerful incentive towards improved foreign relations; while international companies sought new opportunities, sometimes to the embarrassment of critical governments, most notably Canada's which found itself caught between one of its largest oil companies, Talisman, and an active NGO sector which was very critical of Sudan's human rights record. More importantly, with US sanctions blocking American oil majors from working in Sudan, the way was open to look East – to Malaysia, India, and especially China. The new economic opportunity also encouraged the regime in Sudan to seek greater political stability by negotiation with the SPLM/A, which was to lead in time to the 2005 CPA, though not before a fresh revolt had occurred in Darfur.

The new economic links to Asia and to the Gulf, now augmented by an interest in Sudan's agricultural potential as a source for food security, have become an increasing issue though different in their implications from those of the past. In the Cold War, in particular, Sudan's relations to the wider international community were essentially strategic and driven by superpower rivalry (Sudan joined Egypt, Ethiopia and Somalia in being on both sides in the Cold War, as the superpowers played checkers in north-east Africa). At the same time, relations with neighbours largely reflected domestic politics and especially armed conflicts, which so often degenerated into tit-for-tat support for rebel groups. Sudan's development of relations with Asia, however, reflected a different character. Asia was too far away to be involved significantly in regional politics, and none of the Asian states sought to project military power into the area for strategic reasons. Instead, it was much more a marriage founded on economic interests: Asia was in search of resources, especially oil, and Sudan was politically isolated from the US and under sanctions that effectively deterred Western oil majors, in addition to their doubts about security. For Sudan, the gamble is that rapid oil-led economic growth can overcome the political divisions: for the Asian investors, the gamble is that those political divisions do not in the end have such centripetal force that conflict once more destroys that resource source, as it did for Chevron in the early 1980s.

Should the two Sudans become more stable in the future, a more balanced foreign policy between reaction and assertion may prove possible. An end to conflict would reduce the need to be reactive, while more stable political systems might reduce the possibility of the seizure of power by a radical group with an aggressively assertive agenda. A more balanced and stable foreign policy would open up the possibility of more cooperative relations with neighbours: with rising populations across north-east Africa and an increasingly fragile regional environment, cooperation will become increasingly important if domestic and international tensions are to be contained.[17]

[17] John Markakis, *Resource Conflict in the Horn of Africa* (Oslo: International Peace Research Institute, 1998).

2

The Oil Boom
& its Limitations
in Sudan

LAURA M. JAMES

Sudan's economy has been transformed since the early 1990s by Asian investment, particularly in the oil sector. This chapter argues that the Sudanese economy in the twenty-first century is largely driven by oil – and the oil sector is dominated almost entirely by investment from Asian countries. Historically, Sudan depended on agriculture for most of its economic growth and export earnings. But the discovery of oil, and the simultaneous expansion of internal political tensions that left traditional Western partners largely unable to participate in its exploitation, offered a number of Asian state oil companies their first major opportunity to invest heavily in Africa. The result was a very rapid transformation in some parts of Sudan's economy. However, this left other parts, particularly subsistence agriculture in more remote regions, struggling to adjust.

The current level of Sudan's dependence on oil is highlighted by the fact that, in 2009, the commodity accounted for over 90% of the country's export earnings and almost 50% of central government revenue.[1] In that year, average daily production was 475,000 barrels per day (bpd), which came from four producing concessions, all majority-owned and managed by investors from China, Malaysia and India. Asian interest in the Sudanese oil sector also extends beyond current production. Of the most hopeful exploration areas, with the exception of Block B in Southern Sudan, a concession owned by France's Total, most are again allocated to CNPC and Petronas. Asian investment also extends to the downstream oil sector. The Al Jeili refinery in Khartoum is a 50:50 joint venture between CNPC and Sudapet, and Petronas has been considering the construction of a second refinery near Port Sudan, although this now looks unlikely to go forward. In addition, there is a significant knock-on effect on related

---

[1] The main sources for all of the economic data in this chapter are the Central Bank of Sudan (CBoS) annual and quarterly reports, and the national budgets, supplemented by the IMF Article IV reports. Most oil production figures are from the Ministry of Finance *Government of Southern Sudan Oil Production Share* monthly publications. Other statistical sources are cited where used. Most of the statistical data on the Sudanese economy should be handled with care. Collection difficulties mean that the south and other outlying areas of the country are largely excluded from numbers published at a national level, and the informal economy is inadequately captured. International sources generally draw on national official statistics.

sectors, such as infrastructure (for example, roads, bridges, power stations and dams) and even services – many targeted at Asian oil workers. Consequently, as well as being the major recipients of Sudanese exports – China took 58% and Japan 15% in 2009 – Asian partners are also increasingly significant providers of imports to Sudan. China was the source for 22% and India for 6% of the country's total imports in 2009. In contrast, nearby Saudi Arabia, the second-largest import source, provided 7%.[2] In a relatively short time, Asian dominance has been firmly entrenched.

The new investment had important implications for GDP growth, the balance of payments and fiscal developments. It also had a strong impact on the non-oil economy, with different sectors responding in a variety of ways. But Sudan's 'new' oil economy is already showing signs of trouble ahead. Both production and prices have faced problems, with major knock-on economic implications. As oil is a finite resource and may already be declining in Sudan, the bulk of investment in that sector is likely to be withdrawn in the coming years. Moreover, it is not clear how much of the broader Asian and Gulf investment in other sectors will continue in its absence. The future economies of both North and South Sudan are likely to look very different from both the near and distant past – and the role of Asia has yet to be defined.

This chapter views the role of Asian investment in the Sudanese economy through a number of different prisms. First, it provides a brief summary of the historical development of the Sudanese economy before the advent of oil. Together with the second section, which outlines the impact of the discovery of oil, and the political complications that followed, this lays the background for the beginnings of a closer relationship with Asian partners. Next, the chapter takes a slightly different tack and looks directly at the impact of oil on the Sudanese economy, detailing the massive transformations seen in GDP and growth, the balance of payments, the public sector and fiscal pressures, and the various main economic sectors. In each of these areas, the oil-related influx of Asian investment had a significant impact. Finally, the chapter takes a more dynamic view, and looks at the implications of current trends for the future of the Sudanese economy.

Historical Background

I. Before oil

Both the importance of the oil sector and the strong links with Asia are relatively recent phenomena in Sudan. In 1979, when the discovery of oil in the country was confirmed, it was by a US company, Chevron, which had undertaken a longstanding exploration programme. At that time, the Sudanese economy was predominantly agricultural, with cotton as the

---

[2] International Monetary Fund, *Direction of Trade Statistics*, 2009.

principal export commodity – as well as some sesame, livestock and groundnuts. This meant that economic growth fluctuated, depending on droughts, floods, harvests and global non-oil commodity prices. Sudan's main trading partners then were Saudi Arabia and some Western countries.

In the early twentieth century, under the Anglo-Egyptian Condominium (1899-1956), the British took the lead in the establishment of commercial agricultural projects – in particular, a large irrigated cotton-growing scheme in Gezira. The UK colonial administrators hoped that this scheme would be the foundation of Sudan's new economy. However, global economic trends instead highlighted the risks of national dependence on a single commodity.[3] At the time the scheme was designed, in the 1920s, as a means of sourcing raw cotton to feed the textile industry in Lancashire, international prices were high. However, the Great Depression of the 1930s saw a collapse in international trade. In addition, servicing the massive debt owed by Sudan to British bondholders financing the scheme put a large burden on government finances, with service payments worth the equivalent of as much as one-third of government revenue in the 1930s.

Agricultural diversification beyond cotton saw little progress during the Anglo-Egyptian period. There was some development in the livestock sector, and other cash crops, such as gum arabic, sesame, groundnuts and sugar, were produced. However, the colonial government sought to protect its revenue from import taxes by discouraging the development of processing industries or even the planting of a greater range of cash crops like coffee and tobacco, especially in southern Sudan. Fluctuating international commodity prices in the 1930s, moreover, made any new investments extremely risky. Sudan's dependence on cotton therefore persisted. A number of smaller-scale schemes were added to Gezira, including rainfed cotton-growing in Nubia and Equatoria and an irrigated project at Tokar.

Cotton formed the basis of Sudan's relatively rapid economic growth after the Second World War, with further new cotton projects, such as the Zande Scheme in the south. However, international prices remained unpredictable and, combined with variable harvests, led to large annual fluctuations in government revenue and strong inflationary pressures. Growth and investment remained heavily focused in northern central Sudan, while Darfur, the south and most of the east remained poorly developed. This remained the case even as successive governments sought to move from cotton to wheat in the 1970s. Arab and other investors funded new irrigated and rainfed mechanised farming schemes designed to turn Sudan into the 'breadbasket' of Africa and the Middle East. A new fall in commodity prices and poor implementation caused

---

[3] For historical background, see M. W. Daly, *Empire on the Nile: The Anglo-Egyptian Sudan 1898-1934* (Cambridge: Cambridge University Press, 1986).

most of these plans to fail, leaving Sudan with an extremely large public debt burden. The result was a debt crisis in 1977-78, with US loans (which later became part of the problem) being used to bail the government out. The 1980s were consequently years of austerity, with fewer development projects and a minor privatisation push, aimed at balancing the government budget. Agricultural projects continued but by this time a new and much more valuable natural resource was about to be made available.

II. The discovery of oil
Following Chevron's initial commercial discovery at Abu Jabra in 1979, there were several other discoveries in the Muglad Basin in the early 1980s, with the British-Dutch oil major Shell showing sufficient interest to buy 25% of Chevron's concession in 1983. After much negotiation, the consortium agreed plans with the government to build a small refinery and export pipeline. However, the security situation complicated exploration, as the country's long civil war revived. The new oil discoveries were located almost exactly on the fault-line between north and south. In February 1984 southern fighters attacked a Chevron camp near Bentiu, killing three workers, and all oil exploitation plans were put on hold for security reasons. Following the 1989 military coup that brought to power the current Sudanese regime, Chevron was asked to give up its licence and ultimately agreed, transferring all the land leases to the Sudanese government through the intermediary of ConCorp, a Sudanese oil firm.[4]

In the 1990s, the Sudanese government focused on finding a new international partner to replace Chevron, but both security and political concerns meant that there were few takers. A small refinery was built at El-Obeid to produce domestic fuel, and a Canadian oil company, State Oil, took over the Chevron concession, but lacked the capacity to develop it. Another Canadian firm, Arakis, soon bought out State Oil, but it again struggled to develop Chevron's former concession. As a result, in late 1996, the Sudanese government found further investors by signing a deal with an Asian-led consortium, GNPOC, dominated by CNPC and Petronas, with Arakis taking a 25% share and Sudapet a non-paying 5%. These firms were less deterred by the ongoing armed conflict in the area and international complaints of human rights abuses. As a result, oil sector exploration and development proceeded quickly, with the construction of an export pipeline and processing facilities. In 1995, CNPC had already bought another one of Chevron's former concessions, Block 6, in southern Kordofan and southern Darfur. But its leadership of GNPOC was its most substantial investment in Sudan in the 1990s. The weak link in the consortium, however, was the Canadian connection.

Talisman, yet an another Canadian company, purchased Arakis in

---

[4] Sherief El Tuhami, 'Oil in Sudan: Its Discovery and Industrial Development', in Peter Gwynvay Hopkins ed., *The Kenana Handbook of Sudan* (London: Kegan Paul Ltd, 2007).

1998. Sudan began to export oil in late August 1999, following the inauguration of the new export pipeline, but the ongoing war and the activities of international campaign groups increased the pressure on Talisman. In late 2002 it agreed to sell its share in GNPOC to India's ONGC Videsh, and the sale was accomplished in 2003, completing the triumvirate of state-owned Asian oil firms. By this time, production in the concession was averaging around 280,000 bpd - near to its peak level. Plans for new projects in blocks 5A and 6, as well as in the Melut Basin, were also proceeding apace, despite the fact that international oil prices remained relatively low, at under US$30/barrel. Nevertheless, the experience of Talisman demonstrated that, however good the prospects, the political costs for Western companies of involvement in the Sudanese oil sector were simply too high.[5]

Oil Transforms the Economy

The advent of oil has fundamentally revised the political economy of Sudan. At the same time, it is important to note that the sheer size of the country and population, and the ongoing importance of subsistence agriculture, preclude the possibility that it could ever turn into the equivalent of an oil-rich Gulf state. Over the past two decades Sudan has seen a massive increase in known oil reserves, to about 6.7 billion barrels at the end of 2009, according to BP's *Statistical Review of World Energy*.[6] Nevertheless, it is worth noting that even this figure represents only one-fifth of the reserves to be found in, for example, Nigeria. Moreover, the government's own estimates of proven reserves are substantially lower, suggesting that, in the absence of large new discoveries, neither Sudan nor the new state of South Sudan (which contains about 75% of proven reserves) may ever become a major global oil producer.

The rapid rise in oil output since the opening of the first oil export pipeline in 1999, from a start-up level of 130,000 bpd to a plateau of around 475,000 bpd in 2007–10, has nevertheless had significant economic consequences. It has been associated with a sharp rise in foreign investment flows. Oil has become the dominant export commodity, as the oil-driven boom also pushed up imports. Sudan's oil output growth coincided with a rapid increase in international oil prices through much of the first decade of the twenty-first century, from an average of US$25/barrel in 2002 to a peak of well over US$100/barrel in 2008 (although prices fell back somewhat in 2009). The combined result has been to boost the development of the industrial sector, as well as national infrastructure. Moreover, the Sudanese government has been enabled to raise public spending sharply.

[5] Luke A. Patey, 'State Rules: Oil Companies and Armed Conflict in Sudan', *Third World Quarterly*, Vol. 28, No. 5, 2007, p.1007.
[6] BP, *Statistical Review of World Energy*, 2010.

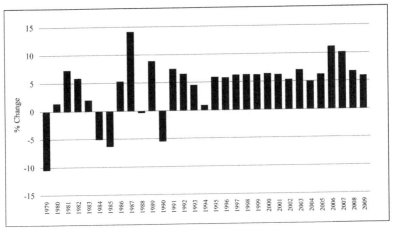

Figure 6 Sudan real GDP growth rate
Source: IMF

I. Growth
The most significant effect of the oil economy in Sudan has been on economic growth: real GDP growth averaged over 7% a year in the decade to 2008, although it fell subsequently as a result of the global economic downturn. This compares with an average of 4% in the previous ten years (see Figure 6). Moreover, as an agricultural economy, Sudan previously saw extremely unstable growth, depending on climatic conditions and harvests, with unpredictable double-digit expansions and contractions. By contrast, in the first decade of oil development, real growth never fell below 5%, despite continued civil conflict.

Following the 2005 North-South Comprehensive Peace Agreeement, which coincided with the beginning of the oil price boom and substantial new production coming on stream, GDP growth peaked at well above 10% in 2006-07. Even so, this impressive economic growth was coming from a very low base, and was largely focused on the capital, Khartoum. Much of the country's massive land area and rural population were left largely untouched by the benefits. As a result, the upshot has been a further concentration of growth and prosperity around a relatively small urban elite.

II. Balance of payments
The rise of the oil sector has also completely changed Sudan's foreign trade profile, driven by new partnerships with Asian countries. The country saw a dramatic increase in annual export revenue, from US$600 million in 1998, before the beginning of large-scale oil export production, to around US$12 billion ten years later. Oil now accounts for over 90% of

export revenue. By contrast, the next-biggest single export earner, sesame, is the source of less than 1% of the total. The oil is sold principally to Asian partners – 58% went to China, 15% to Japan, 9% to Indonesia and 5% to India in 2009.[7]

Import spending, however, has almost kept pace with this rapid rise in exports, leaping from less than US$2 billion to more than US$9 billion over the same decade. Imports were boosted primarily by the requirement for capital goods for oil-related expansion and infrastructure. Initially military purchases associated with the North-South civil war, and then later the need to fund a 'peace dividend' in the wake of the CPA, also drove up spending on imports in the oil years, now that the foreign currency was available to pay for them. By 2008, about one-third of Sudan's import spending was on machinery and equipment; one-quarter on manufactured goods; 15% on transport equipment; and 5% on wheat, despite the country's massive agricultural potential. These imports come from diverse sources, but again China is the biggest single partner, providing 22% of the total in 2009.[8]

In consequence, the advent of oil development has dramatically altered the country's current-account structure. Sudan has frequently posted a trade surplus in recent years, albeit a fragile one, given the volatility of international oil prices. However, this is invariably offset by rising flows of money out of the country, owing to the repatriation of large profits by foreign oil firms, as well as increased spending on trade-related services. These debits have been only partly mitigated by the regular transfer of remittances home by the large Sudanese diaspora. Consequently, the current account has posted a sustained deficit in the oil decade, peaking at about 15% of GDP in 2006 and then fluctuating in line with oil prices in subsequent years.

In order to achieve an external balance of payments, Sudan has needed to finance its persistent current-account deficit by attracting increased capital inflows. Much of this has been provided by new foreign direct investment (FDI), mostly in the oil sector, but also in infrastructure, including transport and power, as well as in parts of the services sector, particularly finance and telecommunications. As a result, in addition to China, Malaysia and India, many of the nearby Gulf Arab countries have become increasingly important investors in Sudan. FDI rose steadily until 2004 in line with oil sector growth, and saw an even sharper increase thereafter to a peak of US$3.5 billion in 2006, following the signing of the CPA and the beginnings of the oil price boom.

A warning signal was sounded in 2007, when FDI dropped back to US$2.4 billion, and remained at similar levels in 2008. The global economic downturn in 2008-09 depressed what might otherwise have been strong investment growth, as well as lowering oil prices and reducing the

[7] The Economist Intelligence Unit, *Sudan Country Report*, September 2010.
[8] *Ibid.*

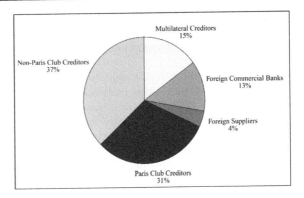

Figure 7 Sudan
debt (end 2009)
Source: Bank of Sudan

availability of loans. With foreign-exchange reserves already very low
(around two months of import cover at the end of 2008), the result was to
demonstrate Sudan's extreme vulnerability to the prospect of a severe
balance-of-payments crisis, with substantial foreign-exchange shortfalls.
In order to maintain a stable exchange rate against the dollar, the Central
Bank had to put in place new exchange controls in early 2009, and to
tighten them throughout 2010, while maintaining an extremely low level
of reserves. The periodic foreign-exchange crises were even more acute for
the Government of Southern Sudan (GoSS), given its heavy dependence
on imports and lack of direct access to foreign currency.

III. Public sector
Sudan's government revenue and spending profiles have been equally
transformed by the advent of oil. Again, however, expenditure has overall
more than kept pace with rising government earnings, resulting in an
ongoing struggle to balance the budget. After facing a ballooning deficit in
the early 1990s (which peaked at more than 12% of GDP and drove inflation up into triple-digits), in 1997 the government committed to a strin-
gent IMF reform programme, the implementation of which fortuitously
coincided with the beginning of oil exports. Advised by the IMF, the fiscal
and monetary authorities made good progress on improving revenue
collection (including through a significant tax reform programme), tracking
government spending and privatising a number of state-owned companies.

The main issue affecting the Sudanese economy that the series of IMF
programmes has been unable to address is the massive external public
debt, which was estimated at almost US$36 billion, or the equivalent of
more than 50% of GDP, in 2009 (see Figure 7).[9] This debt, now composed
in large part of interest arrears, was built up in a series of failed development programmes since the 1970s. Sudan is in theory eligible for debt
relief under the Heavily Indebted Poor Countries initiative, and has been
making token payments of up to US$50 million annually to the IMF to

[9] IMF, *Sudan Debt Sustainability Analysis*, 2010.

show good faith in preparation for this process. However, the likelihood of debt relief has been repeatedly derailed by a number of factors, principally the international community's attitude to the ongoing crisis in Darfur.[10]

As a result, Sudan has sought to fulfil its development needs by seeking financing from Asian partners, principally China and India, as well as from the Gulf Arab countries. Sudan has made every effort to service these new, predominantly non-concessional loans. They are, however, problematic in two respects. First, their contraction is likely to create new problems for the country in negotiating any eventual debt relief, with older creditors objecting to the fact that newer ones will be repaid. And secondly, they became much more difficult to access under the conditions of tightening liquidity associated with the global financial crisis. At the same time, however, new sources of concessional multilateral funds intended to assist crisis-hit poor countries remained inaccessible to Sudan because of its defaulter status. There are concerns that similar constraints could hinder international assistance to the adjustment to the South's secession.

This one major gap aside, the successful IMF programmes enabled the country to bring inflation under control, at an average of just under 8% in 2000–07. Sudan also succeeded in converting its structural fiscal deficit into a small surplus averaging just over 1% of GDP in 2003–04. From 2005, however, budgetary discipline began to slip, owing to a combination of delayed increases in oil output, the need to show a post-CPA peace dividend, and over-confidence driven by the meteoric rise in oil prices.

The result was a renewed series of fiscal deficits, widening to more than 4% of GDP in 2006 and resulting in a build-up of domestic arrears, as government bodies were unable to pay contractors.[11] These contractors, in turn, defaulted on their loans, creating substantial problems in the banking sector, risking the collapse of some large financial institutions, and putting depreciatory pressure on the currency in late 2006 and 2007. Although the deficit narrowed, given high oil prices in 2007-08, enabling some of these arrears to be repaid, it widened again to an estimated 2.6% in 2009, owing largely to the oil price drop and political constraints preventing spending cuts, creating some new financing problems.[12]

The concern is that the structure of the oil economy makes Sudan much more vulnerable to budget fluctuations. When oil prices peaked in 2008, the Government of National Unity (GoNU) depended on the oil sector for over 60% of its total revenue. At the same time, spending patterns had become more rigid, as a result of the decentralisation process implemented since the signing of the CPA in January 2005. Half of net

---

[10] See also Benjamin Leo, 'Sudan Debt Dynamics: Status Quo, Southern Secession, Debt Division, and Oil – A Financial Framework for the Future', Center for Global Development Working Paper 233 (Washington, DC: Center for Global Development, December 2010).
[11] IMF, *Article IV Report*, 2008.
[12] The Economist Intelligence Unit, *Sudan Country Report*, September 2010.

revenue from oil produced in the south (around 40% of total fiscal revenue) was transferred to the GoSS, according to the terms of the peace deal, after 2% had been allocated to the producing states. Block transfers to the northern states also increased steadily over the three years. However, apart from – in theory – the allocations to the east and Darfur under the terms of two additional peace agreements signed in 2006, these remained at the discretion of the central government. As a result, they have tended to be allocated in a politicised manner.

Moreover, the semi-autonomous Southern government still depended almost entirely for its revenue on oil transfers from the north. In 2010 well over 95% of GoSS earnings still came from this source, as the under-developed private sector and administrative inefficiencies meant that incomes from taxes and customs remained negligible. International aid is also an important source of funding in Southern Sudan, although the Multi-Donor Trust Fund set up under the CPA and administered by the World Bank was slow to begin operations, facing a number of problems with disbursement.

Southern government spending is also relatively inflexible, being heavily dominated by salaries, which accounted for 50% of spending in 2007 (of which 70% went on the army). In 2008, a boom year, the propor-tion of spending on salaries went down to 33%, but it bounced back up towards 50% in 2009, underlining the inflexibility of the large public-sector wage bill, which increasingly came to be seen as the main 'peace dividend' in the south. By contrast, capital spending has suffered, and the progress of infrastructure development has been disappointing. Although the GoSS has come up with detailed, well-thought-out strategic plans – presented, for example, at the Oslo Donor Forum in May 2007 – they have proved difficult to implement. The young government has been con-strained by a massive lack of capacity, poor internal co-ordination and absent commitment control mechanisms, as well as ongoing allegations of corruption.

IV. Economic sectors

Despite the massive scale of its post-oil economic transformation, oil still only accounts for around 7% of Sudan's nominal GDP – a proportion that is likely to contract rather than expanding in the coming years. Data from the Central Bank for 2009 showed that services, at 48%, and agriculture, at 31%, remained much more important.[13] Furthermore, by filtering out some of the effect of elevated oil prices, the calculations of GDP at constant prices demonstrate that the vast majority of economic activity across Sudan remains unrelated to oil. Indeed, given the importance of the informal economy in both services and agriculture, and the difficulty of obtaining information from the country's more remote regions, these figures may well be under-estimates.

[13] Bank of Sudan, *Annual Report*, 2009.

Industry beyond the petroleum sector remains a relatively minor component compared with many countries, at around 14% of GDP, despite some spillover from the oil price boom. The manufacturing sector, which historically struggled as a result of chronic under-investment, has benefited in recent years from Sudan's rising growth and some economic reforms. Among the more successful industries have been those based on food processing: for example, sugar refining. The construction sector has also seen strong localised growth in recent years. This has been based in part on Gulf Arab and Asian investment enticed by an oil-associated real-estate boom. Although largely confined to central Khartoum and, to a lesser extent, the Southern capital, Juba (where much of the investment has been from neighbouring African countries), this boom drove construction-sector growth averaging above 8% in 2006-07. Moreover, after a short pause owing to the global economic downturn, it re-emerged in 2009-10 with, for example, the huge Qatari Diar complex being built on the banks of the Nile in Khartoum.

Growth in the services sector was even more robust in the years of the oil boom. Moreover, although some clearly came directly on the back of oil activities, other sub-sectors seemed to demonstrate independent growth. Financial services, for example, have increased rapidly in recent years, despite a flawed regulatory environment and intermittent problems among local banks. In northern Sudan, there is an exclusively Islamic financial system, enforcing *shari'a* prohibitions on the charging of interest. There are around thirty commercial banks, and a growing Gulf Arab presence, which, although largely focused on investment banking, has also seen major Dubai-based firms buy up local institutions. The Bank of Khartoum, for instance, is part-owned and managed by Dubai Islamic Bank, as is the smaller Emirates and Sudan Bank.

Foreign investment in the financial sector is still far from being on a large scale, however. The banking system still suffers from major domestic weaknesses, including the lack of a credit bureau and the prevalence of name-based lending. These contributed to the severe problems encountered in 2006-07, on the back of the temporary fiscal crunch, from which Sudan's banks have still not fully recovered. The failure of government departments to pay suppliers caused a number of them to default on their loans. The proportion of non-performing loans rose sharply, to at least 26%, concentrated in a few of the larger banks especially closely associated with the state, especially the Omdurman National Bank, which required huge cash injections from the Central Bank to prevent its collapse. Even so, access to finance remains vastly easier than it is in the south, where Islamic banking has been prohibited in the CPA, but success in encouraging the growth of a conventional system to take its place has been extremely limited, and the nascent microfinance industry has suffered notable teething problems.

The financial sector in the north – and indeed, the economy as a whole – is also affected by the imposition of US sanctions on Sudan. These and other factors, such as the US-led divestment campaign from firms operating in Sudan, have over the years meant that economic relations between Sudan and not only US companies, but also other Western firms with any interest in operating in the US, have become fairly minimal. Since Sudan has been able to establish effective relations in most sectors with Asian and Gulf firms instead, the direct impact of the sanctions is now, paradoxically, minimal. However, they have the ongoing indirect impact of reducing competition, so that Sudan is likely to get less good terms from investment and trading partners than some other countries. And their most important consequence, especially for banking, is the way in which they complicate access to US dollars and mean that Sudan cannot be connected to the international Visa network. Some banks have made a good business out of charging firms to bypass these problems, but for most it raises costs and creates risks in other markets, to the extent that some banks and commercial companies have pulled out of the country.

Nonetheless, despite recent growth in industry and services, agriculture (much of which, as already mentioned, is subsistence-based) in many respects remains the most significant sector of the Sudanese economy. There have been some changes since the colonial era. Cotton – traditionally the largest non-oil export earner – has in more recent decades been displaced by livestock and sesame. Other export staples include gum arabic and sugar. Owing to the advent of oil, agriculture is much less important to the balance of payments than formerly, having dropped as a proportion of export earnings from 80% to 5% in ten years. While this is to be expected in a new oil producer, it also partially reflects continuing exchange-rate policies that have disadvantaged non-oil exports (the so-called 'Dutch Disease', whereby foreign currency influxes into the economy are allowed to drive exchange-rate appreciation, making domestic industries uncompetitive).

Despite this, however, agriculture still accounts for a substantial proportion of GDP. More importantly, it provides jobs for about two-thirds of the working population and thus represents the principal hope for future broad-based, regionally balanced growth. This would require careful planning, partly owing to the diversity of the sector, based on Sudan's highly varied geography and topography. The south of the country and the peripheries continue to be dominated by nomadic pastoralism and small-scale, rain-fed farming. In the central northern States, however, massive mechanised projects (as in Blue Nile) and irrigation schemes (following on from the huge colonial-era Gezira development) attract the bulk of state investment and assistance. Overall, agriculture still faces massive constraints, especially in the south, ranging from poor infrastructure, lack of financing and unpredictable taxation to low levels of human capital and insecurity.

There are also concerns over the issue of foreign (mostly Arab and Asian) investment in the Sudanese agricultural sector, which is growing rapidly. The Ministry of Agriculture talks of a huge increase to US$7.5

billion by 2010. Deals covering over 1.5 million hectares have been signed with South Korea, Kuwait, Qatar, the UAE and Egypt, among others. Some see this as a means to promote economic growth through large-scale commercial projects. Government officials point to side-benefits of improved inputs and technology, better transport infrastructure, marketing synergies and lower energy costs. However, there is also the risk that a key national asset may be sold off cheaply, to the detriment of subsistence farmers, many of whom have problems establishing land tenure. Foreign companies may bring in their own workers and ship up to 70% of their crops home – potentially problematic in a country with large food-aid imports. It is possible that even the immediate impact on macro-economic balances may not be as large as claimed: some countries are investing relatively cheaply in land, but remain unwilling to commit money to develop it while food prices remain low and Sudan's future political situation remains uncertain. In other cases, development has proved more difficult than expected in the Sudanese environment, which has seen a series of failures of large foreign mechanised farms (notably in the 1970s).

More generally, the business environment in Sudan is relatively poor, discouraging high-quality long-term investment. This is true in both the north and the south, although for some different reasons. The country as a whole comes 154th in the World Bank's 'Ease of Doing Business' rankings, putting it below Nigeria and Sierra Leone. It scores particularly poorly on ease of closing a business and on protection of investors.[14] Processes can be slow and bureaucratic, corruption is a concern and the state (or at least security organs linked to the state) is heavily involved in the economy. Although there are certainly profitable opportunities in Sudan, particularly for Asian and Middle Eastern firms that are not hindered by domestic regulations on competition and payoffs, the overall result is that Sudan as a country does not get the best terms – although some individuals may do very well out of it. Moreover, at times when global investment is low, as during the global economic downturn, there is a very limited range of partners to which to turn.

The Future of the Oil Economy

Oil is a finite resource. An oil economy is therefore necessarily time-limited. The bulk of the Asian investment in Sudan's oil sector will be withdrawn at some point, most likely within the next couple of decades. Moreover, there remains an unanswered question over how much of the broader investment driven by the oil boom will remain viable in the longer term. This is a problem all oil producers face, but the dilemma is potentially more acute for Sudan, for three reasons. The first is that,

[14] World Bank, *Ease of Doing Business*, 2011.

although there is still substantial uncertainty over reserve levels, Sudan may in fact have less untapped oil than was previously thought, limiting the time available for adjustment. Second, both the poor quality of some of the oil and Sudan's dependence on a limited pool of buyers (owing to US sanctions) increase the threat of price volatility. And thirdly, the complexity of the politics surrounding the oil sector, including the prospect of South Sudan's secession, has an impact on management efficiency and future investment.

I. Production and prices
Beyond the political risks, neither the output levels achieved nor the prices received by Sudan have lived up to expectations over the years. The country's hydrocarbon profile seems much less promising than was once hoped. The more valuable 'Nile Blend' oil from GNPOC's concessions in the Heglig Basin, has been declining steadily since 2005, as older oilfields mature, with limited opportunities for enhanced oil recovery techniques. The Petrodar concession in the Melut Basin began production, after long delays, only in April 2006, and the first shipment was exported in September 2006. However, there were initially severe problems with the quality of the oil, a relatively heavy and low-value crude known as 'Dar Blend'. These difficulties were largely resolved in 2007 with the construction of the new Bashayer 2 export terminal, and production has since been rising steadily. However, it has continued to fall below projections (perhaps reflecting a lack of investment by companies) and prices have been extremely volatile. In the absence of new discoveries, it now seems possible that Sudan's output may never rise consistently above 500,000 bpd.

New discoveries, of course, remain the major unanswered question for Sudan. There is plenty of scope for further exploration within the country. There have been recent additional finds in the Melut Basin, including some higher-quality oil. There is a certain amount of optimism about concession block 8, and offshore gas in blocks 13 and 15. Most of the other blocks, however, are seen as outside chances, being explored by relatively small firms. The exception is the massive Total concession in the south, which has long been the focus of high hopes. But exploration has been slow, and there has been some concern over wells in likely spots coming up dry. Furthermore, even for the likelier prospects, the likelihood of a big find, while acceptable from the point of view of an international oil company with diversified interests, is low from the perspective of a national government with an economic transition to manage.

Sudan's dilemma is made more acute by rising oil price volatility in recent years. International oil prices are inherently unpredictable, and dependence on a single commodity will always constitute a vulnerability. This was made very clear to a number of countries through the impact of the global economic downturn in 2009. Sudan has been hit particularly hard, through fluctuations in demand (and international refinery capacity) for Dar Blend. This tends to fall particularly sharply when spare capacity in the market increases, as lighter, easier-to-refine crudes become more readily available. It also faces the risk that rising production costs (for instance, for security in the face of political instability, or more advanced techniques in difficult fields) could cut into profits. In all, lower prices, combined with relatively stagnant production, suggest that the oil boom in Sudan may already be well and truly over.

II. Oil and politics

The future of the oil sector in Sudan is very much bound up with the fallout from the strained relations during the CPA period (2005-2011) between the Government of National Unity in Khartoum and the semi-autonomous GoSS in Juba. Most of the known reserves are either in the South or on the North-South border. However, as the South is landlocked, the oil has to be exported through the North, via the pipelines to Port Sudan. Under the CPA, during the 'interim period' before the southern referendum, with temporary arrangements for revenue sharing of net revenue from oil produced in the South, after 2% has been allocated to the oil-producing states themselves, 50% has been transferred to GoSS. The sector was supposed to be overseen by the National Petroleum Commission (NPC), jointly chaired by the president, Omar al-Bashir, from the northern NCP and the first vice-president, Salva Kiir, representing the southern SPLM. It had an even number of permanent members from north and south and temporary members drawn from the relevant states for specific discussions. However, there were substantial delays in setting up the NPC, and throughout the CPA period it lacked the robust Technical Secretariat that might have enabled it to exercise substantive oversight over the management of the petroleum sector. As a result, there is continued potential for disagreement and uncertainty.

Many in the south still suspect that they have been cheated of their full share, despite provisions to increase the transparency in the sector, such as monthly bulletins explaining oil revenue calculations published by the Ministry of Finance and National Economy.[15] There have been arguments over allocations from concession blocks 1, 2 and 4, near the North-South border, especially in the disputed region of Abyei. Although the borders of Abyei were finally agreed in July 2009, there is still the potential for quarrelling over related arrears and the wider border delineation. Similarly, the low prices sometimes received for the 'Dar Blend' oil from blocks 3 and 7, in the southern state of Upper Nile, have caused some to allege that full details of oil marketing contracts might not be disclosed, with the government selling crude oil to traders at below market prices. The question of transparency in Sudan's oil sector is a hugely complex one, given the variety of oil exploration and production-sharing agreements; the diversity of oil grades and prices; the distinction between

---

[15] See Global Witness's report, *Fuelling Mistrust* (Washington, DC: Global Witness, 2009).

exports and domestically used petroleum; the uncertain impact of sanctions; the problem of determining the relative shares of the federal, southern and state governments; and the unclear North-South border. Whatever the truth of southern suspicions, the reality is that their very existence presents a serious political problem for the oil sector, including in the post-secession era, when the need for cooperation will continue in a more volatile political environment.

There has also been a degree of uncertainty over oil exploration licences. The CPA states that existing concessions will be reviewed but remain valid, with resolution mechanisms through the NPC for any disputes over contracts said to have been signed with the SPLM during the civil war. This process has been put into effect, but slowly and painfully. For example, part of Block B, a large concession area in the South, was disputed between France's Total, with a longstanding contract with the national government, and a UK-based company called White Nile, which had begun explorations on the back of agreements with SPLM leaders. It took until July 2007, however, for the NPC to decide that Total would maintain its stake, and the amount of White Nile's promised compensation was still not agreed. Another part of Block B was claimed by Jarch Management Group (registered in the British Virgin Islands), while ASCOM of Moldova explored Block 5B under a GoSS licence. Nationally, the latter concession had been awarded to the White Nile Petroleum Operating Company (WNPOC), a consortium between Petronas, Sweden's Lundin, and ONGC – which however, eventually decided that the situation merited its withdrawal.

The international divestment campaign has also continued to affect the oil sector. It has had an adverse impact on competition by keeping many of the larger Western firms out altogether, with Marathon of the US, for example, being forced to sell its stake. Some services and engineering firms also eventually withdrew, such as Britain's Weir Group and Rolls Royce. This has been blamed for the relatively slow pace of exploration and construction delays within the sector. Moreover, those firms that remain have been forced to pay much more attention to issues of corporate social responsibility in order to divert negative attention. If north Sudan continues to benefit from southern oil after the south's secession, then South Sudan could also be affected by some of these dynamics.

Finally, in the longer term, companies continue to be concerned about the risk of conflict affecting oil production. Many of the more important fields are still in the volatile North-South border area. Block 6 has also seen attacks across the border from Darfur, and Chinese oil workers have been kidnapped and even killed in Southern Kordofan. There are suggestions that community and tribal action around some of the oil fields has deterred the Asian national oil companies from new investment. However, the biggest risks about which the oil companies are concerned centre on southern secession in July 2011. The prospects of border instability around the oil production areas, or a breakdown of

North-South relations that causes the closing of the pipeline, are both highly uninviting for commerce. Moreover, even in the best-case scenario, when the South becomes independent, oil firms that have previously dealt almost exclusively with the national government face the prospect of uncertainty about whether their contracts will be considered valid and the need for a rapid reorientation in the context of the new regime.

Conclusion: What Next for the Two Sudans?

With the due date for the secession of South Sudan fast approaching as this chapter was being written, and the future of oil development as ever uncertain, there are many question marks over the future shape of the two Sudanese economies. However, some general points can be made.

First, in the absence of new oil discoveries, northern Sudan is going to have to focus increasingly on agriculture and services to drive economic growth. This will involve a major and painful adjustment process, especially to the balance of payments, given the importance of oil exports in terms of access to foreign currency. Nevertheless, there remains some dynamism in other sectors, and the country's underlying potential is large. Existing relationships with Gulf Arab and Asian partners could be built on to encourage investment even in the absence of oil. In the longer term, education will be key to developing the services sector still further. The more immediate determinants of a successful transition will be concerted efforts to manage the exchange rate so as to make non-oil exports more competitive, and to improve the predictability of the business environment. If US sanctions were to be lifted, that might also provide a boost as the country became more integrated into the global economy.

Second, in South Sudan, the area's huge economic potential – with plenty of water, fertile land for agriculture and the likelihood of substantial undiscovered mineral resources – must be set against serious structural problems. Without improved security, improved infrastructure (especially roads and markets) and better access to finance, inputs and training, agricultural activity is likely to remain unprofitable. Unless efforts are made to encourage longer-term, socially responsible investors, rising social tensions (for example, over land issues) may accompany any diversification into commercial agriculture.

As oil declines, the problem of what to do with the massively bloated public sector (including army salaries, which account for a large chunk of the budget) will become critical. Until that problem is tackled, private-sector development is likely to continue to be depressed. And although the South may retain substantial oil income for longer than the North, it is likely to continue to depend on the northern oil export pipeline, creating a major vulnerability. However, in the longer term, if existing trade relations with both the Arab-linked North and African neighbours are developed and fostered, the region could potentially become an important gateway.

For both of these two future scenarios, the relationship between Sudan and the future state of South Sudan will be one of the key determining factors. The driving force behind that relationship, for some years, will be the need to export southern oil through the north – and the strong financial interest of the Asian-led oil consortia in keeping that route open.

3

Local Relations of Oil Development in Southern Sudan

Displacement, Environmental Impact & Resettlement

LEBEN NELSON MORO

The official end of fighting between the Government of Sudan and the SPLM/A marked a halt to the egregious human rights abuses, including massacres and mass civilian displacement, associated with Sudan's oil sector. But a significant improvement in the quality of life for local people in and around the oil areas remained elusive. Instead, old problems, including the destruction of property, uncompensated land expropriations and environmental pollution, have persisted, serving to fuel resentment against the oil companies, which have been accused of complicity in the abuses committed during the war.[1] This chapter examines local experiences and conditions in Southern Sudan's oil-bearing regions, particularly after the October 2002 ceasefire, which culminated in the signing of the CPA in January 2005. It focuses on the local relations of oil operations, rather than the role of the national or Southern governments, arguing that the situation of local people has remained precarious mainly because of the failure of oil companies to comply with all the terms of the CPA.[2]

What is particularly troubling for local communities is the failure of oil companies to properly consult and involve them in their activities. Rather, during the post-war period, oil companies have boosted their own activities without regard for the safeguards of local communities, resulting in worsening hardships in the oil areas and deepening distrust of oil activities.[3] Consequently, the livelihoods of many local people, particularly returnees, have been disrupted. No wonder, then, that some returnees from camps around Khartoum found life in the oil areas unbearable and returned to northern Sudan.[4] Nonetheless, oil companies claim to have

[1] For example, oil facilities, including roads and airstrips, were allegedly used by the SAF and allied militias to launch devastating attacks on civilians in Unity State. See John Harker, 'Human Security in Sudan: The Report of a Canadian Mission: Prepared for the Minister of Foreign Affairs,' (Ottawa: January 2000).

[2] For example, the CPA (Chapter III, Section 3.1.5) states that: 'Persons enjoying rights in land shall be consulted and their views shall duly be taken into account in respect of decisions to develop subterranean natural resources from the area in which they have rights, and shall share in the benefits of the development.'

[3] 'Atem Garang Enjoins the Building of Trust Between Citizens, Oil Companies,' *Sudan Tribune*, 19 July 2006, p. 6.

[4] Interview with the head of the Red Crescent, Bentiu, 23 February 2009.

built schools, healthcare centres, veterinary clinics and water wells in the oil areas, and hence that their activities are beneficial to local people.[5] Moreover, companies claim to observe high operational standards.[6] As will be discussed, most of these claims are disputed by local people, who perceive the projects implemented or financed by oil companies as small-scale interventions that have limited positive impact on their lives.

This chapter explores the major problems facing local populations in oil-producing areas, focusing on the experiences of the Dinka in Paloich and Maker in Melut County, and of the Shilluk in Manyo County. Both Melut and Manyo counties are located in Upper Nile State, where Asian oil companies are heavily involved in oil exploration and extraction.[7] It will also devote some attention to rising tensions in oil-rich Pariang County, Unity State, where local Dinka accuse ruling northern elites of plotting to incorporate their land into the neighbouring state of Southern Kordofan. Some of the claims by oil companies about development in the oil-bearing areas are also considered. Based mainly on research conducted in Upper Nile and Unity States in 2006 and early 2009, the chapter offers a different approach from that of Sudan's oil industry, which is mostly examined from a macro, national perspective, or through the lens of the oil companies, and without regard to local circumstances. It begins by providing an overview of local perspectives towards oil development before 1983 and the onset of the second North-South civil war. Secondly, it explores the local experiences with major oil companies after the CPA was signed, paying special attention to the experiences of the Dinka of Paloich and the Shilluk of Manyo. The third section discusses the difficulties facing displaced persons returning to the oil areas, many of which have been occupied by oil companies. Finally, the development projects implemented by oil companies under the banner of 'corporate social responsibility' are addressed.

Pre-war Attitudes towards Oil Development

The discovery of oil in Sudan in the late 1970s by the American corporation, Chevron, was warmly received, but its development was associated with serious local resentment against the oil companies. Most local people nonetheless approved of Chevron's oil development operations carried out before the outbreak of hostilities in 1983. Oil activities during the war were blamed for the escalation of violence and mass displacement. Violent

---

[5] For example, GNPOC reported that it had constructed more than 40 schools and 70 artesian wells in southern Sudan and formed an Oil Industry-Affected People Compensation Committee. S.K Kuwal,'Oil Industry-Affected People Compensation Committee,' *Sudan Vision*, 12 March 2007.

[6] GNPOC's mission statement, for instance, says that its operations 'maintain high health, safety and environmental standards' and ensure '[development of] a competent Sudanese workforce.' For details about GNPOC operating standards, see www.gnpoc.com.

displacement ended after fighting between the Sudan Armed Forces (SAF) and the SPLA ceased in 2002, but subtle displacement, environmental pollution, and other negative repercussions continued. This section focuses on the background to current local perceptions of the activities of various companies, focusing on those carried out by Chevron.

Chevron, which carried out most of Sudan's pre-war oil activities, was mostly concerned with oil, but was widely viewed as a good company. Chevron workers reportedly operated in the *khalla* (bush), paid compensation to local people negatively affected by oil activities, and provided employment opportunities. As Makwac, a Jikany Nuer local leader from Adok Bahr, remembered:

> People came from the North to look for oil in our land during President Nimairi's time in power. Oil activities started in 1980 and went on up to 1984. They came to Ler, and then to Benet, Mankien and later to Rik. They never came to the town itself but operated in the *khalla* [bush]. These foreigners were white men and *jallaba* [Northerners]. There were no Southerners amongst them.[8]

The Leek Nuer also did not have any serious problems with Chevron. In 1982, Chevron explored for oil in Durchiem Chuol, a Leek Nuer area northwest of Koch, a Jagei Nuer village, but was forced to leave in 1984. Likewise, local Dok Nuer did not have significant complaints against Chevron. Kau, a Dok Nuer from Ler County, told a story about a Chevron surveyor and a Nuer man called Kiuwok in Bang, an area that became part of the present Block 5A.

> A Chevron surveyor found oil under Kiuwok's *luak* [cattle byre]. He asked Kiuwok, if something valuable is found, *fi sika sakit bi nadi sunu?* [on the road and belonged to no one, what was it called?] Kiuwok replied that in Nuer such a thing would be called *bang*. The Chevron people renamed the place *bang*, and till now that place is known by that name. Then the surveyor told Kiuwok that there was oil under his *luak* and he should tell the value of his property. Kiuwok said it was worth three million Sudanese pounds. Chevron paid the three million and an additional two million, totalling five million, a big amount at that time. Kiuwok used two million to buy cattle, one million to buy a house, and the rest he put aside for his children. He was very happy to leave his old *luak*.[9]

Some particularly appreciated the fact that the Chevron workers did not interfere with traditional ritual sites. Chabbany, then a young Dinka boy in northern Pariang, recalled:

---

[7] The Petrodar oil consortium in Blocks 3 and 7 of Upper Nile is composed of China's National Petroleum Corporation (41%), Petronas (40%), Sudapet (8%), SINOPEC (6%) and Tri-ocean Energy (5%).

[8] Interview with Omda Makwac, Malakal, 12 August 2006.

[9] Interview with Kau, Bentiu, 23 August 2006.

I was still a young boy when Chevron people came to our *luak* and wanted to make a line/path through our shrine, which was situated close to the *luak*. They told our elders to either relocate or destroy the shrine and take money as compensation for the damage. Our elders rejected the demand of the oil workers. The Chevron people heeded the view of our elders and, instead, made the line/path to pass in a different location. This happened in 1982. I still have vivid recollections of the event.[10]

Chevron was also praised for recruiting local people to work as labourers. But not everyone appreciated the company's actions. Some were irritated by the fact that its officials did not fully consult local people, 'appropriated' land and destroyed property.[11] Notwithstanding these concerns, there was widespread support for Chevron activities. This changed after 1983, when the company was seen as allying itself too closely with the central government in the war.[12] In 1984, rebels killed some expatriate staff of the company at its Rubkona base, forcing it to halt activities. In a bid to protect its investments and workers, Chevron increasingly relied on protection provided by the SAF and allied militia forces.[13] This provided southern rebels with more reasons to target oil facilities and workers. In 1992, Chevron gave up operating in Sudan and sold off its assets. Subsequently most unskilled oil workers were reportedly recruited from northern Sudan, fuelling anger amongst local people.

Mounting Local Hardship after the CPA

The Government of Sudan recruited new companies from Europe, Canada and Asia to continue oil exploration and drilling in the midst of the war. Sudan exported oil for the first time in 1999, but violence against civilians reached unprecedented levels. Oil facilities, such as roads and airstrips, enhanced the capacity of the SAF and militia groups to wage war and commit atrocities against civilians, most of whom fled to

[10] Interview with Chabbany, Malakal, 6 November 2006.
[11] Chevron operated within the territory granted by the central government. However, the local people were not fully informed about the arrangement reached between the company and the central government.
[12] Abel Alier, *Southern Sudan: Too Many Agreements Dishonoured* 2nd Edition (Reading: Ithaca Press, 1992).
[13] Chevron reportedly provided financial assistance to Arab militias so as to secure oil activities from rebel attacks. See Deborah Scroggins, *Emma's War: Love, Betrayal, and Death in the Sudan* (London: HarperCollins, 2002), p. 88.
[14] Much has been written on the mass displacement of civilians from the oil areas during the war. See, for example, Amnesty International, *Sudan: The Human Price of Oil* (London: Amnesty International Publications, 2000); Human Rights Watch, *Sudan, Oil and Human Rights* (New York: Human Rights Watch, 2003); Leben N. Moro, 'Oil, War and Forced Migration in Sudan,' *St Antony's International Review*, Vol. 2, Iss. 1 (2006), pp. 75-90.

northern Sudan.[14] After the war, egregious violations of civilians ended but local complaints against the actions of the oil companies did not cease. The central government Ministry of Energy and Mining (MEM) and the oil companies rapidly expanded oil operations, earning the government a fortune but causing hardship for local people. Many southern Sudanese, however, are suspicious of the motives of the MEM and the main companies involved in this oil boom, CNPC, Petronas, and ONGC. One southern Sudanese geologist, for example, remarked:

> The government is trying to drain all the oil in the South before the self-determination vote in 2011. People suspect that the output of oil exceeds the amounts reported and that secret reservoirs have been constructed in the north to store the excess oil. Chinese companies are involved in the deception.[15]

This view is supported by northern Sudanese aid workers active in Upper Nile State in 2006. One claimed that the central government had dramatically increased oil production in order to exhaust the estimated 3 billion barrels of reserves in Southern Sudan before 2011 and the CPA's scheduled referendum.[16] In the meantime, local communities in the oil areas have been venting their anger against the Asian national oil companies, whose burgeoning infrastructure has occupied large tracts of land, destroyed property, worsened land and border disputes, despoiled the environment, and failed to provide local jobs.

Dispossession of land

In the war years, the SAF and allied militias, in a bid to protect the oil companies from rebel attacks, violently displaced civilians from the oil areas. After the CPA was signed, mass displacement of civilians ceased, but the MEM and the oil companies have continued to expropriate land without providing compensation. An attempt to force the inhabitants of oil-rich Paloich, in Melut County of Upper Nile State, to relocate to a place they did not like is a case in point. Paloich used to be an insignificant location along the Melut-Malakal road and is inhabited by Ageer Dinka (Joo subsection). During the war, the area was occupied by the SAF and most of the local people fled to other areas. After the fighting ended, displaced people gradually returned to the area. Moreover, the rapid growth of oil activities in the area attracted jobseekers from near and far, as well as northern traders.

Petrodar Operating Company (PDOC), the operator of Blocks 3 and 7, dug its first exploratory wildcat well in Paloich in 2002. From July 2003,

---

[15] Interview with Southern geologist, Khartoum, 6 July 2006.
[16] These opinions have been more or less corroborated elsewhere. For example, *Africa Confidential* (7 October 2005) reported: 'The Islamist group calling for separation of North and South, led by President Omer Hassan Ahmed el Bashir's uncle El Tayeb Mustafa, is still given free rein, signifying that separation is seen as a policy option, once most of the oil has been sucked out of the South.'

it pressured the residents of Paloich town to leave the area.[17] The MEM and PDOC claimed that Paloich town was situated 'above oil lakes'.[18] An evictions campaign had already been implemented in many locations around Paloich town. After the SAF-SPLA ceasefire in October 2002, it became difficult to evict the Paloich town inhabitants outright.

The MEM and PDOC chose Leweny Alei, a village located about five kilometres south of Paloich, as the new residential area for the people who would be displaced. PDOC built a school, a healthcare unit and a mosque in Leweng Alei, and placed a signpost by the roadside bearing the words 'New Palouge'. It then despatched vehicles, accompanied by the SAF, to Paloich town. No one agreed to board the trucks. According to a member of the National Assembly from Melut County, local people refused to relocate because they had not been consulted; the new location belonged to a rival Ageer Dinka clan and was frequently flooded during the rainy season. Furthermore, there was no promise of compensation,[19] and the locals were very determined to get adequate compensation before leaving their areas. Many had returned from northern agricultural schemes, where they had learned about the more generous compensation packages offered to northerners required by the state to leave their home areas.

The dramatic arrival of trucks guarded by government soldiers only bolstered the opposition to the relocation. It was reminiscent of the violent relocation of displaced southerners from Khartoum to desolate camps on the outskirts of the national capital under the guise of urban renewal. Indeed, rumours spread that the people who carried out the violent relocations in Khartoum had moved to Paloich to do the same thing.[20] The thought that the brutal relocations witnessed in northern Sudan were about to be repeated in Southern Sudan during peace time fuelled violence. Some businesses in Paloich town owned by northern traders were reportedly set on fire.

The relocation plan was unsuccessful. This failure was to be expected, for PDOC had not changed the way it conducted business. Indeed, the company continued to expropriate land with no compensation. The locals, for example, complained that 600 farms had been taken by oil companies in the Paloich area since peace returned.[21] PDOC failed to involve the local people in decisions pertaining to land, and instead sought the help of the SAF to coerce the people into moving. Not only did it violate international standards on the relocation of people from areas of resource extraction, it also contravened the CPA.

---

[17] European Coalition on Oil in Sudan, *Oil Development in Northern Upper Nile, Sudan* (Utrecht: ECOS, 2006).

[18] D.D. Bul, 'Oil Exploration and Exploitation in Northern Upper Nile: An Assessment of the Long-term Impacts on the Area' (Renk: ECS, 2005), p. 7.

[19] Interview with Laila Ajuat, MP in the National Assembly, Omdurman, 15 July 2006.

[20] Annual Nutrition Survey, *Annual Needs Assessment in Shilluk Kingdom and Sobat County* (Malakal: World Food Programme, 2003).

[21] G. Willow, 'Faluj Residents Don't Want to be Resettled,' *The Juba Post* 3 (38), 28 September – 5 October 2005.

Destruction of property

The CPA triggered a surge in seismic activity, putting severe strain on local communities. The suffering of the Dinka of Maker, a small village on the banks of the Khor Adar River in Melut County, and the Shilluk of Manyo County illustrates the considerable danger of seismic activity to the livelihoods of local people, many of them recent returnees from other places. Maker was under SPLA control during the war, and most of the time was cut off from the outside world. After the war ended, PDOC extended oil exploration to the outskirts of the village. In March 2006, local leaders stated that they had no contact with PDOC and would not leave their homes if asked to do so.[22] As more returnees come to their original villages to reclaim their expropriated lands, the prospect of conflicts with PDOC will increase.

PDOC also caused significant difficulties for the inhabitants of Manyo, a county on the eastern banks of the Nile. On the west of the Nile is Melut County. In the north, Manyo shares borders with the state of Southern Kordofan in northern Sudan. According to the county's commissioner, Ayok Agat, the local population numbered about 200,000, most of them recent returnees.[23] The PDOC workers arrived in Manyo in March 2006 and began making many seismic lines. A southern geologist working for GNPOC said 'these paths/lines are problematic because they have to be straight. They go for hundreds of kilometres, destroying crops, fruit trees, and houses in their way.'[24] Indeed, the Manyo inhabitants lost many of their acacia trees, the source of gum arabic, and a few homes. The oil workers reportedly recorded the damaged trees, destroyed homes and other losses and promised to pay compensation. However, the promise was not fulfilled.

Mindful of rising opposition, PDOC held a community meeting when seismic work was already in progress. *Nazir* Ogwal, a paramount chief, said the Chinese oil workers and their Arab colleagues were told to stop work and advised to seek permission from the Government of Southern Sudan in Juba.[25] Commissioner Ayok Agat also said that he repeated the same message to the Chinese. However, the Chinese did not seek permission from Juba but instead went to Malakal, the capital of Upper Nile State, and brought back a letter from the NCP governor of Upper Nile,[26] which reportedly gave them authority to explore for oil in the area. The local people were left reeling with bitterness against the Chinese and their own leader in Malakal.

Environmental pollution

Local inhabitants of oil areas have been complaining about the un-explained deaths of animals and new human afflictions. Commissioner

---

[22] Group interview with Chief Akon Dol and several elders of Maker village, Melut County, 12 March 2006.

[23] Interview with Commissioner Ayok Agat, Manyo, 20 April 2006.

[24] Interview with Southern geologist working for GNPOC, Khartoum, 21 July 2006.

Mabek of Pariang County, for example, claims that animals in his county have been dying of mysterious diseases and a number of people are falling ill with heart problems, which used to be unknown before the arrival of the oil companies.[27]

The MEM insists that the government is aware of the environmental problems associated with the fast growth of the oil sector and has adopted laws to deal with potential problems.[28] The Oil Resources Law of 1998 stipulates that companies intending to operate in Sudan should 'adhere to safety, anti-pollution and anti-ecological risks regulations in addition to compliance with the industry's internationally acceptable technical principles'.[29] The government has also enacted the Environmental Safety Act 2000. Furthermore, the MEM says that regulations regarding environmental protection have been incorporated into oil exploration, production and refining contracts and agreements.[30] Unfortunately, the contracts are secret.

Recent reports, however, have cast doubt on the accuracy of claims by the MEM. Investigations by committees in the National Assembly and Southern Sudan Legislative Assembly (SSLA) have raised additional concerns about the environmental consequences of oil development. These committees found significant environmental problems caused by unsafe dumping of water, mud and other waste in the open. One problem highlighted by both committees was that no one knew – or was willing to reveal – the levels of pollutants found in the 250,000 barrels of water produced from oil extraction and released into Heglig every day. According to an ecologist who conducted an environmental assessment in Heglig, 'produced water requires careful management because it contains harmful chemicals. Unfortunately, safety standards are not complied with because of the rampant corruption.'[31]

Oil companies claim that they carefully 'cleaned' the water through a long process before releasing it into the environment, according to Odwar, a geologist and the deputy chairman of the Energy and Industry Committee in the SSLA. When he asked the oil managers at Heglig whether they would be willing to drink the 'cleaned water', they said no. Moreover, he said that 'crude oil was spilt all over the place, at drilling sites, along pipelines and so on'.[32] Hussein Mar, the chairman of the Energy and Mining Committee in the National Assembly, was also sceptical about safety claims by the oil companies and emphasised the urgent need for scientific studies by reputable and independent experts.[33]

[25] Interview with *Nazir* (Paramount Chief) Ogwal, Athidwei, Shilluk kingdom, 22 April 2006.
[26] Interview with Commisioner Ayok Agat, *op. cit.*
[27] Interview with Commissioner Mabek Mading, Pariang County, 10 September 2006.
[28] 'Ministry of Energy: Environmental Protection Priority', *Sudan Vision* (2007). Available from: <http://www.sudanvisiondaily.com/>
[29] *Ibid.*
[30] *Ibid.*
[31] Interview with the ecologist who carried out the study, Khartoum, 27 June 2006.
[32] Interview with Henry Odwar, Juba, 4 October 2006.
[33] Interview with Hussein Mar Nyuot, Omdurman, 11 July 2006.

The fear of environmental pollution has been made worse by incidents of carelessness by oil company workers. For example, dumping of sacks of poisonous chemicals in Koch, located 70 km south of Bentiu town, led to fatalities. A government official explained what happened:

> There was a problem caused by *sumut* [poisonous material] in Dolwok, Koch County. *Sumut* looks like sugar or salt but is poisonous. It is used in drilling to soften rocks. On 4 June 2006, an oil company driver dropped six bags of *sumut* by the roadside. Local people collected the sacks and took them away. Some persons tasted the stuff, thinking that it was sugar or salt. Immediately, they lost their teeth and tongues. Five people died instantly.[34]

The incident might be blamed on individual carelessness. It could also be a warning of serious but less obvious environmental problems. The Jagei Nuer, who occupy the region where the accidental pollution occurred, have also been complaining about the unexplained deaths of animals and hitherto unknown human afflictions. They claim that more than 1,000 people in Koch have suffered from unknown diseases.[35] In February 2008, a German NGO took water samples from the area for analysis in Germany. The result revealed a very high level of salts, strontium and nitrate and, according to the NGO, children under six who drink water containing this level of nitrate can become seriously ill.[36]

Unfortunately, the oil companies and the government have made no efforts to allay local fears. The government may have an environmental legal framework but there is no credible enforcement mechanism. Although a department has been created in the MEM to deal with environmental matters, there is no information about the implementation of environmental laws and regulations. Until local people can sue an oil company or the MEM and be assured a reasonable chance of receiving a fair judgement, the law will simply be a well-intended paper statute. There is no sign that the return of peace has made it possible for local people to sue the oil companies and the MEM under the current legal framework.

Unemployment
The complaints by people in the oil areas about unemployment and discrimination have grown louder since the return of peace. Unfortunately, the oil companies and government officials have not taken steps to address the problem. Although there are no figures to back up the complaints, it seems that most of the people in Paloich have failed to gain jobs. A local nurse, Ayul, said that women had to brew alcohol to make

[34] Interview with Joseph Reik, Bentiu, 23 August 2006.
[35] Bogonko Bosire, 'Sudan villagers, environment suffer from oil boom', *Mail & Guardian*, 4 March 2008.
[36] Hoffnungszeichen, 'Drinking Water in Oilfields of Sudan Contaminated with Brine', press release, 27 February 2008.

ends meet in many homes because the men were idle.[37] Employment by the *serikat* (companies), she complained, was handled in Khartoum, not Paloich. Unemployment is not limited to Paloich; there were also complaints about the same issue in different parts of Unity and Upper Nile states.

Reactions to this exasperating situation have taken several directions. Firstly, some people gave up trying to look for jobs with the oil companies.[38] Secondly, some took the path of confrontation with the companies by causing disruptions to their operations. One MP said that she had to persuade the angry local people to allow PDOC to operate in the Paloich area.[39] Thirdly, some desperate people migrated to Northern Sudan to work as labourers in agricultural schemes. As a UN report on Melut observed: 'Most people are displaced and working on the mechanized scheme around Renk areas. They have very little opportunities of obtaining jobs in the oilfields.'[40] Some of the complaints against oil companies in Sudan are concerned with unfavourable working conditions. Southerners employed by the companies often felt maltreated by northern employees in managerial positions. One example was a stand-off between southerners and the field management at Thar Jath oilfield, in Koch County. A local official from Ler County explained the problem:

> The oil company divided the employees into two categories: Northern Sudanese received 25,000 pounds per day and lived in the company compound but Southerners received only 18,000 pounds per day and lived outside the company compound. The Southerners became upset and beat up some people in the company. The governor ordered that all employees should be paid 25,000 pounds per day and live outside the company compound.[41]

Altogether, the loss and destruction of land and property, coupled with the environmental degradation and lack of economic benefits from the oil sector in Southern Sudan has fed disdain towards the oil companies among local populations. Conditions for southerners returning to the region after the CPA have been just as dire.

Returnees' Woes

Oil companies have occupied large tracts of land used for human settlement, farming or grazing and, oblivious to local concerns about land, have expanded their operations.[42] As the companies occupy more land,

---

[37] Interview with Ayul, Paloich, 11 March 2006.
[38] Interview with a young Dinka, Pariak boma, Paloich Payam, 3 March 2006, and group interview with young Maban men, Adar Yel, 15 March 2006.
[39] Interview with Laila Ajuat MP, *op. cit.*
[40] WFP Malakal sub-office, *Malakal Kodok Meluit Barge Corridor report,* 7 November, 2005.
[41] Interview with local official from Ler, Bentiu, 23 August 2006.
[42] Leben Moro, 'Over a Barrel,' *New Internationalist,* 401 (June), 2007.

many local people have come under increasing pressure to leave their original locations and some post-CPA returnees have found it harder to resettle in their original home areas. Local opposition to the companies has consequently intensified.

In Paloich town, anger against PDOC has been running high for a long time. Moreover, many local people, including the member of the SSLA representing Melut County, have claimed that some returnees were unable to settle in their original locations due to oil wells, excavation works and oil infrastructure. Paloich Airport, for instance, is built on destroyed villages. Returnees were not allowed to enter the airport area. Only a few people were permitted to plant crops near the airport in the rainy season. According to local leaders, stranded returnees had to live with relatives in Paloich town, swelling the numbers of people needing humanitarian assistance.

Far south of Paloich town, at Kilo Ashra (Wunuong), 239 Dinka returnees from northern Sudan were forced to flee after some 850 Mabaan returnees, who had come from Ethiopia and settled in 2005, destroyed the shelters they had put up in the location in March 2006. These groups of returnees had rival claims to the same location. Dinka officials in Melut, however, blamed Sudan security agents for stirring up the dispute. The security agents had been posted to the location to protect the oil companies, whose activities caused most of the land disputes in the region. Another group of Dinka were not able to return to Leweng, located between Paloich and Kilo Ashra, because the SAF had taken over the village. During the war, the army evicted the inhabitants of the village who then sought refuge in the forests in Maker and Bom. After the war ended, they asked the army to leave their area, according to the local leader of this group of returnees. The army ignored the demand and the returnees had no choice but to settle on the nearby lowland, which is prone to flooding in the rainy season.

At Pariak, situated between Paloich and Renk, a serious land dispute concerned the right of the local people to use a *gezira* (island) in the Nile. A member of the Upper Nile State Assembly from the area said that the *gezira* was shared by Shilluk living on the west bank of the Nile, and Dinka, inhabiting the east bank. During the war, the Shilluk and *defa shabi* (Popular Defence Force) rented the *gezira* to Falata (Ombororo and Fulani) nomads from northern Sudan. After the war, the commissioner of Melut ordered the *omda* (chief) of Pariak to lease the *gezira* to Falata nomads. Some local people rejected the arrangement, insisting on access to the *gezira* to grow crops and graze animals. The *omda* brought in policemen from Melut to suppress the dissent. One protester was taken to Melut, jailed for six months and punished with 40 horsewhip lashes in February 2006. The incident was minor, in reality, but has implications for future disputes over land involving oil companies. If local officials can side with Falata, it is also possible for them to side with oil companies.

Land is also a controversial issue in Unity State. Some people were unable to return to their ancestral homelands because the oil companies had expropriated them. On 14 April 2007, for example, 265 displaced people arrived in Rubkona from Khartoum, to find 'their land is gone'.[43] Moreover, the oil companies had drastically reconfigured local geographies and histories, to the extent that many returnees were unable to identify their places of origin, according to the UNMIS official in charge of the repatriation, reintegration and rehabilitation of returnees in the state.[44] Traditional ritual sites, unique trees and other landmarks had been destroyed, making it hard for people to find their old villages. The Commissioner of Pariang County said that new maps had been produced by the government with different names from the old, familiar ones, and that returnees consequently faced significant difficulties in reaching their original villages.[45]

Even more disturbingly, oil companies, openly and more discretely, barred some people from returning to their villages. In July 2006 some returnees were not allowed to settle in their original villages in the oil-rich Heglig.[46] After pressure by Unity State government, the oil companies reluctantly allowed the returnees to settle in the area. However, in some places the oil companies pressured companies drilling for water to halt operations. Lack of water would discourage returnees from settling in locations where the oil companies do not want people to settle. According to Commissioner Mabek, the government in Bentiu was seeking to hire companies that were not prone to manipulation by oil companies.[47] As refugees and IDPs return to the oil areas, tensions will rise. It is probable that returnees will insist on the return of their original lands or compensation for losses suffered. Development projects carried out by the oil companies have provided certain local benefits but fail to consider their essential needs and demands.

Development Projects

Before leaving Sudan, Talisman and Lundin claimed that their oil operations were beneficial to local people.[48] The companies had indeed implemented community-based development projects under the banner of 'corporate social responsibility'. With India's ONGC Videsh and Petronas of Malaysia buying the abandoned shares of the Western companies, only some of the social projects were continued. Most local people,

---

[43] I. Anthony, 'Rubknona Returnees Come Home But Their Land is Gone', *The Juba Post* 3(15), 20-27 April 2007, p. 17.

[44] Interview with Baptiste Martin, UNMIS returnee, rehabilitation and reintegration Officer, Bentiu, in Rubkona, 7 September 2006.

[45] Interview with Commissioner Mabek Mading, *op. cit.*

[46] *Ibid.*

[47] *Ibid.*

[48] J. Sheppard and R Manhas, 'Sudan Experience offers Corporate-Responsibility Lessons, Opportunities', *Oil & Gas* Vol. 98, 46 (13 November 2000), p. 70.

however, perceive the projects as public relations gestures. Some of the projects in the areas of transportation and electricity, water, education and healthcare can be assessed here.

Transportation and electricity
Most investment by oil companies has gone into improving roads, power stations and other infrastructure essential for oil development. The road system in the oil concession areas is far superior relative to other parts of Southern Sudan. The road connecting Malakal to Khartoum, for example, is usable throughout the year. Moreover, oil companies have been working on the infrastructure in Melut town and other locations. A water purification station has been constructed, as well as a power system. Electricity pylons have been placed along the Melut-Paloich road and along small roads leading to oil wells. However, the signposts on these roads bore foreign names such as ASAD, Teima and Rasan. An elderly man claimed that certain oil wells were named after northern *suhada* (Muslim martyrs), who, in his view, were war criminals.[49]

Unity State has also benefited from oil infrastructure. Several counties are connected to the main towns of Bentiu and Rubkona with regular means of transport. The recent changes in Heglig are truly eye-catching. Many modern electricity pylons have been constructed along the main road linking Bentiu and Heglig. However, these carry electricity to oil company compounds and other oil facilities. In addition, Heglig has one of the best airports in Southern Sudan, servicing mostly local and foreign oil workers.

Aimed mostly at facilitating oil extraction, some of the infrastructure has done more harm than good. The El Salaam Bridge over Bahr al-Ghazal river, for example, caused significant disruption to the local economy of Bentiu and surrounding areas. Local people complained that the bridge has blocked the movement of boats and barges. Oil companies also constructed dams on the river at Wangkei and Abiemnom, which affected the movement of people and goods and caused environmental problems. A senior civil servant in the governor's office claimed that between 40 and 60 streams in Unity State had been blocked by roads, causing flooding in some places and shortages of water in others.[50] The damming of Khor Adar, Melut County, also had negative repercussions for some local communities. I heard bitter complaints by local people about the reduced quantity and quality of the water. The amount of fish in the river has fallen. In addition, some parts of the river have been flooded, while other areas have little water. Satellite pictures have confirmed the negative environmental changes caused by the activities of oil companies.[51] One of the consequences of the environmental changes is low crop production.

[49] Interview with Chuol Awer, a local leader, Paloich, 11 March 2006.
[50] Interview with the senior civil servant at the Governor's office, 4 September 2006.
[51] ECOS, *Oil Development in Northern Upper Nile, op. cit.*

Water
Water shortage is a pressing problem during the dry season in many parts of the oil areas. Oil companies have been assisting some communities by digging wells or using trucks to deliver water, such as by GNPOC trucks to the inhabitants of Pariang town. Moreover, GNPOC claims that it has dug water wells and constructed hand pumps in its concessions.[52] It seems that most of the permanent sources of water are located in areas of Heglig where northern nomads have settled. Dinka communities mostly get water from temporary sources, such as water delivery tankers. Oil companies were reluctant to build permanent water sources for local people; they could not easily turn them off if 'local people failed to behave'.[53] However, the most serious problem with the water delivery tankers was that they carried limited volumes of water compared with the huge demand in the areas covered. The people of Paloich, for instance, received water only once every two to four days. Moreover, this is not a reliable form of assistance, and could easily be withdrawn if oil companies have differences with local people.

Education
Oil companies have provided some support for education in their concession areas. In general, the support has been aimed mainly at furthering the political and religious agenda of the government. One example is Petronas, which played the Islamic card to promote its interests in Sudan, readily promoting the government's Islamisation policies.[54] I visited a basic school in Melut town, and learned from its headmaster about the failure of PDOC to help despite repeated requests for support. PDOC, in which Petronas has a big stake, instead constructed an Islamic school managed by the Da'wa Islamia. According to the school's headmaster, over 70 children and young adults, between the ages of five and 18, lived in dormitories in the school.[55] Although its services were appreciated by some people, Da'wa Islamia was perceived by many as a promoter of the religious policies of the government.

There is also a strong presence of Islamic organisations in Unity State, the most active being Da'wa Islamia, Al Birr (Benevolence) and Salaam Al Isa. Most people in Unity State also have mixed feelings about the Islamic schools. A local leader said that some parents withdrew their children from the Islamic schools and registered them in schools teaching in English after the return of peace.

The MEM built the Machakos Basic School in Bentiu. A relatively good school, it has eight classes and enrols 1,800 pupils, most of them in class one. A Kenyan teacher in the school says that she has been teaching 1,300

---

[52] See, for example, *Oil & Gas*, 8 January 2006, p. 8.
[53] Interview with UN official, Rubkona, 7 September 2006.
[54] 'Oil: Risky Money', *Africa Confidential*, 43 (43), 22 March 2006, p. 6.
[55] Interview with the headmaster of the Da'wa School, Melut, 13 March 2006.

pupils in class one.[56] Moreover, she says that enrolment went up due to the introduction of free education in the beginning of May 2006. Another secondary school in Bentiu town was established with funds provided by White Nile Petroleum Operating Company (WNPOC), in which Petronas had a big stake. The school has three permanent buildings and two temporary structures made of papyrus mats and plastic sheets. Young men studying in the school said that it had 600 students and 20 Ugandan and Kenyan teachers, who managed the English section of the school.

The support by the oil companies and the MEM of education was considered to be insufficient and aimed at Islamisation. The State Minister of Education said:

> Petronas has a department of community development but it works on its own. We do not have information about its activities. Its development projects serve its own interests, including promoting Islam, rather than promoting the good of the community.[57]

The Director General of the Ministry of Education also expressed serious misgivings about the support received from Petronas and other oil companies.[58] He said oil companies had financed the construction of schools in several counties. In Koch County, Petronas built six classrooms, each taking only 25 pupils. In an annoyed tone, he said:

> The classrooms are small. Petronas claims to be introducing modern education but fails to realise that most of our children are out of school because of lack of space. We want all our children to get some education but Petronas thinks differently because it does not consult. We are concerned about educating our people, not the so-called modern classrooms.

It is clear that oil companies supported the education of young people. However, their assistance failed to yield significant positive outcomes because it was meagre and did not actively involve the participation of the local communities and local government institutions.

Healthcare

Petronas and ONGC have supported healthcare programmes in several locations under the banner of promoting community development. Petronas operates a number of primary healthcare units. However, the Unity State Minister of Health had almost no information about the activities of oil companies in the health sector.[59]

The most significant health intervention by oil companies in Unity State is the Heglig hospital, which mainly serves oil workers. The hospital in Bentiu was jointly built by the MEM, Lundin Oil Company and White

---

[56] Interview with the Kenyan teacher, Rubkona, 7 September 2006.
[57] Interview with Dau Majok, the State Minister of Education, Bentiu, 28 August 2006.
[58] Interview with James Yut, the Director General of Education, 29 August 2006.
[59] Interview with Andrea Daod, the State Minister of Health, Bentiu, 29 August 2006.

Nile Petroleum Operating Company.[60] The quality of services provided by the hospital is poor. Moreover, some of the buildings have not been completed. According to the Minister of Health, the State Governor expelled the contractor for refusing to disclose the details of the contract it had signed with the MEM. Corruption might have been part of the reason for the secrecy.[61]

The oil companies have clearly extended much-needed medical support to people. This assistance, however, is a small gesture aimed at winning support from politically powerful people. Socially responsible assistance would have targeted the serious health problems, such as malaria, chest problems and diarrhoea, which afflict the most vulnerable people in the oil areas. Altogether, while there have been numerous development projects undertaken by the oil companies, local communities have had little say in how these projects have been implemented, thus frustrating the ultimate benefit they can provide.

Conclusion

This chapter has analysed the conditions of local people in the main oil areas of Southern Sudan following the 2002 ceasefire. The return of peace in the form of the CPA enabled the oil companies to expand the search for, and extraction of, oil, but the concerns of local people continued to be ignored. Oil companies, mostly originating from Asia, did not fundamentally change the way they operate after the end of hostilities. Not only did they violate some aspects of the CPA regarding consultation with local communities, they also continue to neglect international codes and standards adopted by the oil industry. In Paloich, locals were asked to relocate to another place to make way for oil development, but refused to budge. In Manyo, oil exploration exerted a significant burden on the locals; some lost their homes due to seismic activity. Returnees also ran into serious difficulties, and certain places in which they hoped to resettle had been occupied by oil infrastructure.

Oil companies insist that their activities promote development – in terms of schools, health centres, or water points – and cause no harm to people.[62] Nonetheless, local problems, such as land expropriation, environmental pollution and unemployment, continue to mount. Some development projects have indeed been implemented by oil companies but their positive impacts, if any, are limited. Such projects have been implemented without consultation with the intended beneficiaries, and are mostly small philanthropic interventions. The failure of oil companies to

[60] 'Al Bashir Inaugurates Development Projects in Unity State,' *Sudan Vision*, 21 February 2005.
[61] Interview with Andrea Daod, *op cit.*
[62] International Crisis Group, 'Sudan Comprehensive Peace Agreement: the Long Road Ahead,' *Africa Report* 106, 31 March 2006.

provide significant support to people in the oil areas has fuelled feelings of injustice. Consequently, the frustration of southerners towards the Asian companies is growing.[63] Oil was a curse during the war years, but it could have become a source of hope for development in peacetime. So far, this has not proved to be the case. Rather, the precarious situation of local communities in oil-bearing regions could lead to violence, undermining peace and the future of the oil industry. An independent South Sudan will have to deal seriously with the worsening local grievances so as to avert a communal backlash against the oil companies and the government.

[63] Moro, 'Over a Barrel,' *op. cit.*

4

India in Sudan Troubles in an African Oil 'Paradise'

LUKE A. PATEY

In May 2008, a group of Indian oilmen found themselves in a rather precarious situation. Outside the town of Heglig in Sudan, the four oil technicians had been surrounded at gunpoint. The armed men who attacked them were from the local Misseriya ethnic group living in the oil area of Southern Kordofan state. They had seen little benefit from oil development since the central government in Khartoum first began to export oil from the region in 1999, and now in response were directing their grievances directly towards the oil companies.

After hearing about the kidnapping, the Indian Ambassador in Khartoum, Deepak Vohra, quickly set in motion negotiations to free the hostages through the local authorities. He assured the Sudanese, Indian and international press that the men were 'in fine fettle'.[1] A week after the kidnapping, the Sudanese Ambassador to India was summoned to the Ministry of External Affairs in New Delhi and urged to ensure that the Sudanese authorities were doing everything in their power to resolve the issue.[2] But it was not until 74 days after the ordeal began that the kidnapping came to an end. Two of the Indian oilmen managed to elude their kidnappers, while a ransom was paid for the release of another. The fourth oil technician, however, was thought to have become lost in the wilderness after also escaping, and was presumed dead.

The Indian oilmen were working for a company under contract with the Greater Nile Petroleum Operating Company (GNPOC). India's national overseas oil company, ONGC Videsh, or OVL for short, held a quarter stake in the joint venture. It was not the first time companies in Sudan's oil sector had been threatened since the signing of the Comprehensive Peace Agreement ending the North-South civil war in January 2005. The Darfur rebel group, the Justice and Equality Movement, had attacked a Chinese-run oil field in South Darfur in October 2007.[3] It was also not an uncommon event for Indian oilmen to experience, even when working at home. In the summer of 2002, separatist

[1] 'Four Indian oil workers kidnapped in Sudan's Abyei', *Agence France-Presse*, 16 May 2008.
[2] 'Kidnappings: India calls Sudan envoy', *Indian Express*, 22 May 2008.
[3] Mohamed Osman, 'Darfur Rebels Attack Oil Field, Warn Chinese to Leave Sudan', *The Washington Post*, 26 October 2007.

militants in Assam province of India killed six workers from the Oil and Natural Gas Corporation, OVL's parent company.[4] But it was the first time Indians had been threatened by the often violent politics of oil in Sudan – a sign for the Indian government and its national oil company that Sudan was not just an oil paradise in Africa.

Since entering Sudan in 2003, there was much reason for OVL to be jubilant. In purchasing the former stake of the Canadian oil company Talisman, it gained access to Sudan's main oilfields just when production and international oil prices began to soar. At the 2005 India-Africa Project Partnership Conclave in New Delhi, an annual event to promote business between India and Africa, the executive director of the company, V. Ravindranath, said that OVL was 'looking very keenly at many countries in Africa and hoped to repeat the Sudan experience'.[5] And no wonder; almost overnight OVL's oil assets in Sudan became the most profitable venture in the company's history.

Sudan also represented a boon for the Indian government. It was proof that New Delhi was doing its utmost to ensure India's energy security by providing diplomatic support for OVL to enter Sudan. When the first oil from OVL's concessions in Sudan arrived by tanker at a Mangalore port in May 2003, the then Deputy Prime Minister, Shri L.K. Advani, proclaimed that 'this is not imported oil, this is India's oil'.[6] However, despite the public euphoria over Indo-Sudan relations since oil brought the two countries closer together in 2003, behind the scenes a more troublesome situation exists.

This chapter strives to show that modern relations between India and Sudan surrounding the African country's oil sector have faced a number of political and economic challenges. Rather than analyse the relationship through the prism of Sudanese politics, the chapter focuses on the debates and strategies of the Indian government and national oil company OVL in entering and operating in Sudan. The chapter begins by examining the initial threats to the Indian oil company's ambitions at home in India. Factions in the Indian government opposed OVL's investment. Second, it describes resistance to the investment in Sudan. The Chinese and Malaysian national oil companies already active in the African country made an effort to ensure that their Indian counterpart would be excluded. Third, it explains how OVL's Sudan assets went on to represent the company's most prized assets. Finally, the chapter considers the complications that arose for India's oil interests in Sudan. OVL was not able to capitalise on all its objectives in Sudan and increasingly the risks of operating in the politically unstable and physically insecure country began to materialise.

---

[4] 'Sudan's civil strife doesn't deter Indian oil explorer', *Calgary Herald*, 9 July 2002.
[5] Manish Chan, 'India-Africa: Partnering a new future', *Indo-Asian News Service*, http://www.ians.in/, 5 March 2005.
[6] 'Talisman marks end of era with completion of Sudan sale', *Oil and Gas Journal*, Vol. 101, No. 14 (7 April 2003).

Making the Deal

Entering Sudan was no cakewalk for India's national oil company OVL. Rather, it had to face down opponents both at home and abroad. Oil was strongly associated with armed conflict in Sudan when OVL first won approval to invest from the Indian government's Cabinet Committee on Economic Affairs in late 2002. The killing and displacement of thousands of civilians by the Sudan Armed Forces and pro-government militias in and around southern oilfields, where the majority of Sudan's reserves are located, had intensified the North-South civil war between Khartoum and the SPLA in the late 1990s and early 2000s. But in India the debate over the risks of OVL's engagement in Sudan predominantly focused on the company's safety, not the morality of investing in an area where heinous human rights abuses had taken place.

Two opinion pieces in one of India's leading periodicals, *The Hindu*, depicted the overall ethical debate on entering Sudan.[7] On the one hand, Ninan Koshy, a political commentator and social activist, saw the Indian state as having committed a 'grave error' by entering the 'ethnically-cleansed areas' of Sudan's oilfields. On the other hand, one of India's leading foreign policy experts, Raja C. Mohan, saw the investment as a necessary evil. India needed to improve its energy security position if it wanted to compete with China, and the oil business was not for the faint-hearted. The events that unfolded in Indian political circles following the duelling opinion pieces supported the priority of capturing oil resources abroad; energy security trumped ethical concerns. But opposition to the OVL deal would come from other sources.

Talisman and other Western oil companies were leaving Sudan around the same time as the Khartoum government and SPLA rebels were fostering peace. In late July 2002 the two sides signed the Machakos protocol which provided the framework for the eventual Comprehensive Peace Agreement. Nonetheless, at the time, insecurity was still a major concern among oil companies in Sudan. OVL's request for approval of the $720 million investment from the Cabinet Committee on Economic Affairs faced multiple domestic opponents. Some members of the Indian parliament and ruling BJP Cabinet regarded committing hundreds of millions of dollars of a developing country's budget to a war-torn region as a 'risky venture'.[8] If peace were to fail in Sudan, and it often did, OVL risked losing its investment. Questions were also raised about the rationale of investing in a country ruled by an Islamist government that had once harboured international terrorists such as Osama bin Laden. Having its own problems with domestic security, India did not want to encourage inter-

---

[7] Ninan Koshy, 'India joins Sudan's war'; C. Raja Mohan, 'Sakhalin to Sudan: India's energy diplomacy', *The Hindu*, 24 June 2002.

[8] 'Gift of the Nile', *Outlook*, 1 July 2002.

national terrorism. Furthermore, contractors in the Indian oil sector lobbied that the investment would threaten the scope of ONGC's activities at home if such funding were provided to its subsidiary OVL abroad. Overall, at the heart of the Indian opposition against OVL entering Sudan was a factor common to the process of many foreign policy decisions, domestic politics.

Political rivalries at home threatened to derail the Sudan deal for OVL. At the time, the National Democratic Alliance was in power under the leadership of the Hindu nationalist Bharatiya Janata Party (BJP) and its Prime Minister, Atal Bihari Vajpayee. One of the rising stars of the BJP, Pramod Mahajan, had united in opposition to investing in Sudan with his party rival, Disinvestment Minister Arun Shourie. Both men had political reasons to question the deal. Mahajan saw his position as the potential future BJP leader threatened by the rising importance of Petroleum Minister Ram Naik, under India's new focus on energy security. Sinking the Sudan bid would help to weaken Naik's position. Disinvestment Minister Shourie was also at odds with Naik. They naturally clashed on the question of whether or not India's public oil companies should be privatised. Naik was a proponent of keeping public companies under state ownership for security purposes, while Shourie was steering forward policies of privatisation. If OVL began to make large investments abroad the position of state-owned enterprises might be consolidated. Together, these political grudge matches would jeopardise OVL's Sudan plans. But its corporate parent, ONGC, keen on seeing the subsidiary's international expansion, did not sit and wait for its fate to be decided by politicians in New Delhi.

ONGC Chairman Sabir Raha stepped in to make his case for pushing OVL into Sudan. In his eyes, India was missing a golden opportunity. He argued that if CNPC and Petronas could operate in Sudan as state-owned enterprises surely OVL could do the same.[9] The Ministry of External Affairs also weighed in on the debate in OVL's favour. It did not want OVL's Sudan investment to become a political embarrassment for New Delhi, afraid that the same events that led to the Canadian company's exit would befall OVL.[10] But after some analysis, the ministry pegged Talisman's exit as the result of civil society pressure in Canada and the United States rather than insecurity from the civil war. The fact that CNPC and Petronas did not budge as Western oil companies rolled out was an encouraging sign. OVL as a majority government-owned company, with New Delhi holding 74% of the shares,[11] could avoid the divestment pressures from activists that had plagued Talisman. OVL and the other Asian national oil companies were not influenced in the same manner as Western companies, which were typically prone to divestment

---

[9] 'ONGC seeks to be global oil and gas player', *The Oil and Gas Journal*, Vol. 101. Iss. 11 (February, 2003).

[10] Interview, former government official, New Delhi, 16 December 2008.

[11] J. Mitchell, and G. Lahn, 'Oil for Asia', Briefing Paper (London: Chatham House, 2007), p.5.

pressures through their capital positions and consumer reputations in domestic markets.[12] Actually, activist pressure on Talisman and other Western oil companies presented OVL with a strong bargaining chip in the negotiations.[13] In the end, a compromise was struck between critics and supporters of the deal.

L.K. Advani, the Deputy Prime Minister at the time, subdued concerns over OVL's investment in Sudan by suggesting that the company take out political risk insurance. In response, OVL reported that it had a $1.2 billion insurance policy through the GNPOC consortium with the international bank HSBC's Insurance Brokers Ltd. in London. Furthermore, it indicated that it would seek insurance from the World Bank's affiliated Multilateral Investment Guarantee Agency. These measures helped to quiet opponents of the Sudan deal, and the Indian Cabinet gave the green light for OVL to proceed in finalising the deal with Talisman. However, the company's troubles were not quite over. While the Indian government was bickering over its internal misgivings about the Sudan deal, a familiar opponent was swooping in to claim the prize. The Chinese oil company CNPC already dominated the oil sector in Sudan and was hungry for more.

Overcoming the Chinese Threat

OVL faced fierce competition from its Asian counterparts CNPC and Petronas in its bid to enter Sudan in 2003. The presence of Chinese and Malaysian oil companies in Sudan at first acted as a guiding light for India. The construction of the oil sector under the two Asian firms demonstrated that the international oil industry was in fact not the sole domain of powerful Western oil majors and menacing Middle Eastern and Russian state-owned companies. However, while the Indian oil company portrayed its involvement in Sudan as strengthening the international relationship with its Asian counterparts,[14] CNPC and Petronas had other ideas. Both companies were eager to capture the abandoned shares in the GNPOC consortium.

Asian national oil companies were not just one monolithic structure moving towards investment opportunities where Western oil companies strayed. The Chinese and Indians were the newest and highest-profile players in the international oil industry, but the Malaysians, Japanese and South Koreans were also in the hunt and it was anything but a coordinated landing on African shores. In Sudan, holding a contractual *right of first refusal* in the GNPOC consortium, CNPC and Petronas could technically have initial access to Talisman's abandoned shares. The two companies

[12] Luke A. Patey, 'Against the Asian tide: the Sudan divestment campaign', *Journal of Modern African Studies*, Vol. 47, Iss. 4 (2009), pp. 551-573.
[13] Interview, political analyst, New Delhi, 3 December 2008.
[14] 'ONGC pursues Sudan expansion', *The Financial Times*, 16 September 2003.

already held a 40% and 30% share respectively in the GNPOC venture. The quarter stake offered by Talisman's departure, however, presented the opportunity to benefit further from a consortium that was producing oil and reaping in profits. Partnerships through joint ventures were useful to diversify risk, but if the terms were right and the oil was flowing, which was the case in Sudan in 2003, new partners were better avoided. For the Indian government, the sudden outside opposition fuelled its desire for OVL to win the oil bid.

It was going to be a tremendous challenge for OVL to beat its Asian counterparts for Talisman's stake in Sudan. In particular, CNPC was seen to have a special position on account of the close relationship fostered between the Beijing and Khartoum governments. Since the National Islamic Front – now the National Congress Party – attained power in Sudan through the 1989 military coup, it had moved to win Chinese interest in its oil sector and Beijing's political backing. OVL was in a tight position with both CNPC and Petronas having until the end of December 2002 to initiate their contractual rights of first refusal for Talisman's stake. In the face of opposition, the Managing Director of OVL, Atul Chandra, pleaded his company's case to the Indian government for political support. He hailed the Sudan investment as 'a great leap forward in terms of national oil security'.[15] ONGC Chairman Sabir Raha was to echo this call, saying that there was 'no alternative but to go overseas for equity oil' and that the rapid expansion of Chinese companies offered a lesson for India.[16] Raha implored the Indian Commerce Minister, Arun Jaitley, and the Oil Minister, Ram Naik, to promote OVL's position to the Khartoum government. New Delhi would respond in rapid fashion.

The interest shown by the Chinese and Malaysian companies in increasing their investment in Sudan's oil sector largely dispelled the Indian government's previous doubts about insecurity.[17] If CNPC and Petronas were keen to expand their involvement in the country, then it surely was an opportunity that New Delhi had to capitalise upon. It initiated a diplomatic lobbying mission to urge Sudan to counter rights of first refusal to CNPC and Petronas,[18] jumping on any chance to persuade the Sudanese to lean in its company's favour.[19] For instance, while Sudan's current second vice-president, Ali Osman Taha, was passing through New Delhi in July 2002,[20] he was quickly ushered into meetings with

---

[15] 'Gift of the Nile', *op. cit.*

[16] 'ONGC makes progress in Sudan', *International Petroleum Finance*, Vol. 26 (March 2003).

[17] Vandana Hari, 'India's ONGC Confident it will close Sudan stake', *Platts Oilgram News*, 31 December 2002.

[18] Sanjay Dutta, 'Diplomatic arm-twisting clears Sudan oil deal', *The Times of India*, 14 March 2003.

[19] 'Oil hunt', *Businessworld*, 7 July 2003.

[20] Taha was *en route* to Jakarta in an effort to improve ties with another Asian country, Indonesia; Veeramalla Anjaiah and Ivy Susanti, 'Sudan wants to strengthen ties with Indonesia', *The Jakarta Post*, 25 February 2005.

high-ranking Indian officials.[21] During his six-hour stopover he met with Oil Minister Naik and had a tête-à-tête with Prime Minister Vajpayee in an effort to support the bid of OVL.

The Sudanese Ambassador to India at the time, Abdalmahmood Abdalhaleem Mohamad, was also crucial in facilitating the deal, working diligently with the Indian embassy in Khartoum.[22] His swagger went a long way towards convincing the Indians that Khartoum had security matters under control.[23] In return, the economic and political rewards of a partnership with India promised to fill another piece of the puzzle in countering the American and Western policy of isolation for the Khartoum government. The NCP resembled a more pragmatic regime after shedding the involvement of its spiritual leader and then Parliamentary Speaker, Hassan Turabi.[24] In its foreign relations, while the NCP still considered China its closest international ally, it was nonetheless hesitant to provide Beijing with total influence over its oil sector.

If CNPC and Petronas were to split Talisman's 25% share in GNPOC, it would result in CNPC gaining majority control of Sudan's most important oil project. The NCP decided to rule out any single company owning more than 40% in the consortium.[25] The Indian government's diplomatic support fitted well into Khartoum's pragmatic calculus allowing OVL to enter Sudan. In the end, much to the surprise and dismay of CNPC and Petronas, the Khartoum government would strongly back the entry of OVL.[26] However, it still wanted to appease China and Malaysia. It dispatched Foreign Minister, Mustafa Osman Ismail – or, as he was known in foreign diplomatic and aid circles in Sudan: 'Mr. Smiley' – to both Beijing and Kuala Lumpur to present the government's case. Ismail employed his flair and charm to persuade corporate and bureaucratic officials in both Asian capitals to back down and accept Sudan's political determination. After two months of delay, OVL's bid for the Talisman shares would be approved by Khartoum, a decision reluctantly accepted by China and Malaysia.

In March 2003, Talisman announced that it had finalised the deal with OVL for its stake in GNPOC. The rewards of capturing the abandoned

---

[21] Taha had visited India in both 1995 and 1997 to attend the Ministerial Conference of Non-Aligned Countries; Embassy of India in Khartoum, <www.indembsdn.com/eng/india_sdn_partners.html.com>, (accessed: 19 September 2010).

[22] Interview, political analyst, New Delhi, 22 February 2008.

[23] The outspoken ambassador would later represent Sudan at the United Nations in New York, facing a barrage of criticism over Khartoum's actions in the Darfur conflict.

[24] Emily Wax, 'Sudan's Unbowed, Unbroken Inner Circle', *The Washington Post*, 3 May 2005.

[25] 'Petronas to hit ONGC's overseas investment plan', *The Times of India*, 18 December 2002; Chris Varcoe, 'Sudan sale to close in March', *Calgary Herald*, 1 February 2003; Scott Haggett, 'Out of Africa: Talisman closes the book on Sudan', *Calgary Herald*, 13 March 2003.

[26] There were also hidden costs from the original Talisman purchase. OVL transferred 2% of its Block 5A participating interest and 1% of its Block 5B share to Sudan's national oil company Sudapet in mid-August 2004 as *quid pro quo* for Khartoum's support for the deal; 'OVL transfers stake to Sudapet', *The Hindu*, 12 August 2004.

share would be significant, as GNPOC was producing over 200,000 barrels per day of crude oil in 2002. Farther south of the GNPOC concessions, OMV of Austria also sold its stake in Block 5A and the adjacent Block 5B to the eager OVL the following year. It had been an uphill battle, but OVL had gained its reward. The company was keen to capture overseas petroleum assets to bolster the stagnating domestic production of its corporate parent and to take on the challenge of responding to New Delhi's rising concerns about energy security. The bounty was plentiful.

Paradise Found

After such difficulty in winning oil stakes in Sudan, OVL moved quickly to expand its position. In June 2004 the Indian oil company agreed to construct a 12-inch, 741 kilometre multi-product pipeline from Sudan's Khartoum refinery to the export terminal of Port Sudan on the Red Sea at a cost of almost US$194 million. The pipeline was estimated to take 16 months to complete, and Khartoum was to reimburse the companies in 18 payments over a nine-year period.[27] The pipeline project was OVL's first major infrastructure venture abroad and was completed two months ahead of schedule. Past debates over the risks of entering war-torn Sudan were quashed. In fact, after the Talisman deal had been concluded, it was revealed that the MIGA insurance sought by OVL from the World Bank would not cover risks related to war, terrorism and expropriation.[28] If the company had indeed lost its investment due to armed conflict, it was unclear how it could have recouped the damages. Nonetheless, despite its previous decision requiring the company to find appropriate insurance, New Delhi decided to cancel the requirement in 2004.[29] Political-risk insurance was seen as too high a cost, at nearly $50 million for the pipeline agreement alone. Rather, New Delhi saw stability consolidating in Sudan, with the south receiving regional autonomy with the signing of the Comprehensive Peace Agreement in January 2005.

OVL benefited immensely from Sudan. Its entry was timed perfectly with an exceptional oil boom in Sudan. Total crude output shot up from 305,000 barrels per day (bpd) in 2005 to 480,000 bpd in 2008, and Sudan's crude rose 42% in value on account of enormous spikes in international prices.[30] OVL's investments made Sudan one of India's largest destinations for foreign investment between 1995 and 2005, representing 11% and behind the US at 24% and Russia at 20%.[31] This stood against

[27] ONGC Videsh, *Annual Report 2004-05* (New Delhi: ONGC Videsh), p. 179.
[28] 'ONGC Videsh Ltd's Sudan venture high on risk', *Indian Express*, 5 June 2003.
[29] 'No insurance for ONGC in Sudan', *Indian Express*, 25 June 2004.
[30] BP, 'BP Statistical Review of World Energy' (BP, London, 2009); Ministry of Finance and National Economy (Sudan) <www.mof.gov.sd/> (18 November 2009).
[31] Deepak Nayyar, 'The Internationalization of Firms From India: Investment, Mergers and Acquisitions', *Oxford Development Studies*, Vol. 36, No. 1 (2008), p. 114.

the trend of Indian foreign investment heading towards industrialised countries. The payoffs of the GNPOC concession grew rapidly as OVL raised the Indian tricolour over Heglig base camp in Southern Kordofan in May 2003. The over 3 million tons of Sudanese crude that OVL immediately accessed produced the company's first oil revenues from an overseas project. From 2003 to 2007 OVL's share of Sudanese crude represented over 58% of the company's production.[32] OVL was only producing Vietnamese gas when it won the GNPOC stake. Even when production in its Russian oil and gas field at Sakhalin-I kicked into full gear in 2006, Sudan was still the company's highest producing venture.

Sudan was by far the company's largest producer of oil and primary revenue earner. OVL went from reporting a Rupees (Rs) 589.95 million profit in 2002 to Rs 23,971 million by 2007 (roughly from US$11.8 million to US$479 million).[33] Sudan represented over 40% of OVL's sales in the same period. The hundreds of millions of dollars that Indian politicians had fretted over investing in the war-torn country were rapidly recovered. In 2002, OVL had increased its borrowings to over Rs 47,679 million (US$900 million) from ONGC, primarily to purchase Talisman's stake. But already by 2006, the company was able to begin to pay back its loans from ONGC, basically returning the funds it borrowed to enter Sudan. The original US$720 million investment was recovered a year ahead of schedule at the end of 2004, thanks to rising international oil prices.[34] OVL's venture in Sudan was also providing benefits to its parent company back in India in other ways.

At the same time as its foreign subsidiary finalised the deal to enter Sudan, ONGC became India's first fully integrated oil and gas company when it attained majority ownership in Mangalore Refineries and Petrochemicals Limited. Ownership of the refinery complex north of Mangalore city extended the company's operations from exploration and production in the upstream market to refining in the downstream market. With crude oil first arriving from Sudan in May 2003 thanks to OVL, the internationalisation of its integrated operations awarded ONGC such benefits as bypassing trader margins for crude bought on overseas spot markets when prices were low and cost savings crucial.[35] OVL had the option of bringing Sudanese crude back to Mangalore or selling it on international spot markets.[36] OVL often opted for the latter. By the end of 2003, it agreed to keep the British oil-trading firm Trafigura (Talisman's former marketer) selling Sudanese crude on its behalf.[37] In 2004, only

[32] ONGC Videsh, *Annual Reports 2003–04* to *2007–08*, (New Delhi: ONGC Videsh, 2004–2008).

[33] *Ibid.*

[34] Pratim Ranjan Bose, 'Hike in oil recovery boosts OVL's Sudan field earnings', *The Hindu*, 10 November 2004; Interview, oil analyst, New Delhi, 12 December 2008.

[35] '3 mt Sudan crude – for OVL annually', *The Hindu*, 14 March 2003; ONGC, *Annual Report 2002–03* (New Delhi: ONGC), p. 191.

[36] Vandana Hari, 'Focus: Sudan oil to India', *Platt's Oilgram News*, 1 May 2003.

[37] 'UK's Trafigura to hawk ONGC's Sudan crude', *The Times of India*, 5 September 2003.

0.33 million metric tons of its 3.675 MMT allowance in Sudan went back to India.[38] The Mangalore refinery remained a destination for OVL's Sudanese crude and was a regular buyer of the Nile blend on its own, but OVL could produce higher profits from selling the oil on the market.

Sudan was a crucial investment for OVL and the entire ONGC group, by helping it to evolve into a truly international integrated oil and gas corporation. Succeeding Sabir Raha, ONGC Chairman R.S. Sharma spelt out that OVL was the 'growth vehicle' of the group.[39] OVL was now India's second largest producer behind ONGC in terms of both oil and gas production and reserves. However, it was not a complete shopping spree for OVL in Sudan. There remained plenty of risks on the horizon, upsetting the company's oil paradise.

Diminishing Returns

The Indian Ministry of External Affairs correctly predicted that OVL would evade the same divestment pressures that led the Canadian oil company Talisman to withdraw from Sudan. The growth of activism in the US surrounding the Darfur civil war was to lead to a renewed divestment campaign against oil companies in Sudan. Along with CNPC and Petronas, OVL was one of the campaign's primary targets. But, as a majority state-owned company, the divestment threat was seen as unthreatening by company executives. A warning from the California Public Employees' Retirement System indicating that it would not invest any of its more than $200 billion US portfolio in corporations involved in Sudan's oil sector was brushed aside. Current ONGC head R.S. Sharma said: 'We do not care if CalPERS invests with us or not. We have more than 300 FIIs (Foreign Institutional Investors) as our investors. We will continue our operations in Sudan.'[40] The US-based Save Darfur Coalition in particular sought to exploit the 2008 Beijing Olympic Games as a pressure point to push China to use its strong ties with Sudan to change the Khartoum government's political behaviour in Darfur (see Budabin, Chapter 7 this volume). But along with Malaysia, and Japan as a major buyer of Sudanese crude, India has been able to avoid much of the negative publicity directed at China by activists and the media in the US. There were, however, setbacks to OVL's oil ambitions in Sudan.

OVL was able to avoid the pressures of civil society groups, but the company was never able to pull off a number of other deals in Sudan. In 2004, OVL was wrapping up its purchases of Blocks 5A and 5B from the

---

[38] Planning Commission, The Government of India, 'Integrated Energy Policy, Report of the Expert Committee', New Delhi: Government of India, 2006), p. 59; ONGC Videsh, *Annual Report 2004–05*, (New Delhi: ONGC Videsh, 2005).

[39] James Norman, 'Petrodollars', *Platt's Oilgram News*, 31 January 2005; 'Outlook bright for ONGC's overseas assets', *The Hindustan Times*, 26 June 2006.

[40] 'ONGC, BHEL, VIL foul of CalPERS', *The Financial Express*, 19 May 2006.

departing European companies when stakes in the highly prospective Blocks 3 and 7 in Upper Nile State became available. The blocks were located in the Melut Basin covering over 72,000 square kilometres east of the White Nile river. The joint venture company Petrodar operated the two concessions. The Petrodar consortium was led by CNPC, with Petronas holding a major stake and Sudapet and two Middle Eastern firms, Al Thani and the Gulf Petroleum Corporation, minor interests. At the time, there had been 32 wells drilled in the blocks, with eleven discoveries of Dar blend crude.

The findings in Blocks 3 and 7 gave way to estimates that the concessions would reach production levels of 200,000 bpd by 2005, with 1 billion barrels in reserves at Adar Yale, Agordeed and the giant oilfield of Palogue.[41] OVL entered into talks with the two Middle Eastern firms to buy their combined 11% stakes in the venture and secured acceptance from the Cabinet Committee on Economic Affairs in New Delhi to invest US$360 million.[42] A 5% share of the project alone was set to ensure OVL 10,000 barrels of oil per day.[43] However, in the week that it took the Indian Cabinet to ratify the committee's approval, the Chinese state-owned company SINOPEC managed to make a higher bid and purchase the Gulf Petroleum stake.[44] Following the Chinese oil company's acquisition, the lucrative deal fell through completely for OVL. The Upper Nile oil concessions went on to produce 180,000 bpd by 2007 when the Palogue field came onstream,[45] and roughly half of Sudan's 490,000 bpd in 2009. The Indian media had a field day scolding the company and government for their slow action. It was a stark reminder to OVL of the competitiveness of the international oil industry. Unlike the Talisman deal, the Khartoum government did not impose its sovereign will on the Chinese oil companies. Rather, Khartoum already had the Indians within the fold of Asian political and economic supporters.

There were more missed deals. Shortly after making its Talisman purchase, OVL was offered a contract to upgrade and revamp the Port Sudan refinery by the Khartoum government.[46] Ever quick on the trigger when it came to big international oil stories, the Indian media announced that the deal was in place; OVL had beaten its Malaysian rival Petronas

[41] 'OVL to acquire 11 pc stake in Sudan oil field', *The Times of India*, 21 January 2004.

[42] 'OVL to buy 11% in two Sudan blocks', *The Hindustan Times*, 22 January 2004; 'India's Share of Equity in Sudan may go up by 1 MT', *The Financial Express*, 20 January 2004.

[43] 'India's Share of Equity Oil', *op. cit.*

[44] Anup Jayaram, 'Face-off', *Businessworld*, 16 August 2004; 'Sinopec buys Kazakh oil assets, returns to Sudan', *Reuters*, 22 October 2004; 'Kuwait's Kharafi buys 3 pct stake in Sudan oil co.', *Reuters*, 16 March 2008; 'Egypt Kuwait Hldg buys 5 pct of Sudan's Petrodar', *Reuters*, 25 March 2008; *Businessworld* incorrectly reported that CNPC had captured the block when it was SINOPEC. In the end, Al-Thani would hold on to its stake, later selling to the Egyptian company, Tri Ocean, in March 2008 for US$400 million.

[45] European Coalition on Oil in Sudan, 'Sudan, Whose Oil? Sudan's Oil Industry: Facts and Analysis' (Utrecht: ECOS, 2008).

[46] 'ONGC hits pay dirt in Sudan', *Business Standard*, 4 August 2003.

[47] 'ONGC to build $1.2bn oil refinery in Sudan', *The Times of India*, 3 February 2005.

for the 100,000 bpd refinery project.[47] The Malaysians had protested against OVL's initial entry into the GNPOC consortium, along with the Chinese, and it was time for Indian retribution. Reports of the Port Sudan refinery project in the Indian media carried over to wider analysis of India's growing African engagement. The more than one billion dollar refinery in Port Sudan has been counted as one of the largest Indian investments on the continent.[48] Yet the project never saw the light of day. The rehabilitation and expansion were discussed between the company and the government, and feasibility studies of local demand and export potential were completed. The estimated price tag was US$1.2 billion. In the end, however, in the eyes of Indian and international banks, such as State Bank of India and BNP Paribas, the non-recourse loan OVL was seeking to fund the refinery expansion was felt to be far from secure.[49] Difficulties in finding suitable lenders and the rising financial costs, due to increases in the world price of steel, had put an end to the refinery project early on. Elsewhere, OVL's interests in attaining a 30% stake in Block 8 in Blue Nile State, in which Petronas owned 77%, and in Block B where Total was acting as operator, have also failed to materialise for the company.[50]

Even existing deals in Sudan that were initial successes have hit rough patches. The pipeline OVL completed ahead of schedule in August 2005 ran into trouble in the months following, when the Khartoum government failed to make its payments to the company on time. The agreement was on a lease-to-own basis with the government. However, the government was late in paying the first three instalments and failed to make the fourth altogether by July 2007, sparking worries at OVL's corporate headquarters.[51] Sudan also did not allow OVL to take payments in oil in kind, as had previously been agreed between the two parties should such a scenario arise. It was unclear whether Khartoum was having financial difficulties or was simply being inefficient.

Requests for the pipeline payments sent by OVL to top Sudanese officials were at first met by silence. Some claimed that political motives were behind the Sudanese delay, with rumours in New Delhi suggesting that Sudan was looking for a clear sign of support from India against the possible indictment of President Omar al-Bashir by the International

[48] Sanusha Naidu, 'India's Growing African Strategy', *Review of African Political Economy*. Vol. 35, No. 1 (2008), p. 119.

[49] ONGC group of companies signs pipeline contract with Govt. of Sudan. ONGC Press Release. 1 July 2004. www.ongcindia.com; Archana Chaudhary, 'ONGC approaches bankers to raise $600 m for Sudan project', *The Hindu*, 18 December 2004; Archana Chaudhary and Rukmani Vishwanath. 'ONGC in loan talks for Sudan refinery deal', *The Hindu*, 8 January 2005; In a non-recourse loan the lender can only use the project itself as collateral, not the wider assets of a company.

[50] 'OVL seeks stake in 2 more oil blocks in Sudan', *Hindustan Times*, 6 November 2007.

[51] Sanjay Dutta, 'India-Sudan ties may sour over OVL pipeline', *The Times of India*, 17 July 2007.

Criminal Court.[52] The Indian Oil Minister Murli Deora visited Sudan in January 2010, in part to ensure that the payments would finally be received.[53] It would turn out to be a growing trend. Payment for many of the loans and lines of credit Indian companies and the Indian EXIM bank provided to the Khartoum government have been significantly delayed.[54] Investor confidence in the ability of the Khartoum government to pay for major projects has waned, particularly among large Indian private companies.

To make matters worse for OVL, its other oil stakes in Sudan have also been underperforming. The low quality of oil from Thar Jath and Mala fields in OVL's Block 5A has forced the operator of the concession, the White Nile Petroleum Operating Company (WNPOC), to make an agreement with GNPOC to add only 10% of the crude into its pipeline – a measure taken to ensure that the quality of the Nile blend remained high.[55] In Block 5B, OVL became caught between the Khartoum government and the regional government in Southern Sudan over its ownership rights to the concession. WNPOC was forced to give up a large portion of the block to the Moldovan oil company ASCOM, as the Government of Southern Sudan demanded its presence in the oil sector. Kuol Manyang, the Governor of Jonglei State where the concession was located, told WNPOC representatives not to carry on their operations east of the White Nile river.[56] Regardless of the political intervention by the GoSS, the result was the same for both WNPOC and ASCOM. West and east of the river only dry holes were found. In late April 2009, WNPOC abandoned its interest in the concession.[57] OVL had spent close to US$90 million on its share of the consortium's exploration costs. Ever an ally of the oil company, the Indian government agreed to write off the company's accrued expenses. But New Delhi could not turn around the fleeting longevity of OVL's main oil assets in Sudan.

The oil sector in Sudan may never reach the production levels to which its architects had aspired. The lofty predictions of Sudan's former oil minister Awad Ahmed al-Jaz that total production would reach 1 million bpd by 2009 did not materialise. Rather, Sudan produced only 473,000 bpd that year and is not set to average more than half a million bpd until after 2011.[58] The main reason for the stagnation was the rapid

---

[52] Interview, political analyst, New Delhi, 12 December 2008; Bashir was charged by the International Criminal Court prosecutor in July 2008.

[53] 'Deora in Sudan: Seeks to resolve OVL payment dispute', *The Business Standard*, 25 January 2010.

[54] Interview, senior Indian official, Khartoum, 12 October 2010.

[55] Interview, political analyst, Khartoum, 11 October 2010.

[56] Interview, former oil official, Khartoum, 15 October 2010.

[57] 'Swedish Lundin fails to find oil in the third Sudanese well', *Sudan Tribune*, 30 October 2008; Sanjay Dutta, 'OVL to quit block in Sudan', *The Times of India*, 27 April 2009; 'Flop Sudan oil venture results in $89m loss', *The Telegraph* (Calcutta), 27 April 2009.

[58] 'Sudan reports sharp oil revenue drop for November', *Sudan Tribune*, 13 January 2009; 'Interview: Sudan oil output falls short of estimates – minister', *Reuters*-India, 25 October

decline of the GNPOC concession in Blocks 1, 2, and 4 of the Muglad Basin in Unity and Southern Kordofan states. Production levels of the high-quality Nile-blend crude fell from a peak of nearly 271,000 bpd in September 2006 to 124,766 bpd in June 2011, a drop of 54%.[59] Oilfields in Blocks 3 and 7 in Upper Nile State have quickly become Sudan's main producers. But the geological shortcomings of what were once Sudan's key oilfields in Unity State and Southern Kordofan were not just a work of nature. In the lead up to south Sudan's independence vote in January 2011, security issues surrounding the oilfields, which straddle and lie near to the disputed North-South border, have dissuaded investment needed to ward off sharply declining production.[62] OVL and its Chinese and Malaysian counterparts in the GNPOC consortium that operates Blocks 1, 2, and 4 were unwilling to invest the required hundreds of millions of dollars in enhanced recovery techniques.

Heading towards the separation of Southern Sudan, the Asian national oil companies remained uncertain about the future political situation with border demarcation still pending in the region and questions surrounding contract renegotiation hanging in the air. Both northern and southern officials assured India, along with China and Malaysia, that the oil investments were safe and that existing agreements would be honoured.[61] But fighting in Abyei and Southern Kordofan in the months before southern independence told a different story, continuing to hamper production in the GNPOC oil concessions.[62] In the meantime, OVL's most prized international asset has steadily declined in value – a result reflected in OVL's total company revenues. When Managing Director, R.S. Butola, announced in early 2010 that the company's production for 2010-11 would be lower than the previous year, he placed the blame on the falling GNPOC oilfields.[63] India's oil assets in Sudan were producing less and less as the African country prepared for major political upheaval in 2011.

Conclusion

Sudan will certainly go down in the history books of India's national oil company OVL as an unprecedented success. It represented OVL's first major international foray, capitalising on both the exit of Western oil companies in 2003 and the rising urgency in the Indian government to support the overseas activists of its national oil companies in the name of

[58(cont.)] 2009; EIU, *Sudan Country Report* (London: EIU, March 2010), p. 8.
[59] EIU, 'Sudan: Country Profile, 2009', pp. 22–3; Republic of Sudan, Ministry of Petroleum, Sudanese Petroleum Corporation, <http://www.spc.sd/> accessed 15 June 2011.
[60] Interviews, oil company representatives, Khartoum, October 2010.
[61] Sandeep Diskhit, 'Both Sudans assure India on energy front', *The Hindu*, 30 April 2011.
[62] Peter Martell, 'Oil workers returning to south Sudan after clashes', *AFP*, 27 April 2011.
[63] 'ONGC Videsh sees output dip', *Upstream* 15 April 2010.

energy security. It was not, however, a seamless venture. On top of the threats faced by Indian oilmen operating in the country's oilfields, a number of political and economic challenges ate away at the stability and profitability of India's Sudan venture. There was opposition to OVL's interest in buying Talisman's abandoned stake both at home in India and among other Asian national oil companies that were already active in Sudan. New Delhi's quick action to come to its company's aid in Sudan represents one of the first instances of the Indian government flexing its diplomatic muscle to win an overseas oil deal. But if Chinese threats can be overcome, it will take much more financial investment to sustain the company's declining oilfields and political fortitude to navigate the political intentions of Khartoum and Juba.

India was ready to recognise South Sudan after the official date of independence on 9 July 2011. Its consulate in Juba was to be upgraded to embassy status. In the months before its independence, Indian officials were indicating to southern Sudan that further investment in agriculture, health and education was to come, while at the same time stressing to northern Sudan that it would remain a 'development partner'.[64] Yet outside the diplomatic glad-handing, the threat of armed conflict between the two Sudans was on the rise, particularly in the border areas of Unity State and Southern Kordofan. This complicated political climate that will surely follow southern independence, at least in the short term, will represent the next challenge for India's oil ambitions in Sudan.

[64] 'India's oil contracts will be honoured: South Sudan', *Indo-Asian News Service*, 28 April 2011.

5

Malaysia–Sudan

From Islamist Students to Rentier Bourgeois

ROLAND MARCHAL

China is usually cited as *the* outstanding partner of Sudan's governing regime. But other East Asian state partners have also been playing important roles in relations with Khartoum. Although not as important as China, three in particular deserve attention. Japan and South Korea share a low profile and, although diplomatically allied with the West – both are members of the OECD and South Korea joined its Development Assistance Committee in 2010 – have dealt with Sudan in an autonomous manner, not willing to damage their own interests. They remained silent when their Western allies were vocal about the crisis in Darfur and the alleged reluctance of the Sudanese regime to be a fair player in the implementation of the CPA that ended the North–South civil war between Khartoum and the SPLM/A. In addition, neither Tokyo nor Seoul has had to face any prominent activism or domestic public pressure concerning Africa in general and Sudan in particular, despite the fact that both have economic relations with Khartoum. Japan has often been the second-largest buyer of Sudanese oil, and Sudan is a market for Japanese goods. South Korea has a history of engagement in Sudan, with significant business and agricultural interests today (see Introduction in this volume, for further details).

Malaysia, Sudan's third Southeast Asian partner, has maintained a completely different attitude from both Japan and South Korea, at least under Prime Minister Dr. Mahathir Mohamad, who governed between 1981 and 2003. Instead of keeping a low political profile and focusing strictly on business interests, Malaysia's former leader repeatedly made bold anti-Western statements and mentioned various conspiracies against the Third World. As this chapter seeks to demonstrate, the links between Malaysia and Sudan, however, go beyond rhetoric, and the nature of their relations in the 1990s sheds light on less known aspects of Sudan's modern history. Most observers, of course, rightly associate Malaysia with the development of Sudan's oil sector and the role of Malaysia's state oil company *Petroliam Nasional Berhad*, or Petronas, in this. This is justified, given the role of Petronas in Sudan and the fact that oil constitutes 99% of Malaysian imports from Sudan.[1] Moreover, Petronas is one of the most successful international oil companies, active in most African oil-producing countries.[2] This chapter, however, does not examine this prominent dimension (though it touches on trade relations), but instead explores a neglected but significant dimension of Malaysia's relations with Sudan.[3]

Top-down processes of Islamisation were implemented in both Sudan and Malaysia from the early 1980s onwards. There were contacts between Islamists in both countries in the 1970s, who, as explained below, engaged in a fruitful dialogue on their common problems. Both Islamisation processes failed, however, and the reasons for this deserve analysis. As this chapter explores, the two movements became associated with state power and built their own business constituencies at the same time as claiming to establish an Islamic State. Their achievement was limited, however, since they built up a rentier class and were delegitimised because of their massive use of coercion.

This chapter begins by comparing the ways in which the respective Islamist movements in both countries pushed for political and economic change in the late 1970s and early 1980s. Relations between these movements started long before they came to power (or attained their share of it). It goes on to underline a number of patterns showing how Sudan in the 1990s not only sought oil-sector partnerships but also imitated, in its own way, the achievements promoted by the Malaysian state in terms of creating its own business class and containing confrontation with the West. Although not of paramount importance, these bonds demonstrate how the different Islamist elites were trying to define and forge an Islamic modernity without highlighting an 'Arabian model'. Both regimes, for their own reasons, tried at one point to claim an Islamic State rooted in modernity, and both failed to deliver it.

Two Different Islamisation Processes

The governing regimes in Sudan and Malaysia had to take into account a growing Islamist movement in the late 1970s and early 1980s. The 1979

---

[1] For instance, oil represented US$51.120 million out of a total of US$52.124 million worth of imports in 2008 (according to the Department of Statistics, Malaysia). The importance of oil compared to other potential exports means that the Malaysian involvement in Sudan is that of ultimately Petronas', which raises interesting points of discussion about the success of Dr. Mahathir's African policy.

[2] See the webpage: http://www.petronas.com.my/internet/corp/centralrep2.nsf/frameset_corp?OpenFrameset (accessed 7 November 2009).

[3] This chapter, for reasons of limited space, is not able to explore an important social dimension of relations between the two countries. Malaysia hosts more than 20,000 Sudanese, who are settled with families, and many went because they wanted a better education for their children in a Muslim society. Malaysia provides this slightly conservative environment and has a good educational system. Many also say that life is easier in Malaysia than in Sudan: even modest salaries are sufficient to sustain a family, a drastic contrast with Khartoum.

Iranian Revolution had repercussions beyond the Middle East, stimulating a resurgence of Islamist actors in Muslim societies around the world. The governments of both Sudan and Malaysia pursued a policy of co-option, not confrontation, towards Islamists within the regime, and of moving, at least symbolically, towards the Islamisation of certain aspects of society.

In both cases, the state apparatus and its social policies were used as channels and mechanisms to undertake top-down Islamisation processes. These aimed, first of all, to cut off the leadership of political oppositions, while also reinserting the regime into a broader context where it could mobilise support from the Middle East and elsewhere for the purpose of enhancing its own domestic legitimacy. These policies have been successful, to a certain extent: Malaysia today has become a global hub for Islamic finance,[4] and Sudan, despite its messy internal political situation, can aspire to a regional role connecting the Greater Horn of Africa and the Arabian Peninsula. When it comes to a more detailed assessment, the reality, however, is bleaker.

When Dr. Mahathir Mohamad stepped down in 2003, his critics labelled him a pharaoh (or 'Mahafiraun', to cite the Malay term), comparing him to Mohammed Suharto of Indonesia and Ferdinand Marcos of the Philippines. While his former deputy, Anwar Ibrahim, was contesting a dubious legal case, he had lost touch with his own community and no longer appeared to be a credible defendant of other communities in Malaysia (Indian, Chinese). His last speeches were full of bitterness towards the Malay community, which had suddenly become unwilling to reward him with any support for his deeds, and towards his allies, who felt that his authoritarianism was increasing the gap between the various Malaysian communities.[5]

The prospect of a modern Islamic state in Sudan had drowned itself in the development of a heavy security apparatus, coercive social policies, corruption, and/or mismanagement of oil revenues. The strongest criticisms of the regime today, as in Malaysia, come from those who were at its forefront in the early days, like Hassan al-Turabi. In the early 1990s, they justified the construction of a police state for the sake of educating the Sudanese people and protecting their Islamic experiment from the West. They would become the victims of their own creation, and their heirs rule now one of the most corrupt, unequal and violent countries in Africa.

Reluctant Islamisation as a political weapon

In 2003, when Dr. Mahathir Mohamad left the post of Malaysia's Prime Minister after more than two decades in power, the Sudanese President Omar al-Bashir delivered a vibrant speech congratulating his colleague

---

[4] See, for instance, the Malaysia International Islamic Financial Center (http://www.mifc. com/).
[5] Khoo Boo Teik, *Beyond Mahathir: Malaysian Politics and its Discontents* (London: Zed Press, 2003).

and reminding the audience that he went to Malaysia for the first time in 1983 (as part of a Commonwealth programme) to be trained at the Malaysian Military Academy. There is little doubt that the young Sudanese military officer, who was already an Islamist, was puzzled by the political situation he observed in Malaysia: co-option more than coercion seemed to frame state policy towards local Islamists, and Sudan's ruler adopted this policy.

Jaafar Nimairi and his leftist allies came to power in Sudan via a coup in October 1969. In contrast to Khartoum's previous military coup in 1958, Sudan's traditional political parties were adamantly opposed to him and his Communist allies. Riots and violent protests were organised in response. The repression was brutal and bloody, and featured the bombing of Aba Island, where the new regime's opponents had been regrouping in 1970. Being isolated in the political arena, Nimairi seemed weak and vulnerable. A faction within the Sudan Communist Party (SCP) attempted to trigger a palace coup, but thanks to the intervention of the new Libyan leader, Muammar Qaddafi, Nimairi survived the badly planned coup attempt and eliminated most cadres of the SCP. Seeking new allies, Nimairi made peace with the southern Sudanese Anyanya rebel movement through the 1972 Addis Ababa agreement. By agreeing to a devolution of power to southern Sudan, a loose federal structure and the integration of many Anyanya fighters into the Sudan Armed Forces, he consolidated his grip on the military apparatus and was able to cope successfully with several coup attempts organised by the remnants of the opposition from Libya. Political infighting grew in the south, however, while regional pressure for an accommodation with his opposition became more pressing at a time when Sudan needed direct investment. In 1977, he thus decided to strike a deal and offer an amnesty for a section of his opposition, then in exile and mostly encamped in Libya.

The Sudanese Muslim Brothers had reorganised themselves after 1964 into a new organisation, the Islamic Charter Front (ICF), led by the charismatic Dr. Hassan Abdallah al-Turabi. This group was adamantly anti-Communist and succeeded in prohibiting SCP activities until the 1969 coup. After the coup, it was the SCP's time for revenge; the leaders of the Islamic movement were arrested and the movement repressed. In 1977, however, the ICF emerged as a quasi-winner: the SCP had been destroyed by Nimairi's repression after 1971, while the Islamists were allowed to restart their activities under the umbrella of Sudan's then sole political party, the Sudan Socialist Union (SSU). Hassan al-Turabi and other leaders were offered positions in the Cabinet (the former became Attorney General) or in the state apparatus.

The importance of the changes that took place before the overthrow of Nimairi in 1985 cannot be underestimated. First, by infiltrating the army and the security apparatus, the Islamists prepared the ground for a new coup that would eventually take place in 1989. Second, they built a larger constituency for themselves, using state facilities and providing business opportunities for their followers. The newly established Islamic banks received special treatment. Able to operate in Khartoum with extraordinary fiscal privileges, these became one of the main channels of Islamist influence. Led by Hassan al-Turabi, the Islamists also built a range of relationships with international players (notably Iran at the time) that eventually helped them counter the isolation they faced after their June 1989 coup. Hassan al-Turabi and his colleagues were also instrumental in the implementation of what became known as the 1983 September Laws (a superficial Islamisation of Sudan's Penal Code). This decision, after many other rifts, became a further argument for the southern Sudanese to justify a new outbreak of hostilities that had started a few months before, in May 1983.

Nimairi made one last attempt to identify the Islamists with the complete failure of his regime, jailing Hassan al-Turabi and some of his colleagues in March 1985, but it was too late. A few weeks afterwards, a coup left no option but for Jaafar Nimairi to go into exile in Cairo. The internal situation in Sudan became more confused, despite a newly elected government taking power in 1986. Its inability to act to stop the war in the south prepared the ground for another coup in June 1989. Despite some of its leadership being in jail, and the country being led by a military junta, the successor of the ICF, the National Islamic Front (NIF) was the real backbone of the new power and undertook a project to achieve a radical, coercive reform of Sudanese society on behalf of Islam.

Islamisation by default?
Malaysia also witnessed the development of a significant Islamic opposition in the late 1970s. Its ruling National Front (*Barisan Nasional*) coalition was an unbalanced gathering of political parties representing the three main communities in the country: the Malays, through the United Malays' National Organisation (UMNO), the Chinese community, through the Malaysian Chinese Association; the Malaysian Indian Congress, and other, smaller movements. It had to cope with a vocal Islamic opposition led by two groups: the *Parti Islam Se-Malaysia* (Pan-Malaysian Islamic Party, or PAS),[6] and the *Angkatan Belia Islam Malyasia* (Islamic Youth of Malaysia, or ABIM), a youth organisation established in 1971.[7]

Dr. Mahathir Mohamad, who had been appointed Prime Minister in 1981, was celebrated as a staunch Malay nationalist and came to power as the result of his talented leverage among UMNO's leadership. His

---

[6] The PAS was set up in 1951 in Penang. Many of its founding members were from UMNO Religious Bureau, who defected as a result of differences of opinions about the nature of the state after independence from Britain. At one point, the PAS was part of the ruling coalition in 1973 but left in 1977.

[7] See K. S. Jomo and Ahmad Shabery Cheek, 'Malaysia's Islamic Movements' in Joel S. Kahn and Francis Loh Kok Wah eds., *Fragmented Vision: Culture and Politics in Contemporary Malaysia*, (Kensington: Asian Studies Association of Australia in Association with Allen & Unwin, 1992).

promotion (like that of Anwar Ibrahim later on) illustrated a genuine democratisation of Malaysian politics.[8] Mahathir's Islamic thought would put him alongside many 'lay Salafis' of the nineteenth century in the sense that, while he showed little inclination for discussions on *fiqh* (jurisprudence), *tafsir* (interpretation of the Holy Quran) and *Sunnah* (Islamic tradition), or debates with the *ulema*, in most of his discourses he complained that the Malays should be better entrepreneurs, scientists and engineers.[9] Islam, for him, was compatible with modernity and lay development. While his bitter, recurrent criticisms of Israel aroused attention, prompting accusations of anti-Semitism in the West, few international observers took note of his long-term commitment to advancing the Malay understanding of Islam and his opposition to a narrow scriptural approach to religion.

It was in this context that very early in his first term as Prime Minister he announced the creation of an International Islamic University and an Islamic Bank, as well as a prohibition against Muslims gambling in casinos and serving alcohol at official functions. He also introduced a 'Look East' policy that used Japan and South Korea (but not Singapore or Taiwan, where the Chinese influence was very evident) as models for Malaysia. Coupled with his 'Buy British last' policy, these decisions were seen as a break with the past.

Despite vocal Islamic opposition in the late 1970s and the likely surge of a more radical Islamic movement stimulated by Iran's Islamic Revolution, as witnessed in many other Muslim countries, the Malaysian political system remained stable in the 1980s. This capacity to digest such an event can be mostly ascribed to the 'entente cordiale' between two of Malaysia's leaders, Dr. Mahathir Mohamad and Anwar Ibrahim, the leader of ABIM since 1974. When he shifted sides to join UMNO in 1982, the latter provided the regime with the Islamic credentials to defeat the Islamic opposition.[10]

At the time, Anwar Ibrahim was considered the most talented politician in the Islamic movement. He was quickly appointed Deputy Minister in the Prime Minister's Department, elected UMNO Youth President and Minister of Culture and, by 1987, was already Mahathir's heir apparent. This move created such disruption and confusion within the Malaysian Islamists that Dr. Mahathir was able again to take the initiative and gain credibility for his own Islamisation programme. What retrospectively may appear to be an alliance of convenience lasted until the 1997/98

---

[8] As a Malaysian researcher underlines, Mahathir was the first Prime Minister not to be born into an aristocratic family or able to play golf. Like his then deputy, Musa Hitam, he came from a commoner family and had been educated in a local university. See Farish Noor, 'Islam et politique en Malaisie: une trajectoire singulière', *Critique Internationale* No. 13 (October 2001).

[9] Patricia Sloane, *Islam, Modernity and Entrepreneurship among the Malays* (New York: St. Martin's Press, 1999).

[10] Although the PAS lost the parliamentary elections (with only one MP being elected), the competition did not end there and eventually the state resorted to violence to contain them.

Asian financial crisis, and ended in court where Anwar Ibrahim, stripped of all his responsibilities, had to defend himself against accusations of alleged sexual crimes, after witnessing the dismantling of his own faction within UMNO.

Anwar Ibrahim's decision to join the ruling party in March 1982 may have surprised most of his followers, but not his Sudanese friends (as explained below). In previous months, he had expressed hostile views against the 'Look East' policy on the grounds that Japan and South Korea could not be models for an Islamic nation. As a student, he had also campaigned against the use of English for campus inscriptions. Later, Anwar visited Ayatollah Khomeini in Neauphle-le-Chateau in 1978 and was decorated by the Pakistani dictator, Zia ul-Haq, as the Malaysian Islamic movement was attentive to the situation in both countries.[11] Most observers thought that he would eventually take over the PAS; throughout the 1970s, many of his predecessors had found their way to the PAS leadership.[12] Yet this shift had major consequences for the Islamic movement. His successor was unable to stop the haemorrhaging of activists, who were defecting either to UMNO or PAS. While this event contributed to the radicalisation of the Islamic opposition, Anwar Ibrahim greatly helped to sabotage the latter's propaganda and the PAS was heavily defeated in the subsequent elections. ABIM also redefined its stance on crucial issues to the extent that it became known as the 'Anwar bin Ibrahim Movement' by his critics.

The following two decades were characterised by a systematic policy to contain the PAS and label it a reactionary, backward-looking movement. The impact of this negative propaganda, however, should not be overestimated. As revealed by incidents between Christians and Muslims in Penang in January 2010, a creeping Islamisation of the Malaysian state was produced by decisions made at the top and fostered by the increased proximity between local UMNO branches and PAS activists.

Early Commonalities and Genuine Disagreements

Relations between Sudanese and Malaysian Islamists started in the 1970s and initially developed in Britain, Canada or the Gulf States more than in their respective countries. The main actors and sites for these contacts were student associations and university campuses, which also reflected the coercion these movements had to cope with back home. Being in opposition was not easy in states that had talented security apparatuses,

[11] Later on, the issue of *velayat-e faqih*, referring to a book by Ayatollah Khomeini, sometimes known as *Islamic Government*, which supported government by sharia, provoked another strong division among PAS and ABIM, with the young generation of PAS leadership endorsing it against the older one.

[12] Yet, as K. S. Jomo underlines, the ABIM leaders were increasingly concerned that the cooperation with PAS was more beneficial to the latter than to them.

highly repressive laws and obedient judges. Judging from what Sudanese Islamists stated during interviews at that time, their fellow Malaysian Islamic students were very impressed by the level of organisation reached by their colleagues from Africa in terms of funding, internal solidarity, and ability to mobilise beyond their strictly natural constituencies.

Beyond a repressive domestic environment, both groups also shared commonalities. Prior to Dr. Mahathir's appointment as Prime Minister, Malaysia's Internal Security Act allowed two previous Prime Ministers, Tun Razak and Hussein Onn, to jail not only those allegedly working for the Communists but also all those, like journalists and trade unionists, who tried to make their grievances public. It was only when Mahathir took over that Malaysia's prisons became less populated by political opponents. In 1980, there were 1,200 political prisoners, fewer than 100 in 1985 and 27 in 1987, but repression against PAS and other activists never stopped.[13]

In Sudan, as already mentioned, the 1969 coup mounted by Nimairi and his allies was the start of a very repressive decade against the traditional parties and the Islamists. The ICF, led by Hassan al-Turabi, had started a genuine *aggiornamento* by getting into politics and, for the first time and despite modest electoral gains, thinking of itself as a political movement, rather than a lobbying group, that would use tactics or personal connections to persuade leaders of Sudan's traditional political parties to move towards an Islamic State, i.e. a full implementation of *Shari'a*.[14] This strategy suddenly had a much higher price as the ICF was targeted as such.

Apparent commonalities
Certain commonalities need to be underscored here, although their relevance was not the same for both groups. While these common features were debated at the time by Islamist intellectuals, it is unclear how these discussions reshaped their internal understanding and the policies they tried to enforce in their home countries.

First and foremost, they claimed an Islamic identity but had to do so in plural societies, in which the status of other groups was a colonial legacy and an expression of an economic setting they could not fundamentally change. In Sudan, the 'southern problem' was interpreted as a consequence of the isolation ('closed districts' policy) of the south that had been enforced by the Anglo-Egyptian colonial authorities to contain Islamic and nationalist influences from Egypt and northern, urban Sudan. The first solution promoted by the Islamists was to let Islamisation

[13] Farish Noor, *Islam Embedded: The Historical Development of the Pan-Malaysian Islamic Party Pas (1951-2003)*, Vols. I and II (Kuala Lumpur: Malaysian Sociological Research Institute, 2004).
[14] Roland Marchal, 'Eléments pour une sociologie du Front national islamique soudanais', *Les Etudes du CERI*, No. 5 (1995); Abdelwahab al Effendi, *Turabi's Revolution: Islam and Power in Sudan* (London: Grey Seal, 1991).

succeed, although the issue of separation was discussed during a 1987 NIF conference.[15] This understanding, of course, hardly reflected the complexity of the North-South issue and the ambiguities of northern Arab Sudanese identity that was so often implicit in references to Islamic identity.[16] In Malaysia, the leading coalition, the *Barisan Nasional*, was made up of UNMO, Chinese and Indian parties claiming to represent a fair share of their respective communities. After the 1969 anti-Chinese riots, the government enacted a new policy to promote Malays within the economic realm. The situation was different from Sudan in the sense that Chinese and Indian people were well represented in bureaucratic and business elites. The question of identity did not have the same resonance compared with Sudan because the political representation was more democratic and the regional context more conducive to a peaceful handling of these tensions.

A second commonality was the internal ideological diversity of these movements. Although they read texts by the same Islamic thinkers, and were both influenced by the growing financial support provided by Saudi Arabia and the Gulf states, Islamic NGOs, or militant benefactors, they did not endorse the Wahhabi school of thought that became dominant among the Egyptian Muslim Brothers and their associates in the 1960s. Both the Sudanese and Malaysian Islamist movements were reflecting complex local histories and also wanted to distinguish themselves from groups that shared neo-Salafi ideologies. In Sudan, Hassan al-Turabi had had problems enough in the 1960s with the Muslim Brothers and the Ansar-e Sunna, a Wahhabi organisation, not to simply adopt their ideology. He also pretended to develop his own new system of Islamic thought, which prompted him to be open-minded on important social issues (if compared with debate among Islamist or Salafi-Jihadi 'revolutionary groups' in 2009). The situation was both different and very similar in Malaysia. ABIM was pluralistic, which was also a way to confront PAS, the main component of the Islamist movement. As with Sudan's Islamists, it also promoted a more modern reading of the situation to be heard by a constituency that was already benefiting significantly from policies in favour of the *Bumiputra* (people of the land). The leadership personalities were also very important, as demonstrated in Anwar Ibrahim's March 1982 shift to UNMO.

A third commonality is the marginal position both movements occupied in the world Islamist movement at that time. Sudanese Islamists, as mentioned before, were condemned to exile; some leaders were imprisoned for most of the 1970s. Due to the highly ambivalent relations between the Egyptian Muslim Brothers and their Sudanese branch, Hassan al-Turabi expressed a contrasting view on the international Muslim

[15] Abdelwhahab al-Effendi, '"Discovering the South": Sudanese dilemmas for Islam in Africa', *African Affairs*, Vol. 89, Iss. 356 (July 1990), pp. 371-389.
[16] A problem that became palpable in the 1990s in the behaviour in front of non-Arab groups in Sudan (from the *fellata* to the Darfuris or the Nuba Mountain people).

Brotherhood very early on. He was adamantly opposed to having the international organisation controlled by the Egyptian branch simply because it was the country in which the movement had been founded. In addition, he never envisioned this organisation to be Arab-centred and always made clear that all Muslims in the world, including African and Asian, should have their share in the organisation and its leadership. Such a stance could only be enthusiastically endorsed by Anwar Ibrahim, an ambitious and highly articulate politician.

These structural commonalities were also reflected in the personal contacts of Anwar Ibrahim himself. While preparing his PhD thesis in the UK, for instance, he was a close friend of Ahmed al-Turabi, a nephew of Hassan al-Turabi and a leading businessman in Khartoum today. When Dr. Mahathir offered him the chance to join UMNO, another key figure in Sudanese Islamism, Yassin Omar Iman, travelled to Malaysia to discuss the proposal with Anwar. This came at a time when the ICF had joined the SSU in Sudan, and the Sudanese Islamists were advising the same move for Anwar. Pragmatism was the defining mood of the day.

Confronting the reality of power
These relations continued in the 1980s but significantly cooled after 1989 for a while. Anwar Ibrahim, to his credit, challenged his Sudanese friends and criticised the repression and huge human rights violations that took place after the June 1989 coup in Khartoum. Were these policies expressing the open-mindedness and free discussion promoted by Hassan al-Turabi while in opposition?[17] It took time to reconcile the different viewpoints, but Anwar was clearly more strategic in his thinking than his fellow Sudanese Islamists, who were naïve and short-sighted in their belief in governing by coercion. This situation in Sudan eventually created the conditions for adventurous policies and international sanctions. With hindsight, some Sudanese Islamists came to believe that their Malaysian counterparts were more serious in the implementation of the same ideas. While Anwar had a quite vibrant and articulate discourse on cultural change, the Sudanese were too quickly satisfied by rhetoric more than action. One example is the establishment of the Popular Defence Force in northern Sudan, whose role was initially to provide greater Islamic knowledge and better education to the less educated youth. This became a coercive institution to control university students and provoked severe rows between the regime's civilian and military figures.

These connections between the two Islamist groups played a role when Petronas became involved in Sudan's oil sector but, fundamentally, state interests on both sides were decisive, even if the Malaysian Islamists, who were working within Petronas, helped to narrow differences in the numerous discussions that took place.[18] When Anwar Ibrahim was

[17] Interview with Mahbub Abdisalam, Paris, 20 November 2009.
[18] Interview with Omar Yassin, Sudan's first Ambassador to Kuala Lumpur, Khartoum, August 2009.

dismissed by Mahathir and sent to court, the Sudanese regime was not in a position to do much as it also was cornered and required Mahathir's support to deal with the IMF.[19] However, Anwar Ibrahim was not let down completely: certain people, including the late Ahmed Osman Mekki, went to talk to Mahathir and visited Anwar Ibrahim in jail. When he was released and went to Germany for medical care in 2004, Anwar Ibrahim was also visited by Ali el-Haj (at present the assistant Secretary General in Hassan al-Turabi's current political organisation, the Popular Congress), Dr. Alamin Osman (his old friend from his student days) and other Sudanese Islamist cadres to show their solidarity. The relationships are not substantial today, especially because Sudan's jigsaw concentrates most of the energy of its politicians.

Malaysia as a Model? Homologies and Lessons Learned

Malaysia was a potential model for Sudan in many ways. First, connections with Anwar Ibrahim, and then Mahathir's strong character, were good incentives to promote a Sudanese interest in the political dynamics of Malaysia. In the 1990s, despite focusing on their own internal problems, Sudan's Islamist leaders reasserted their interest for two main reasons. Throughout that period, Kuala Lumpur decided to play the Islamic card in its international relations. Contacts with the Gulf States were fostered, and Malaysia became involved in peacekeeping operations in Muslim countries such as Somalia and Bosnia.[20] Furthermore, the involvement of Petronas was also a clear signal that friends were helping. This interest was illustrated by different measures. Several Sudanese Islamist cadres were sent to Kuala Lumpur's International Islamic University, and the ambassadors appointed there from 1990 on had evident connections with the Sudanese security apparatus. This interest was also reinforced by the proximity of Singapore and the alternative this banking sector offered to the Sudanese Islamists after international sanctions were adopted in 1996 (linked to the attempted assassination of the then Egyptian President, Hosni Mubarak, in June 1995 in Addis Ababa).

The fascination Malaysia exerts on many other Third World countries is linked to a number of features that clearly oppose the mainstream conditionalities those countries had to accept from donors in the 1980s, when the debt crisis reached its peak. Two are relevant here and certainly caught the attention of Sudan's would-be Islamist rulers.

---

[19] The IMF estimated that Sudan was $1.7 billion in arrears on its loans in 1996. It had reduced its monthly instalments from $4 million to $250,000, but Sudan still had difficulties keeping up the payments. *Africa Confidential* reported that Malaysia paid instalments for Sudan in autumn 1996 and January 1997. The transactions had to be disguised, it being against IMF rules for one state to pay another's debts. See *Africa Confidential* Vol. 38, No. 5, 28 February 1997.

[20] Shanti Nair, *Islam in the Malaysian Foreign Policy* (London: Routledge, 1997).

A new business class attached to a developmental state
Nimairi emphasised his ambition of making Sudan self-sufficient and transforming the country he ruled into the 'breadbasket of the Arab world'. The notion of the 'developmental state' was very popular, especially among Sudanese Islamists. It fitted their nationalism and highly instrumental notion of the state, identifying it as the magic tool to reform and reshape society as a whole. While this notion was a core concept in the theory of African socialism (which has nothing to do with Marxist socialism), it was regarded with suspicion by the donors and Bretton Woods institutions very early on, and flatly opposed after 1975.

Despite this negative international stance, Malaysia under Mahathir was a clear example of a 'successful developmental state', at least as seen from outside. Mahathir, moreover, was hardly shy about his choice. Despite several financial scandals exposing corruption in the parastatal sector, UMNO's oligopolistic control of business, and 'crony capitalism', Malaysia was able to stick to this policy, albeit with noticeable amendments after 1991.

An offshoot of this policy was the support provided to the Malays to go into business and become successful entrepreneurs (though the debatable success of this policy over two decades cannot be properly assessed here). The appointment of Mahathir as Prime Minister was one consequence of the growing influence of a Malay middle class benefiting handsomely from public contracts. For years, Dr. Mahathir's trips to Africa were an opportunity provided – and sometimes even ordered – to Malay companies to access new business arenas and expand overseas. Internally, they were the backbone of the support provided by the Malay community to UMNO and the ruling coalition.

Mahathir's decision to step down in 2003 was to a large extent the result of the failure to build such a self-sustaining class. No one became more critical of this policy's lack of achievement than Dr. Mahathir himself. Yet, the new Malaysian bourgeoisie – even if it was rentier by nature, as Mahathir eventually acknowledged – appeared to be both a staunch critic of the Mahathir era and a leading opponent of a more radical Islamisation that would jeopardise relationships with the West (the US being Malaysia's top trade partner) and other key non-Muslim countries in the region (i.e. Japan, the genuine driver of Malaysia's industrial development).

Many Third World or African leaders never explore the intricacies of parastatal firms' accounts and the real financial costs of Malaysia's development. The image of modernity that Kuala Lumpur projected was such that no critic could challenge the assumed success of Mahathir's policies. This was also the case because it was congruent with ideological precedents cultivated in the African continent by potential rulers and also broadly corresponded to several privatisation experiments under IMF and World Bank tutelage, as illustrated, for instance, in Mozambique or the Ivory Coast.

In Sudan, the question of developing a more indigenous bourgeoisie was not at the forefront in the 1990s. The Nimairi era (1969-1985) had witnessed the closure of many foreign businesses and the reduction of the 'compradore' bourgeoisie to a cluster of Greek, Lebanese, Syrian and Egyptian businesspeople. The main challenge for the Islamists was to root out the bourgeoisie that was symbiotically connected with the traditional parties as part of the 'colonial pact' framed in the 1910s and 1920s with the reintegration of the Mahdi family into the political arena and the containment of Egyptian nationalism.[21]

This reshaping of Sudan's business elites was achieved through coercive tactics and macro-economic policies in the three years following the June 1989 coup. The concept then, as in Malaysia, was to promote a new business class made up of commoners, rather than members of the old, great trading families associated with the traditional political parties. Being rich or getting richer, as in Malaysia, was not a contradiction of the ethos prevailing at the time: it was a way of strengthening the regime, and, as in Malaysia, the real costs of this choice should not be underestimated. Many new entrepreneurs were at best amateurs, some were fond of embezzlement, and quite a few were unsuccessful despite the state's support.

What made things different was the nature of the regimes. The non-Malay business realm in Malaysia reacted by adapting to the new challenges, mostly by 'corporatising' its assets: non-Malay shareholders were controlling companies that had Malay CEOs acting under the scrutiny of skilled deputies. In a nutshell, they lost precedence, but not pre-eminence: they were no longer the public faces of the companies, but still controlled them. The dynamics of growth was more opportunistic in Sudan, as it was fundamentally linked to the edging out of certain economic actors, opportunities created for Islamic NGOs, and the grip of the security apparatus on segments of the most profitable contracts, especially those linked to import-export trade, the oil sector and information technology. This difference relied on the contrasting legitimacy enjoyed by the two regimes. While Sudanese Islamists never risked returning to fair political elections until the CPA and 2010, the Malaysian parties have been competing in several elections. One should not be naïve: many Malaysian elections were rigged, and activists were imprisoned. Yet nothing is comparable to the December 2000 elections in Sudan when Omar al-Bashir was re-elected with a Brezhnevian score, despite a very low turnout.

A further striking comparative element concerns the oil sector's autonomy vis-à-vis other businesses owned or managed by the ruling party. In both countries, oil revenues constitute the main share of the national budget, but the autonomy of the oil sector is noticeable. Petronas

---

[21] Tim Niblock, *Class and Power in Sudan: The dynamics of Sudanese Politics 1898-1985* (New York: State University of New York Press, 1987).

looks very much like a state within the state and provides its accounts only to the Prime Minister. Under Mahathir, the regime's leading figures tried to interfere with the company's contracting practices or lobby to get their 'protégés' promoted in its hierarchy. None were successful. This was not the sole responsibility of the CEO, who maintained an unshared authority over the management of the company, but also the unquestionable political support he always enjoyed from Mahathir. This was not without conditions, as demonstrated by the aftermath of the Asian financial crisis, when Petronas was asked to pay for a large share of the debts created by the poor management of some public companies such as Proton. In Sudan, nothing could sum up the situation more revealingly than the following fact: during negotiations to the create the Government of National Unity in September 2005, the SPLM requested control of the Ministry of Energy and Mining, which was responsible for oil, but was told that that request was not realistic because the then minister, Awad al-Jaz, considered the ministry his own child.[22] Even his colleagues had no leverage over the way his ministry recruited and defined its relations with outside players.

Opening up to claim a more global role

Malaysia and Sudan were ambitious in the way they sought to assert their own importance in the international arena beyond Islamic circles. Both could develop their strategy according to several areas of economic potential and talented politicians, yet they were markedly unable to mobilise the same scale of means and offer the same signals of success.

The usual way to promote a country was to acquire new friends and keep old ones. Dr. Mahathir came to be perceived in Africa and beyond as a Third Worldist and a prominent advocate of South-South cooperation. It should not be forgotten, however, that he was very heterodox in his personal relations (he also became a close friend of Margaret Thatcher and Ronald Reagan) and that his anti-Communism was based both on Malaysian history (the Malaysian Communist guerrillas were mostly Chinese) and a firm commitment to the West. Dr. Mahathir, nonetheless, could still make speeches denouncing imperialism or the undue domination of the North over the South and shake hands with unsavoury rulers like Zimbabwe's Robert Mugabe.

It took a long time for Sudan's Islamists to actually think to do the same. To be fair, they understood very early on that they would not get much sympathy from the West. After Nimairi was overthrown, the Islamists rallied under the National Islamic Front, a new organisation. Confident that sooner or later they would return to power, they therefore looked for scenarios and likely international support. China was seriously considered, which explains why the NIF sent a huge delegation to Beijing in

---

[22] Awad al-Jaz moved to the Ministry of Economy and then, in 2010, to the Ministry of Industry in the GoNU but maintained the upper hand on his former ministry.

1987 to meet with the Communist Party of China. This delegation was made up of leaders, including Hassan al-Turabi, representatives of the various, NIF-linked social organisations, and business representatives. A Chinese delegation visited Khartoum in 1988 and the first contacts were cultivated, especially because, at that time, the NIF was participating in the government under Prime Minister Sadiq al-Mahdi. While the real discussions on oil exploitation started later, these two moments can be considered the start of a lasting relationship between the current regimes in Khartoum and Beijing.

Relations with the West were more problematic. For over a decade, France was a friendly listener; other European countries were often pragmatic in their relations with Sudan as far as business was concerned. The NIF leadership crisis in December 1999 was the real turning point. The removal of Hassan al-Turabi from power was used as proof that the regime wanted to normalise relations with the West. Contacts and cooperation started early in 2000 with Washington but were acknowledged only after 9/11. The conflict in Darfur and the reluctant implementation of the CPA, however, underlined the fragility of these developments.

While Malaysia's rulers were able to play both cards – the West and the global South – at the same time, Sudan's Islamists seem to have had difficulty in keeping their new friends. Today many amongst the ruling elite in Khartoum disagree with betting only on China and Russia, as both countries have already shown that they could abandon Sudan for higher stakes. A few, led by a leading NIF/NCP member of and Presidential Advisor in Sudan's Government of National Unity, Nafie Ali Nafie, are convinced that any reconciliation with the West would come at too high a cost and that Asian countries can be the alternative. Malaysia may see this differently.

Promotion does not only proceed through politics and diplomacy, however, and educational facilities can dramatically increase a country's prestige. Both regimes, indeed, wanted to promote their country as an educational hub for the global Islamic Ummah, but were not in the same situation to implement such ideas. The International Islamic University, located in the outskirts of Kuala Lumpur, is a vast complex resembling any US university campus. The staff is truly international and the system of grants and scholarships allows the university to have a large spectrum of lecturers and students. Although Malaysia committed resources to this institution over time, it was also able to secure funding from various sources, notably the Gulf States.

Islamists possessed the same ambition in Sudan but were operating in a much more difficult environment. Sudan was perceived for decades, firstly, as a very poor country that backtracked when foreigners were interested in investing, because of political mismanagement and a deeply rooted culture of corruption. The Islamic African Center, established south of Khartoum in 1977,[23] was not impressive in terms of infrastruc-

[23] Visit its website for more information: http://www.iua.edu.sd/history.htm

ture, though it actually played an important role in identifying religious military personnel attending training sessions there until 1985. Its main function was to provide a higher religious education and vocational skills that would allow the trainees, who were supposed to be African, to spend part of their time making *daw'a* and being able to have a normal job.

After the 1989 coup, this limited scope was re-evaluated and the Center became the International University of Africa, a higher educational institution. Although its name does not mention any religious reference, the main aim has not changed and the backbone of the teaching remains connected to Islamic sciences. This institution has been successful, attracting students from West Africa and the Horn (especially Somalis), but does not compare very favourably with its counterpart in Malaysia. In Kuala Lumpur, students come from all over the world.[24] In Khartoum, the scope is more limited, the facilities are not equivalent, and lecturers do not offer the same variety of nationalities and expertise.

It is not known for sure whether Dr. Mahathir had a premonition of the future global development of the Islamic financial sector when he announced in 1981 that an Islamic bank would be operating in Malaysia. Yet he was right on this point. At that time, the decision might have appeared as a way to channel funding from the Gulf to Malaysia, but the actual outcome was to promote Malaysia as a centre for Islamic finance in Asia. The Islamic financial sector emerged as a key element of the Malaysian economy following the establishment of a single national *Shari'a* Advisory Council within the Central Bank, Bank Negara Malaysia, which also oversees the country's parallel conventional financial system. Malaysian Islamic banking assets account for about $65 billion with *takaful* (Islamic insurance) assets of about $2.6 billion and Islamic capital market stocks with a market value of about $235 billion.[25] The country is also a centre for *sukuk* (Islamic bonds) and is developing an Islamic commodities market. According to Bank Negara, Islamic assets under management globally amount to about $750 billion and are growing at between 15 and 20% a year. Malaysia has signed agreements with a number of countries, including Bahrain, Dubai and Qatar, to collaborate on developing Islamic finance, including mutual recognition of common standards.

The introduction of Islamic banks in Sudan in the late 1970s, notably Faisal Islamic Bank and Barakat Islamic Bank, was both a consequence of the huge flows of petrodollars invested by the Gulf States and a way of promoting an Islamic economic agenda. They greatly benefited from advantages not given to local private banking institutions and from the political support provided by the Islamists who had positions within the state. These banks were not as successful as their equivalents in Malaysia, for several reasons. The Sudanese state was often near to bankruptcy but

---

[24] As the author has personally witnessed.

[25] For further details, visit the website of the Association of Islamic Banking Institutions Malaysia: www.aibim.com

was also the only significant economic actor up to the latter half of the 1990s, when major international oil companies became involved. Because of the political climate, the Islamic banks could hardly grow; Sudan was under heavy UN and US sanctions after 1996.[26] Moreover, as demonstrated by successive IMF reports from the late 1990s, bad loans were too common in certain banks not to see patterns of corruption and embezzlement. Old habits die hard. Again, one may judge that Sudan very superficially promoted an Islamic banking sector but did not seek to regulate or expand it beyond what was strictly necessary for the state of the economy. Some in Khartoum in 2009 even mentioned that those Islamic banks still functioning were often also ready to offer conventional banking services to keep or gain new customers.[27]

Conclusion

From the early 1980s, Malaysia and Sudan became involved in Islamisation processes decided upon by their governments and pursued, at first, to weaken political opponents. The Islamists in both countries became part of the ruling elites and were able to push their own agendas. In these processes, the struggle for power provoked the defeat of the faction that claimed to be more Islamic (Anwar Ibrahim in Malaysia, Hassan al-Turabi in Sudan). Their policies, however, have had drastic, lasting impacts on the social fabric of their respective countries. The strongest commonality in the early days of their relations, the wish to build an inclusive modern Islamic State in a plural society, has evaporated. In Malaysia, Anwar Ibrahim has been fighting for over a decade to be cleared of dubious charges of sexual crimes and to compete for the leadership of the country. At the social level, tensions between communities and among Malays have increased, and mobilise the rhetoric of militant Islam. The elites that prospered under Mahathir seem reluctant to stabilise these processes. Despite the apparent prosperity of ruling elites in Sudan, inequalities have increased to the extent that internal peace could be challenged tomorrow and not just in Darfur. Coercive policies – more brutal and less targeted than in Malaysia – seem still the panacea for a regime that is unable to reform itself, despite the impressive challenges it faces at home and internationally.

The division of the country and the birth of a new state of South Sudan constitute a new challenge for the Sudanese Islamists. These events throw the Sudanese nationalism that informed Islamism into crisis and therefore create further problems (and tensions) concerning the definition of being (north) Sudanese. The attempt to continue business as usual by reasserting a coercive vision of the state and Islam would only provide

---

[26] Sanctions actually started in the early 1980s because of the non-payment of interest on the IMF loans.

[27] Interview with international financial expert, Khartoum, August 2009.

new motives for further fragmentation. It is far from sure that the Malaysian Islamists may be in a better position to advise their Sudanese counterparts on a way out. In their own manner, they may opt for a more conservative attitude toward the state and their plural society as a means to gain a grip on their potential constituency. In both cases, a window of opportunity on to a greater commitment to democratic values seems to be closing because of local and more global dynamics.

6

'Dams are Development'

China, the Al-Ingaz Regime & the Political Economy of the Sudanese Nile

HARRY VERHOEVEN

'Why do we need dams? Because dams are development' (Chief Technical Advisor to the Sudanese Minister of Water Resources and Irrigation)[1]

'[The] Merowe Dam's contribution will be as great as the oil...It is the greatest developmental project in Sudan's modern history' (Awad al-Jaz, Al-Ingaz economic 'czar')[2]

Hydro-electric dams have long fascinated policy-makers, who have equated them with 'development'. In recent decades, they have attracted criticism because of the ecological, social and cultural costs associated with their construction. No country in the world has more experience with dam-building than China, currently involved in the construction of more than 250 dams outside its borders. Beijing does not simply provide the capital and technical expertise for these 'temples of modernity', but increasingly its growth model, heavily reliant on infrastructure and state control, fascinates its partner countries and many African regimes crave Chinese-built dams as symbols of civilisation and prestige.

China's excellent relations with Sudan have been a critical factor, directly and indirectly, in the development of the latter's ambitious Dam Programme. Together with the Agricultural Revival Programme, big dams are an integral part of Khartoum's 'hydro-agricultural mission', the Al-Ingaz regime's high modernist attempt at recalibrating northern Sudan's political economy and dealing with the imminent secession of South Sudan.[3] They offer the possibility of mass electricity generation and are critical

[1] Interview with the author, Khartoum, September 2009.
[2] Website of the Dam Implementation Unit, http://www.merowedam.gov.sd/en/testimonials.html
[3] The Al-Ingaz – 'Salvation' – regime came to power on 30 June 1989 via a military coup, which installed a Revolutionary Command Council for National Salvation and a shadow government of Islamists that took all important decisions. The term 'Al-Ingaz' will be used throughout the chapter to refer to the regime, including in the post-2000 and post-2005 period. It is useful to continue using this specific term for two main reasons. Firstly, the regime continues to refer to itself in this way, informally but also formally on a regular basis; secondly, it underlines important continuities about the regime that are central to the argument over the entire 1989-2011 period. Despite major political changes, large swathes of the political-economic vision and normative assumptions made by the regime leadership remain fundamentally unaltered.

for irrigation, thus helping to feed Sudan's growing population and Arab-African markets further afield. The old dream of extensively damming the Nile was financially impossible until the advent of the Sino-Arab-Sudanese partnership in the 1990s, involving an intricate mix of technical assistance, diplomatic protection, arms transfers, cash crops and petro-flows. However, Al-Ingaz' hydro-agricultural designs are generating local and regional resistance that might well turn violent in the future.

This chapter begins by sketching the deeper political-economic and ideological trends in which Sudan's Dam Programme must be situated, with special attention to China's role in reshaping the international landscape of dam construction. It explains why dam-building matters to China and how Chinese companies matter to Sudan. The chapter then proceeds to analyse Khartoum's 'hydro-agricultural mission', setting out both the historical context of the link between development, politics and hydropower in the Nile Basin and the political-economy of Sudan's water resources today. Finally, the analysis turns towards the role of China, Egypt and several Gulf Arab states in the hydropolitics and agro-investments around the Nile and the local and regional fall-out of these rapidly expanding developments. Dams, as will be shown, are definitely development to some, but not to all.[4]

The Resurrection of Dam Building in the Global South: China as a Dam Superpower

In the imagination of many developmentalists, dams have long occupied a prominent position as symbols of man taming the forces of nature, bending the course of rivers to put them at the disposal of irrigation planners and industrial forces. One of India's founding fathers and first Prime Minister, Jawaharlal Nehru, famously referred to dams as the country's 'temples of modernity'. Nehru considered them critical for domestic industry-powered growth and for Delhi's international status, putting newly independent India in the category of 'advanced' countries able to muster the expertise to build such icons of progress.[5] Development ideology in the 1960s and 1970s, as embodied by Robert McNamara's World Bank, prioritised big infrastructure works and especially megadams in national economic strategies: the idea was that

---

[4] This chapter relies heavily on elite interviewing, particularly with the past and present leadership of the Al-Ingaz regime and the intellectual driving forces behind Al-Harakat Al-Islamiyyah, including Dr. Hassan al-Turabi, Dr. Ghazi Salah-ud-Din, Abdelrahim Hamdi, Dr. Mustafa Osman Ismael, Dr. Abdelrahman Khalifa, Prof. Ali Geneif, Prof. Abdulla Ahmed Abdulla, Dr. Abdelhalim Al Muta'afi, Mohamed El-Amin Khalifa, Prof. Hassan Makki, Prof. At-Tayeb Zain Al-Abdin, Prof. Mustafa Idris and many others between July-August 2009 and March 2011.

[5] Edward Luce, *In Spite of the Gods: The Strange Rise of Modern India* (London: Abacus, 2006), pp. 27-28.

dams did not just produce electricity and facilitate irrigation through flood control, but that they were 'game changing' infrastructure – the kind of intervention that would help turn around a poor country's economic fortunes with one master stroke. Drawing inspiration from the American Hoover Dam and the Tennessee Valley Authority, dams were credited with almost magical powers of economic revival, particularly in areas long considered to be 'backward' or 'barren'.[6]

The most illustrious example in the Nile Basin was the Aswan High Dam, which, together with the Suez Canal, was at the heart of the 1956 geopolitical crisis when Nasser's Egypt sought to emancipate itself from colonial over-rule. For Nasser, nationalising the canal and building Aswan were about demonstrating technical prowess and regional autonomy. They were also about transforming Egyptian agriculture, which would no longer have to suffer the uncertainty of the annual Nile floods as it had done for thousands of years.[7] The dam enables reliable, all-year-round supply of irrigation water, thus allowing for massive increases in food production, much needed given Egypt's soaring population. Aswan was a Pharaonic project of personal prestige for Nasser and underlined Cairo's ambitions to lead the Arab world out of the century of colonial humiliation. Scientists emphasised that huge evaporation rates and accumulating sediment made the dam deeply problematic in ecological terms. This was deemed unimportant, however, as was the mass displacement of tens of thousands of Sudanese Nubians, whose ancestral lands were flooded. The upstream countries were simply not consulted when Cairo and Khartoum signed the 1959 Nile Treaty, effectively dividing the waters between them and leaving only a few drops for Ethiopia and Uganda. Aswan symbolised Egypt taking its destiny into its own hands: it was declared a civilisational milestone that would brook no opposition.[8]

Resistance to big dams gradually emerged in industrialised countries but the dam industry overcame the loss of OECD markets by migrating to the global South. Western donors financed dams as aid, under the banner of sustainable development and apolitical poverty alleviation, with local elites as eager partners.[9] Yet, particularly from the 1980s onwards, local communities began contesting the costs, which included the loss of fertile land, displacement of millions of often voiceless people, destruction of ecosystems, lack of democratic debate and cost over-runs, corruption and underperformance of the dams. The resultant complex social

---

[6] Erik Swyngedouw, 'Technonatural revolutions: The scalar politics of Franco's hydro-social dream for Spain, 1939-1975', *Transactions of the Institute of British Geographers*, New Series 32(1), (2007), pp. 9-28.

[7] Timothy Mitchell, *Rule of Experts: Egypt, Techno-Politics, Modernity* (Berkeley: University of California Press, 2002), pp.43-44.

[8] John Waterbury, *The Egypt of Nasser and Sadat: The Political Economy of Two Regimes* (Princeton: Princeton University Press, 1983), pp. 297-298.

[9] Ann Danaiya Usher, *Dams as Aid: a political anatomy of Nordic development thinking* (London: Routledge, 1997).

conflicts involve national governments, international financial institutions, multinational corporations, regional states, powerful landowners, tens of millions of poor farmers and radical social movements.[10] What often began as 'green' megaprojects supposedly providing irrigation water to smallholders has unleashed nation-wide discussions about the developmental model elites in Delhi and elsewhere have pursued since independence. Academics and activists have situated dams within the broader context of utopian attempts to forcibly modernise the countryside, favouring politically privileged constituencies at the expense of the voiceless (and tribal groups in particular).[11] For many, resisting dams is not just about the particular problems associated with hydro-infrastructure *in situ*; it means opposing top-down developmentalism posing as technocracy in general.

Dams largely went out of development fashion after 2000. The World Commission on Dams called for fundamental reforms of the entire dam business and the practices of international partners and national governments.[12] In recent years, however, dams have been staging a comeback. Whereas the World Bank, battered by criticism, remains cautious in the projects it funds, China has emerged as the world's dam superpower. China is home to the record-breaking controversial Three Gorges Dam as well as thousands of smaller ones. Beijing sees hydro-infrastructure as an essential factor in its growth miracle. The flood control and irrigation that big dams enable, as well as the thousands of megawatts of power they generate, have been critical inputs as agriculture and industry have grown at breathtaking rates. It might not be a coincidence that the Communist Party of China's politburo is dominated by engineers; the combination of Marxist-Leninism and engineering science leads to deeply held beliefs about social transformation through grand top-down interventions and qualitative leaps forward that tame nature.[13] Beijing accepts that there is a price to pay for damming its rivers and has made serious efforts to improve compensation schemes for displaced populations (one million people alone in the case of the Three Gorges Dam).[14] There is no question, however, that the

[10] Jean Drèze, Meera Samson, Satyajit Singh eds., *The Dam and the Nation: Displacement and Resettlement in the Narmada Valley* (Oxford: Oxford University Press, 1997); John Wood, *The Politics of Water Resource Development in India: The Narmada Dams Controversy* (New Delhi: Sage Publications, 2007).

[11] James C. Scott, *Seeing like a State* (New Haven and London: Yale University Press, 1998); David Mosse, *The Rule of Water: Statecraft, Ecology and Collective Action in South India* (Oxford: Oxford University Press, 2003); Arundhati Roy, *The Algebra of Infinite Justice* (London: Flamingo, 2002).

[12] World Commission on Dams, *Dams and Development: a New Framework for Decision Making* (London: Earthscan, 2000).

[13] Richard McGregor, *The Party: The Secret World of China's Communist Rulers* (London: Allen Lane, 2010).

[14] Michael M. Cernea and Hari Mohan Mathur eds., *Can Compensation Prevent Impoverishment? Reforming Resettlement through Investments and Benefit-Sharing* (Oxford: Oxford University Press, 2008), pp. 82-90.

benefits far outweigh the costs in the eyes of the transformers of 'backward' China: dams are development.

As China has dramatically scaled up its economic interactions with other developing countries, its role in dam-building in Latin America, Asia and Africa has often been overlooked, with petro-dollars and the import of copper, uranium and food crops attracting plenty of attention. Chinese companies are now involved in more than 250 different foreign dam projects, thus potentially being at the forefront of an energy and agriculture revolution, including in the Nile Basin.[15] Chinese enterprises are building dams in some of the world's most challenging locations, often accepting contracts that were turned down by the traditional donors, and thus emerging as a veritable alternative to Western conditionality and geopolitics. Chinese banks have lavishly funded African hydro-infrastructure, contributing to fears about the growth of a new debt mountain just when Western countries have made serious efforts to finally cancel longstanding Third World arrears.

Beijing's export of its dam model is led by the Sinohydro Corporation, the world's number one hydroelectric company and leading dam-builder in China and across Africa. It has a self-declared market share over 50% of the new dams being built worldwide. Sinohydro is a state-owned conglomerate working on the entire spectrum of dam-related activities, from building and engineering consultancy over investment and maintenance to R&D. As part of the Chinese government's preference for extensive, multi-year package deals with African partners, Sinohydro, through its myriad companies and headed by the powerful party loyalist Fan Jixiang, is Beijing's privileged partner to rehabilitate hospitals in Angola, build housing schemes in Libya, implement irrigation projects in Algeria and construct railways in the DRC. Dams, however, remain the jewels in its crown: Sinohydro proudly claims to have installed 130000MW in hydropower capacity – 20000MW just in 2009 – and has broken all records in terms of size, construction speed and cost of dams.[16] Sinohydro's African operations account for 42% of its non-Chinese profits.[17] Besides Sudan, it has built – or is building – dams in 25 other African countries.

Sinohydro is also the leading partner of Khartoum for its Dam Programme. The conglomerate sees its activities in Sudan and Angola as models for its 'go-out' strategy in other developing countries. If Sudanese oil was once the jewel in CNPC's crown, then today the Merowe Dam in northern Sudan is Sinohydro's shining example. Beijing spares no costs to back this aggressive push into new markets: Sinohydro's triple-A credit rating is underpinned by the full support of the China EXIM Bank, the China Development Bank and the Construction Bank of China.

---

[15] International Rivers, 'China Overseas Dam List', see overview sheet on the IR website; http://www.internationalrivers.org/en/node/3110

[16] Sinohydro website, http://eng.sinohydro.com/en/

[17] Official Sinohydro Company presentation, to be found on http://eng.sinohydro.com/en/

Unsurprisingly, in Sudan and elsewhere in Africa, it is thus Sinohydro that has been both celebrated and vilified because of its controversial, 'game changing' role in hydropower development.

Finally, there is also the softer, subtler influence China is exerting on African political elites: the high modernist idea of 'economic growth through big infrastructure' is making a comeback.[18] Sinohydro's engineering prowess and readiness to take on even the most questionable dam projects matter to Beijing: they are good business and underscore that China's engagement with Africa is about more than dumping second-class goods on a secondary market, as critics often allege. Complex technical achievements, such as Sinohydro's dams, boost Chinese confidence and impress African partners who often equate 'progress' with big projects of the dam variety. Fed up with decades of (post-) Washington Consensus policies and the failure of the liberal political-economic Western agenda, Luanda, Addis Ababa and Algiers (to name but a few) have fallen in love with a simplified narrative of China's growth miracle: political authoritarianism and mass investment in roads, bridges and dams. They are reproducing a high modernism that is often obsessed with the material products of modernity but engages very little with the 'software' (institutions) that really drive systemic societal change. Big dams symbolise not only the rapid intensification of ties between China and African countries but also the growing 'ideological' influence of Beijing on the political-economic vision of African elites.

Khartoum's 'Hydro-agricultural Mission': The Context for Sudan's Dam Programme

Sudan ranks among the poorest countries in the world but nevertheless eyes an ambitious expansion of its infrastructure. Its Dam Programme is an absolute developmental priority for Khartoum's Islamists, who have been in power since 1989. Dreams of damming the Nile and controlling its flows are not new, as illustrated by Nasser's Aswan High Dam. Egyptian civilisation, of which northern Sudan (Nubia) formed an integral part, was built on a nexus of water and agriculture, and the ability of a surprisingly decentralised system of water control and irrigation to regularly produce huge surpluses that underpinned Egypt's political and military strength.[19] Napoleon's enlightened *savants*, the scientific elite Bonaparte brought on

---

[18] 'High modernism' is defined here as an often implicitly held belief in the virtues of modernity and techno-scientific innovation and the concrete expression of that belief through politics (e.g. government-led social engineering) and culture (e.g. austere, abstract and 'futuristic' architecture). For an excellent critique of high modernism, see James C. Scott, *Seeing Like a State, op. cit.*

[19] Fekri Hassan, 'The Dynamics of a Riverine Civilization: A Geoarchaeological Perspective on the Nile Valley, Egypt', *World Archaeology.* 29, 1 (1997), p.69.

his colonising mission, believed that only 'rational' water management – the building of canals, dams and irrigation infrastructure – could revive Cairo's lost greatness, and they drafted ambitious modernist plans. Muhammad Ali, the nineteenth-century founder of modern Egypt, drew inspiration from that top-down vision of a simultaneous centralisation of water control and political-economic power to revolutionise Egyptian agriculture.[20] His 1820/21 invasion of Sudan was in part a bold attempt to control the Nile from its sources to the Mediterranean.

Sudan's water resources also played a key role in the British imperial system. Sudan fulfilled the strategic role of keeping the Nile in British hands and producing cotton for the Lancashire textile factories. British engineers developed the 'Century Storage' plan for the Nile to balance low flow years by high ones through over-year storage in a series of dam reservoirs all along the river, trying to reach an optimal equilibrium through centralised water management.[21] The world's biggest irrigated scheme was set up in 1926 in Gezira, between the White and Blue Niles, and involved a pivotal role for the Sennar Dam. The scheme generated incredible wealth – for the imperialists. Gezira was an enclave for which canals, housing schemes and transport infrastructure were built, but locked in nefarious patterns of accumulation in the hands of privileged elites, while most of the country was ignored.[22]

That this had nothing to do with development of the Sudanese population was also evident after independence. Khartoum depended for 80% of its export earnings on cotton (now oil) and has struggled ever since to develop a more balanced relationship with the global system. This asymmetry is mirrored in the internal, *de facto* colonial structure of Sudan's political economy: investment in industry, agriculture and public services has been disproportionately concentrated in Khartoum and adjacent areas, while a violent mix of neglect and selective extraction of resources regulates interaction with the peripheries – the south, Darfur, the east, and the high north.[23] Control is maintained through violence, patronage, and notions of cultural-racial supremacy of the riverain elite, the so called *Awlad al-Balad*.[24] Despite paying strong lip service to the ideal of Sudan as a possible agricultural superpower, Khartoum's multiple attempts at becoming the 'breadbasket' of the Middle East have faltered due to incompetence, the disregard for smallholders and, above all, the prioritisation of political goals, like patronage and resisting decentralisation of power, over

[20] Timothy Mitchell, *The Colonisation of Egypt* (Cairo: American University Press, 1989).
[21] Robert O. Collins, *The Waters of the Nile: Hydropolitics and the Jonglei Canal 1900-1988* (Oxford: Oxford University Press, 1990), pp.198-202.
[22] Tony Barnett, *The Gezira Scheme: An Illusion of Development* (London: Frank Cass, 1977).
[23] Douglas Johnson, *The Root Causes of Sudan's Civil Wars* (Oxford: James Currey, 2003), pp.16-19.
[24] Literally meaning 'Sons of the Land' or 'Boys of the Land', this Sudanese expression refers to the dominance of the Shaigiyya, Ja'alyin and Danagla tribes in political and economic life. These tribes were privileged during the colonial era and have wielded disproportionate power since 1956 in independent Sudan.

the economic and ecological prerequisites of a green revolution.[25]

The Al-Ingaz regime, which seized power on 30 June 1989, has also been fascinated by the control over water and land. Its Dam Programme should not be understood as a new idea to develop Sudan, but as the continuation of old notions of centralisation, man-nature relations and the link between political power and water infrastructure. Just like previous governments, it mixes high modernist visions of the top-down engineering of Sudanese society and agriculture with sophisticated political-economic strategies of further entrenching itself in power. In the first decade of their rule, the Islamists were unable to implement their agenda for the hydro-agricultural transformation of Sudan and no dams were built. Sheikh Hassan al-Turabi, the regime's godfather, was too busy trying to export the revolution from Khartoum; the army and paramilitaries were caught up in the bloody civil war with the SPLA; and the economic team was preoccupied with guiding Sudan out of the crisis that impoverished the entire nation. Under the aegis of Abdelrahim Hamdi, the Minister of Finance, the Programme for Economic Salvation combined bold price liberalisation with debt defaulting and command-and-control to increase food production in eastern and central Sudan. Trade unions were crushed and subsidies were removed. Despite the regime's break in relations with Washington, the IMF and the West's Gulf allies (and the associated sanctions and refusal of assistance), the food and fuel shortages that had brought even Khartoum to its knees, disappeared. A big propaganda victory in this respect was Turabi's declaration in 1992 that Sudan had become self-sufficient in wheat production: to the Islamists, it demonstrated how effective their unorthodox recovery programme was (at least for those people deemed worthy of being fed; 'the honour of living' was not extended to the famine-stricken regions of South Kordofan, Jonglei and Bahr al-Ghazal).[26]

The convergence of three developments enabled Al-Ingaz to move away from a survival strategy into regime consolidation. Following the Mubarak assassination attempt in 1995, and the 1998 plane crash of Vice-President Zubeir, a power struggle broke out between the Sheikh and his lieutenants. Hardliners in the security services and army teamed up with disgruntled Islamists under the leadership of Omar al-Bashir – long a mere figurehead – and defeated Turabi.[27] A key role was played by Turabi's deputy, Ali Osman Taha, who shifted the balance of power in Bashir's favour in 1999-2000. Turabi's fall crucially enabled Khartoum to declare that it was ending attempts at spreading the Islamist flame to

[25] Harry Verhoeven, 'Climate Change, Conflict and Development in Sudan: How Neo-Malthusian global narratives help win local power struggles', *Development and Change* Vol.42, No.3 (2011).

[26] 'Denying the Honor of Living' was a phrase used by Omar al-Bashir in 1989 for those deemed enemies of the Salvation Revolution. See Africa Watch, *Denying "The Honor of Living": Sudan: A Human Rights Disaster* (New York: The Africa Watch Committee, 1990).

[27] Philip Roessler, 'Internal Rivalry, Threat Substitution and Civil War: Darfur as a Theory-Building Case' (manuscript, University of Oxford: Oxford, 2010).

neighbouring countries, leading to a partial restoration of ties with Egypt and Saudi Arabia, and freeing up the possibility of re-engaging substantially with Gulf Arab capital.

The escalation of intra-regime tensions coincided with Sudan's emergence as an oil exporter in August 1999, the key link in extensive political and commercial partnerships between Khartoum and several Asian emerging economies (China in particular), which exploited the absence of possible Western rivals. Thanks to the Port Sudan pipeline and a Chinese-built oil refinery, petrodollars began flowing to Al-Ingaz. While initially the money was spent on containing the American regime-change strategy and the advances of John Garang's SPLA, as the hostilities were scaled down and peace negotiations began that would culminate in the Comprehensive Peace Agreement (CPA), funds increasingly flowed to a frontal Islamist attempt at destroying the traditional power base of the Hizb al-Umma and the Democratic Unionist Party. The old sectarian patronage networks, which had enabled both parties to dominate Sudanese politics for decades, were largely taken over. An investment spree facilitated the rise of new business elites, mostly from Khartoum, River Nile State and, to a lesser extent, North Kordofan, who have become staunch regime supporters, combining external piety, nationalist rhetoric and economic connections. The oil money – US$7 billion in 2008 alone – has been spent on the security services and on a construction boom in Khartoum and northern Sudan, leading to a spectacular expansion of the road network, hospitals and schools built and refurbished ministries and bridges.

The best funded policy has been a hyper-ambitious (and exceedingly expensive) Dam Programme, which integrates many of the short-term and long-term goals of Al-Ingaz. Under the impulse of Taha, Hamdi and Awad al-Jaz, the Islamist economic 'czar', Khartoum launched a self-declared 'hydro-agricultural mission'. The goal was to try to transform Sudan, once again, into the breadbasket of Africa and the Middle East and diversify its economy away from a dangerous dependence on oil.[28] The risks associated with the latter were underscored by the spectacular drop in international oil prices in 2008-2009, setting off a foreign-exchange scramble by Sudan's Central Bank, and by the imminent secession of the south, which holds about 75% of Sudan's proven oil reserves. Regime strategists have therefore advocated a second economic engine – dam construction and irrigated agriculture – which, both in itself and through its links to the wider economy, should increase growth rates.[29] Dams are critical: they do not just help with flood control, but are able to provide a constant irrigation supply for capital-intensive agriculture and to generate the megawatts needed for industrial expansion. The electricity produced can improve and expand the current grid, ending power cuts

[28] Interviews with senior Al-Ingaz politicians and government technocrats, Khartoum, 2009, 2010 and 2011.
[29] Agricultural Revival Programme; interview with Minister Abdelhalim Muta'afi, February 2011.

and bringing long awaited services to marginalised communities across northern Sudan who, since the CPA, have become increasingly assertive in calling for more and better public goods delivery. Demand, particularly in the cities, is rising rapidly – at almost 10% per annum – and Khartoum is dreaming about Chinese growth levels of the economy; in that case, power generation levels might have to quintuple, or so the economic rationale for the Dam Programme goes.[30]

The rapprochement with Egypt and the Gulf Arab states, the rapid intensification of relations with China and the availability of petrodollars formed the material and political enabling conditions for Al-Ingaz to carry out its plans of damming the Nile. Sudan was already home to the Sennar, Jebel Aulia, Khasm al-Girba and Roseires dams, but under Islamist rule it has embarked on what is the most ambitious infrastructure project in its history. The massive Merowe Dam was built between 2003 and 2009 at the fourth cataract on the Sudanese Nile, in the impoverished heartlands of the Nubian people in Northern State. It adds 1250MW power-generating capacity to the Sudanese grid, which at current network consumption levels actually means that supply outstrips demand. The Merowe Dam alone, the costs of which probably exceed US$3.5 billion, took up 40% of *total* government investment spending between 2005 and 2008, underlining just how critical the Dam Programme is to Khartoum.[31] Even before Merowe was finished, work also began to heighten the 1965 Roseires Dam in Blue Nile State, aiming to increase power generation further, but above all enabling the irrigation of a massive 1,5-2 million feddans through an extension of the existing Rahad and Kenana agricultural schemes.[32] Roseires' heightening is also not cheap; after initial estimates of a price tag of US$500 million, US$1 billion seems more likely. These are huge numbers for a country like Sudan, where hunger and disease are widespread and more than half the population lives on less than one dollar a day in most of the peripheries. Education, health care and famine relief have never received such political backing, or such massive financial injections.

Moreover, Bashir and Taha are pushing ahead with yet more dams in the next couple of years. In the midst of the electoral campaign of April 2010, a US$838 million contract was signed for the Siteit Dam and a dam on the Atbara River. The Islamists are excited about hydro-infrastructure on the second cataract (the Dal Dam) and third cataract (the Kajbar Dam). Kajbar is being trumpeted as necessary to expand the country's power supply by several hundred megawatts, and will cost US$700 million according to conservative estimates; preparations for the dam have picked up again after an unexpected pause. A deal was also inked in for

---

[30] Interviews with senior Islamists, Khartoum, April 2010.
[31] Finance Minister Ali Mahmood announced the $3.5 billion figure in Sudan's National Assembly in late 2010; other (government) sources suggest even higher estimates (interviews at the Ministry of Water Resources and Irrigation, Khartoum, March 2011).
[32] A faddan is 1.039 acres or 0.420 hectares.

the Shreik Dam on the fifth cataract, with a similar price tag to Kajbar, seeking to generate an additional 420MW.[33] All of this adds up to a push unprecedented in scale, ambition and cost. Al-Ingaz is dead serious about its hydro-agricultural mission.

Al-Ingaz and the Recalibration of Sudan's Political Economy: The Dam Programme's Deeper Domestic Logic

The central organisation driving Sudan's Dam Programme is the Dam Implementation Unit (DIU), headed by Usama Abdallah, a personal friend of Bashir and now, according to the accounts of other leading Islamists, one of Al-Ingaz's most powerful figures. The DIU started off as an ad hoc entity to build the Merowe Dam.[34] Since 2005, it has been transformed into a body that does not just execute the Dam Programme, but also controls multibillion dollar budgets; runs road, education, health-care and other development projects across northern Sudan; employs its own security forces; and is only accountable to the President himself. Recently the DIU became a Ministry in itself, though this does not normalise the unit in any way. Technocrats in other government institutions speak enviously of the ways in which the DIU has systematically marginalised alternative views on the water-agriculture nexus in Sudan and has usurped policy areas that used to fall under the Ministry of Water Resources and Irrigation, the Ministry of Agriculture and the Ministry of Public Works.[35]

The DIU is a highly secretive organisation that refuses almost all engagement with outside observers or Sudanese critics, and shares very little relevant information, even with its formal collaborators. Consultants who worked with Usama Abdallah and his team describe one-way data flows to the DIU. Information on the environmental, social or economic damage that DIU projects could cause to local communities, their livelihoods and the ecosystems in which they live, was deemed classified.[36] Both in the cases of Merowe and Roseires, systematic pressure was exerted on the DIU's international partners to adjust findings, with the threat of the withdrawal of the contract if absolute silence vis-à-vis the outside world was not upheld. The *cause célèbre* is the removal of Nasir Awad, the former secretary-general of the Higher Council for the Environment and Natural Resources (HCENR), who tried to implement the law by insisting on a proper environmental and social impact assessment for Merowe. After refusing to succumb to intimidation, Awad, one of Sudan's top civil servants, found himself removed within 24 hours by presidential decree from his position at the HCENR, allowing the dam to

---

[33] Website of the Dam Implementation Unit, http://www.diu.gov.sd/en/admin-en/newspublish/home.viewdetails.php?news_id=192
[34] Interviews with senior Al-Ingaz leaders, December 2010-March 2011.
[35] Interviews in northern Sudan with technocrats and politicians, April-December 2010.
[36] Interviews in Khartoum and Damazin, August 2009-December 2010.

be built without any systematic examination of its potentially devastating impact on riverain ecology and people.[37] A positive environmental and social impact assessment for Merowe was ultimately prepared by Lahmeyer International, previously heavily implicated in fraud surrounding dams in Lesotho and for that reason on the World Bank's corporate black list.[38] Lahmeyer's document was described by several of Sudan's leading scientists as 'laughable and short on nothing but science'.[39]

The extraordinary political and financial backing that the DIU has received in the past couple of years suggests that Sudan's Dam Programme is not just about increasing electricity supply and is much more than business-as-usual infrastructure spending. Al-Ingaz is attempting to undertake a profound transformation of northern Sudan, hoping to entrench itself more firmly into power as the south secedes and the ideological agenda of the Revolution is put on the back burner. Politicians like Taha, Hamdi, al-Jaz and Usama Abdallah, but also more academic regime voices like Ali Geneif and Abdullah Ahmed Abdullah,[40] are the driving forces behind the 'hydro-agricultural mission' that is vital to the long-term survival of Sudan and the current government, or so they argue. The regime is convinced it needs to 'deliver' economically in the so-called Hamdi Triangle of Dongola–Sennar–(North) Kordofan, the core areas of northern Sudan, or that otherwise it will lose support quickly and the country will find itself short of economic options. Building infrastructure, bringing electricity to people and re-launching agriculture (the breadbasket idea) are the basic ingredients of this self-styled 'competence agenda': the bottom line is that, even if the northern Sudanese do not like *Shari'a* or the political authoritarianism of Al-Ingaz, they should appreciate its economic performance.

Sudan's ruling Islamists are convinced that output legitimacy is critical in fostering a new middle class of pious businessmen and civil servants who owe their success to Al-Ingaz policies. Turkey's mildly Islamist AK party famously represents the rise of openly Islamic entrepreneurs from the Anatolian heartland; the AK is both an exponent of the declining hold on power by Turkey's traditional secular elites in Istanbul and Ankara, and a factor in itself that has contributed to the surging influence of new 'Islamic' centres of political and economic power.[41] The

---

[37] Interviews with many of the protagonists involved in the Merowe-Awad saga, northern Sudan, 2010.

[38] International Rivers, *German Company Brought to Justice over Abuses in Sudan Dam?* IR website, 5 July 2010, http://www.internationalrivers.org/en/blog/peter-bosshard/2010-5-7/german-company-brought-justice-over-abuses-sudan-dam

[39] Several interviews with members of the Sudanese National Academy of Sciences and some top civil servants, Khartoum, April 2010 and December 2010.

[40] Two former ministers of agriculture, each still very influential in Khartoum: Abdullah Ahmed Abdullah is the deputy chairman of the National Electoral Commission, while Ali Geneif is the author of the Agricultural Revival Programme and the key economic advisor to Ali Osman Taha.

[41] William Hale and Ergun Ozbudun, *Islamism, Democracy and Liberalism in Turkey: the case of the AKP* (Abingdon: Routledge, 2009).

mutual reinforcement of political and economic power is something Turabi has always been interested in. The removal of the Sheikh from power has not altered the fascination of his former disciples with the mechanisms at work and their belief in developing a pro-Islamist economic class that underpins political hegemony.

The enduring high modernist ideas held by people in Islamist Khartoum about social engineering and spreading 'civilisation' and 'progress' through top-down approaches inform this vision, as well as the developmental experiences of China and Malaysia.[43] Al-Ingaz has always prided itself on having brought about a revolution – a claim vigorously denied by its opponents – and under the banner of *mashru al-hadhari* (the civilisation project), the regime went all out in its assaults on the fundamental pillars on which Sudanese society had hitherto been built.[42] The argument here is that the post-Turabi regime has indeed downplayed many of the important cultural-religious transformation attempts and is steering a pragmatic course in its foreign policy, but that social engineering in less obviously confrontational ways has not been abandoned by Khartoum.

In this context, key Islamist Dr. Ghazi Salah-ud-Din revealingly spoke of a 'Sino-Sudanese model of development'.[44] Khartoum's engagement with the deeper drivers of the Chinese economic miracle is, as is the case for most African regimes, relatively shallow, but there is clearly a fascination with some of their key manifestations. Regimes like Angola's ruling MPLA and Sudan's Al-Ingaz emphasise the combination of a strong authoritarian state, an export-oriented economy and continuous party-led investment in massive infrastructure projects. There is a belief in the virtues of selective liberalisation – politically and economically – and, particularly relevant to the Sudanese case, the transformational power of dams and engineers.

It was no coincidence that Omar al-Bashir campaigned for the Sudanese presidency in April 2010 with a picture of himself in front of the Merowe Dam, the symbol of civilisation and progress delivered by Al-Ingaz, as his main electoral poster. The 'taming' of nature by specialists; the power of tall buildings and water infrastructure to impress a poorly educated population and other developing countries; the disregard by a central, 'rational' elite-led state of the 'backward' locals inhibiting 'development'[45] – high modernism is recognised as an essential characteristic of the Chinese experience. On a more general political level, perhaps the most important lesson Bashir, Taha and Ghazi have learned from China is the idea of output legitimacy: given the continuing absence of real democracy and accountability in Sudan, the government derives

---

[42] Interviews with key regime members, Khartoum, 2009-2011.
[43] African Rights, *Facing Genocide. The Nuba of Sudan* (London: African Rights, 1995); African Rights, *Food and Power in Sudan* (London: African Rights, 1997).
[44] Interview with Dr. Ghazi Salah-ud-Din, Khartoum, April 2010.
[45] Scott, *Seeing like a State*, op. cit., pp. 88-97.

its legitimacy from the tangible results it produces *for* the population (i.e. services, security, or national pride) rather than the input side of public policy. This further underlines the political importance of the Dam Programme: it is critical in delivering the public goods to Khartoum's vital constituencies.

The International Political Economy and Local Impact of Dams on the Sudanese Nile

Al-Ingaz's hydro-agricultural mission has important diplomatic conse- quences, as lucrative contracts – for construction, agriculture and long- term investment – associated with the Dam Programme and Sudan's Agricultural Revival accrue to privileged Chinese and Gulf Arab partners. Plans for a big expansion of dam and irrigation infrastructure may not be new, but without foreign technical expertise, political support and finan- cial backing, they could not be realised. Khartoum has worked hard on turning this dependence on external partners into an advantage, trying to use its ambitious plans to tie itself closer to vital allies as it remains isolated from the West.

China's physical role in the Dam Programme is critical. Beijing's role as a dam superpower influences the regime on the ideological level, but also means that several state-owned enterprises have signed lucrative deals to implement Sudan's Dam Programme. Sinohydro is the DIU's leading technical partner, flanked by the China International Water and Electrical Corporation, China National Water Resources Hydropower Engineering Corporation and Harbin-Jilin. Sinohydro's expertise took the lead in building the Merowe Dam; the contract is said by insiders to have amounted to much more than the official US$500 million.[46] It has also been at the forefront of heightening Roseires; large numbers (probably thousands) of Chinese engineers and labourers have moved to Sudan to carry out the work. China's Exim Bank is one of the main financiers of Sudan's rapidly expanding power sector, which includes fossil fuel plants at Rabak and Port Sudan, but more importantly the big hydro- electric dams. Exim Bank played an important role in the funding of Merowe (US$520 million according to official statistics),[47] in effect sub- sidising some of Sinohydro's economic expansion, a classic ingredient of China's 'go global' strategy. Sinohydro also got the US$700 million Kajbar Dam contract in November 2010, while other Chinese consortia clinched deals of close to US$1 billion each for the Upper Atbara/Siteit Project and the Shreik Dam.

Egypt is another key actor in Al-Ingaz's hydro-agricultural mission, and plays a role as important as China's. Egypt has been obsessed with

[46] Interviews in different ministries, Khartoum, December 2010-February 2011.
[47] Dam Implementation Unit, 'Merowe Dam Project: A Battle of Dignity and Independence of Decision' (Khartoum: DIU, 2010), p. 5.

controlling the Nile for millennia, rightly considering the river to be its key national security interest, as almost 100% of its water use is related to the Nile. Egypt dominates Nile Basin politics and has done so through the 1959 Treaty with Sudan, which allows it to consume 55.5 billion m³ of water (with 18.5 billion m³ going to (northern) Sudan and 10 billion m³ lost due to evaporation at Aswan). This leaves very little for consumption or irrigation by eight other upstream countries, which have been clamouring for a renegotiation of the 'colonial' 1959 agreement. Ethiopia in particular has been vocal in the Nile Basin Initiative negotiations, and, given the lack of a multilateral breakthrough, has threatened unilateral action on the Blue Nile (i.e. building its own dams without Egyptian 'permission'). This led to a dangerous scaling up of bellicose language between the former Egyptian President Hosni Mubarak and Ethiopian Prime Minister Meles Zenawi in late 2010, an explosive situation given the power politics both Cairo and Addis Ababa have historically indulged in in Sudan.[48]

Sudan's Dam Programme could never have taken off without the green light from Cairo, and though the evidence is not definitive, there are strong reasons to believe that the Bashir-Turabi split, and the subsequent rapprochement between Mubarak and Al-Ingaz, secured Egypt's go-ahead.[49] Secular Cairo was long hostile towards the military-Islamist regime in Khartoum, especially after the failed assassination attempt on Mubarak in 1995 in which Turabi's lieutenants played a key role. The Sheikh's removal led to improved, though still not cordial, relations, and an informal understanding: Khartoum would cease attempts to export the Revolution (ending its partnership with Ayman al-Zawahiri's Al-Jihad Al-Islami Al-Masri and Al-Gama'a Al-Islamiyyah, previously hosted by Al-Ingaz),[50] fully respect Egypt's share of Nile waters and perhaps give Egyptian farmers access to fertile plots in northern Sudan. In exchange, Egypt offered normalisation of relations and an Egyptian-led rapprochement between Sudan and the Gulf Arabs.

Cairo's go-between diplomacy was an important element, as Bashir and Taha sought Saudi, Kuwaiti and Emirati funds that could enable the hydro-agricultural mission. It is also worth noting that, though Mubarak

---

[48] For an extensive discussion of Nile Basin geopolitics, see Harry Verhoeven, 'Black Gold for Blue Gold? Sudan's Oil, Ethiopia's Water and Regional Integration' (London: Royal Institute of International Affairs/Chatham House, 2011).

[49] Interviews with senior Islamists, security service personnel and former government ministers, Khartoum, December 2010 and February-March 2011.

[50] Al-Gama'a Al-Islamiyyah is an Egyptian terrorist organisation, formerly under the spiritual leadership of Sheikh Omer Abdul Rahman and allegedly involved in assassinating Anwar Sadat. It also played a key role in the failed assassination attempt on Hosni Mubarak in Addis Ababa on 26 June 1995. A dissident extremist faction of Al-Gama'a Al-Islamiyyah broke away when more mainstream voices ended their holy war against the Mubarak regime. They teamed up with Ayman al-Zawahiri, Al Qaeda's No.2 for almost 15 years now, who headed the Al-Jihad Al-Islami Al-Masri and fused several radical organisations into Al-Qaeda under the leadership of Osama Bin Laden and himself. All these movements were active in Sudan throughout the 1990s.

demanded a high price for better Egyptian-Sudanese relations, Sudan's Dam Programme has strategic and practical advantages for Cairo. The dams in northern Sudan help reduce the sedimentation problem that is said to erode Aswan's capacity (as well as helping to prevent acute problems with salinity facing Egyptian farmers), by transferring the issue to Sudanese territory where Merowe, Kajbar and Shreik might quickly lose capacity due to alluvial sediment.[51] Moreover, Al-Ingaz's big push for dams helps to lock in the share of the two upstream countries in the Nile Basin and ties them closely together, making a renegotiation of substantial amounts of Nile water very unlikely.[52] Egypt and Sudan are citing historically acquired water rights and argue that they have the expensive infrastructure in place that they need for irrigation, given how little rainfall there is for their agriculture. Merowe and the heightened Roseires Dam will allow Sudan to use its full quota of 18.5 billion m^3 of Nile water: any renegotiation of the 1959 treaty would lead to developmental cuts that are 'too painful', according to Cairo and Khartoum.[53]

The final key players in the hydropolitics of Sudan's hydro-agricultural mission are the Gulf Arabs. Rapprochement with the latter was needed because they had been alienated by Turabi's hosting of Osama bin Laden and support for Saddam Hussein in the first Gulf War. Their extensive credit lines were invaluable to fund the dreams of Khartoum politicians and engineers alike and, with Cairo's help and the important personal contacts of Abdelrahim Hamdi in the Gulf region,[54] this obstacle was largely removed after the Bashir-Turabi split. According to official data, about half of the Merowe Dam was funded by the Arab Fund for Economic and Social Development and several pools of national capital from wealthy Middle-Eastern oil producers.[55] These are, by and large, not grants, but loans (in some cases at commercial, not concessionary, rates reflecting the unfinished rapprochement in 2001-2002, when the financial package was put together). This seems to have changed somewhat, however, for Roseires (with the Kuwaiti National Development Fund as the main foreign partner, on better conditions for Sudan) and possibly also for the Kajbar, Upper Atbara/Siteit and Shreik projects which are also being funded by Gulf Arab partners.[56]

Similar to the situation in the 1970s, international fears about climate change and rising global food prices are propelling Gulf Arab and other Asian countries to try to control directly the areas of food production of

[51] Seif al-Din Hamad Abdalla. '*Al-qudra al-takhzīniyya l'il-sudūd 'ala al-nīl wa rawāfidihī dākhil al-Sudan*', Paper presented at a workshop of the Middle East and African Studies Centre, 'Towards a National Strategy of Water in the Sudan', Khartoum, September 2007.

[52] Verhoeven, 'Black Gold for Blue Gold? *op. cit.*

[53] Interviews with technocrats and leading figures in the NCP and government of Sudan, 2009-2011.

[54] Interviews with key Islamists, including Hamdi, Khartoum, February 2011.

[55] DIU, 'Merowe Dam Project', *op. cit.* p.5.

[56] Website of the Dam Implementation Unit, http://www.diu.gov.sd/en/admin-en/newspublish/home.viewdetails.php?news_id=195

the future.[57] Africa is seen as harbouring large untapped potential, with Sudan in particular rated a possible regional 'breadbasket', reminiscent of the *'fata morgana'* dreams of the Nimairi era. Al-Ingaz's Agricultural Revival Programme, closely associated with its Dam Programme, relies hugely on foreign direct investment to improve the low productivity of Sudanese agriculture. The simple recipe remains largely unchanged since the 1970s: 'free' water; dirt cheap labour; abundant land; capital from Gulf Arab states; and Western technology to break Sudan's dependence on 'backward' production techniques.[58] A nexus is developing in which agro-businesses close to the regime, led by the Kenana Sugar Company, jointly owned by Khartoum and four Gulf Arab countries, work closely together with the DIU and foreign investors to make a big push on irrigated cash crops. Many of these partnerships and deals are notoriously murky, but Egyptian, Kuwaiti, Jordanian, Qatari and Chinese sovereign wealth funds and/or private businesses have concluded agreements regarding hundreds of thousands of acres of land in River Nile State, Gezira, Sennar, White Nile and, increasingly, also in the south (Upper Nile and Unity).[59] According to Sudanese officials, 2800 km³ of Sudanese land is already in Emirati hands and the 2 million acres that will be irrigated thanks to the heightened Roseires Dam are likely to be used for producing Kenana sugar and cash crops for the Gulf Arab market.

The petro-dollars generated by Khartoum's oil sales are thus critical in paying back the loans given by Saudi, Kuwaiti and Emirati creditors for the Dam Programme. There is an interesting triangular relationship at work between Beijing, Cairo-Riyadh-Kuwait-Abu Dhabi and Khartoum that involves oil money, food production, cheap loans, dam construction contracts and mutual diplomatic support. This division of labour – Sudan's land and water, thanks to irrigation through Chinese-built dams, will produce food for the Gulf Arabs who are to be paid back with Sudanese export crops and Chinese petrodollars by Al-Ingaz – is extremely beneficial for all the national elites involved. Its impact on local populations is far more questionable.

The hydro-agricultural plans of Bashir and Taha are generating resistance, not just within the wider context of Nile Basin hydropolitics and Ethiopia-led resistance by upstream countries,[60] but increasingly inside the government and among local communities. The all-powerful DIU's secretive methods, its takeover of the duties of other ministries and its

[57] Lorenzo Cotula, Sonja Vermeulen, Rebeca Leonard, James Keeley, *Land grab or development opportunity? Agricultural investment and international land deals in Africa* (London: International Institute for Environment and Development, June 2009).

[58] Verhoeven, 'Climate Change, Conflict and Development in Sudan', op. cit.

[59] Documents shown to the author at the Ministry of Investment, Khartoum, March 2011.

[60] Ironically, Sinohydro, which is playing a pivotal role in Sudan's Dam Programme, also contributes to Ethiopia's dam-building. Sinohydro leads the Tekeze Hydroelectric project with an installed capacity of 300MW and has also executed nine strategic road projects that are an Ethiopian government priority.

total lack of accountability are widely unpopular in technocratic and academic milieus that form Sudan's water and agriculture establishment. Many 'insiders' are criticising the opportunity cost of spending billions of dollars on dams while other developmental needs are neglected; they also question relying so strongly on Chinese and Gulf Arab knowhow and investment, instead of taking a more bottom-up approach to rural development.[61]

Moreover, the local communities whose interests are sacrificed on the altar of Islamist high modernism are challenging the DIU's designs. The Merowe Dam might be *'considered the project of poverty elimination in Sudan'*[62] by Bashir, but it has displaced 50,000 people and destroyed the millennia-old archaeological heritage of the Nubian people. Despite strong criticism of Merowe's environmental impact – including sky-high evaporation rates, of possibly up to 5 billion m^3 [63] – and myriad anecdotes about the failure of DIU 'model villages' to resettle displaced Nubians and offer them alternative livelihoods, Khartoum dismisses these 'conservative voices'. DIU special forces have repeatedly resorted to lethal violence in the area around Merowe,[64] but also around the new Kajbar Dam, to break the resistance. People in the High North lack a possible foreign patron to back up the threat of armed rebellion, but the violent potential of the discontent around the dams should not be underestimated. This is also the case in Blue Nile, where Bashir and Taha have imposed the heightening of the Roseires Dam, despite the strong disapproval of the local SPLM/A governor Malik Agar and his armed supporters. Initially the compensation scheme for the possibly 70,000 people to be displaced by the new reservoir was nigh on non-existent, but following Agar's pressure and the upheaval around Merowe, the DIU has increased the funds available for decent resettlement.[65] The problem remains that almost all the benefits of the Roseires Dam are for investors downstream, while (not coincidentally) the costs fall on the old local enemies of Al-Ingaz during the Khartoum-SPLM/A war. Some observers reckon that it is only a matter of time before some locals launch attacks on the DIU's Chinese contractors,[66] just as Chinese oil workers have been targeted because of the Beijing-Khartoum alliance and the Darfur situation.

---

[61] Interviews in several Sudanese universities and ministries, including the Ministry of Water Resources and Irrigation, August 2009-March 2011.

[62] Website of the Dam Implementation Unit, http://www.merowedam.gov.sd/en/testimonials. html. Italics in original.

[63] Estimate by Professor Asim al-Moghraby, one of Sudan's leading environmental and engineering scholars, Interview, Khartoum, March 2011.

[64] Organisation Mondiale Contre la Torture (OMCT), *Sudan. Ongoing Violence Against Communities Resisting Dam Construction in the Northern Nile Valley.* (Geneva: OMCT, November 2007).

[65] Interviews in the fieldwork in Blue Nile State and Khartoum between 2009 and 2011; Website of the Dam Implementation Unit http://www.diu.gov.sd/en/admin-en/newspublish/ home.viewdetails.php?news_id=218.

[66] Interviews with local village leaders and NGO workers in Blue Nile State, in areas where dam-induced displacement is foreseen, August–September 2009.

Conclusion

Accounts of China's rise and its impressive scaling-up of interactions with Sudan and Africa have traditionally focused on the extraction of resources, arms trade, surging bilateral trade and labour issues. This chapter has argued that hydro-infrastructure is often overlooked as a key material export for Beijing, the world's real dam superpower. It also symbolises a very particular way of thinking about 'progress' that is once more becoming salient in capitals around the global South, increasingly in Juba (where Chinese companies are exploring the possibility of developing hydropower post-independence) but especially in Khartoum: dams are development. The Islamist Al-Ingaz regime is no longer trying to spread the revolution, but still believes passionately in re-engineering Sudanese society. The Dam Programme both reflects its high modernist idea of what development is and recalibrates Sudan's political economy in ways intended to entrench the regime in power for another 20 years.

The international partnerships integral to the Agricultural Revival and Dam Programme form a complex political-economic web that ties China, key Middle Eastern countries and Sudan closely together in mutually beneficial inter-elite flows of money, resources and technical expertise. At the same time, the DIU and its *modus operandi* are generating a blowback. For critics, the fundamental problem remains that Al-Ingaz's ambitious hydro-agricultural mission is based on a '*fata morgana*'; its assumptions about development, productivity and ecology are, in many cases, literally mirages in the desert that disempower communities and reproduce violence. Sudan's regional cousins, with the exception of Egypt, do not support the Dam Programme and Nile Basin tensions are peaking; technocrats lament the ecological price tag of the dams and highlight the immense opportunity costs; and local minorities are resisting what they see as another round of Khartoum-led violent marginalisation and uprooting of cultures and communities that differ from the riverain, Islamist vision for Sudan. For all these people, Al-Ingaz's dams are not development: quite the contrary.

7

Genocide	How Activists Linked
Olympics	China, Darfur
	& Beijing 2008

ALEXANDRA COSIMA BUDABIN

As negotiations to end Sudan's decades-long North-South civil war progressed closer to a final peace agreement in 2004, a UN Human Rights Coordinator for Sudan cautioned that a region called Darfur in the west of the country now posed 'the world's greatest humanitarian crisis'.[1] Since 2003, the government of Sudan had been waging war against rebel groups in Darfur. Over the summer of 2004, a group of concerned organisations and individuals in the United States formed the Save Darfur Coalition (SDC) to highlight humanitarian concerns and advocate conflict resolution. Expanding the scope of its advocacy campaigns, the SDC sought additional targets beyond the US national arena in order to generate leverage over the government of Sudan. From 2004 to 2008, the SDC highlighted and targeted crucial linkages in the international arena, while staying rooted domestically in the US. Activists identified China as a vulnerable target because it was an ally of the Sudanese government, its status was increasing in the international community, and it was hosting the Olympic Games in 2008.

During the Beijing Summer Olympics of 2008, China welcomed over 200 countries for the quadrennial ritual of competition, fellowship and sportsmanship. China's hosting of the Olympics intensified media attention around its human rights policies. When actors such as the US and the United Nations failed to compel the other members of the international community to respond to the situation in Darfur, SDC advocates in the US began a unique campaign to target China, which I shall refer to as the 'China Campaign'.[2] This Campaign included a lethal re-branding of the Beijing Games as the 'Genocide Olympics'. Overall, the Campaign created a public relations storm that threatened the positive image that China had wanted to project. In light of the campaign's widespread support and

---

[1] Mukesh Kapila, quoted in 'Sudan: Gov't stresses commitment to just and peaceful solution to Darfur conflict,' *United Nations International Regional Information Networks (IRIN)*, 24 March 2004; available at http://www.irinnews.org (accessed 10 July 2009).

[2] The term China Campaign is used here to encapsulate the activities of the many Darfur – and China – related NGOs in the US and elsewhere that were involved with lobbying China on behalf of Darfur. The term is used informally by some in the Darfur advocacy movement.

appeal, China was forced to contend with this unexpected torrent of negative attention connected to a foreign policy issue.

This chapter examines the campaign against China launched by advocates on behalf of Darfur in the frenzied months leading up to the Beijing Olympics of 2008.[3] First, it places China's foreign policy towards Sudan and response to the Darfur conflict in context. Second, it describes the emergence of a US-based advocacy campaign to target China's policies towards Darfur using the Beijing Olympics, mapping the main players and goals of the China Campaign leading up to the 2008 Games and the extent of official US support. Finally, the chapter examines China's interaction with the China Campaign and assesses the impact of this targeted advocacy effort.

China's Foreign Policy on Darfur

China's relationship with Sudan is a notable part of the extensive engagement that has been growing between China and Africa in recent decades.[4] In 2002, Beijing enhanced its 'go out' strategy with the plan to invest heavily in the developing world.[5] Its current position is the outcome of a decades-long cultivation of official ties in certain African states involving diplomatic and economic linkages, a combination that has been dubbed 'resource diplomacy'.[6] China's staunch alliance with Sudan followed a pattern of entwined economic and diplomatic engagement with its African partners. Today, the scope of China's engagement in Sudan encompasses many sectors and areas of development. In the process, however, despite a foreign policy highlighting respect for sovereignty and non-interference as central tenants, China has also begun to embrace multilateralism.

China long sought to host the Olympics as a way of presenting itself positively to the world. The government's first bid for the 2000 Olympic Games was unsuccessful and may have reflected discomfort with China in the wake of the 1989 Tiananmen Square violence.[7] When the International

---

[3] An earlier version of this chapter appeared as 'Genocide Olympics: The Campaign to Pressure China over the Darfur Conflict,' *Central European University Political Science Journal*, Vol. 4, Iss. 4 (December 2009), pp. 520-565.

[4] When China's brutal clampdown on the 1989 Tiananmen Square demonstrations led to Western opprobrium, China reasserted its relationship with the Third World, which included ties to many African countries. At the end of the Cold War, China launched a new era of engagement with the world order under the leadership of Presidents Jiang Zemin and Hu Jintao. The 1990s saw China opening its burgeoning economy to global flows of capital and investment. Following the path of economic growth laid by Deng Xiaoping a decade before, this 'recommitment' to the Third World linked economic and foreign policy.

[5] Martyn Davies with Hannah Edinger, Nastaya Tay, and Sanusha Naidu, 'How China delivers development assistance to Africa' (Stellenbosch: Centre for Chinese Studies, 2008), p. 4.

[6] See Ian Taylor, 'Unpacking China's Resource Diplomacy in Africa,' in *China in Africa* (Uppsala: The Nordic Africa Institute, 2007).

[7] Frank Ching, 'From Mao to Now: Three Tumultuous Decades,' in Minky Worden ed., *China's Great Leap: The Beijing Games and Olympian Human Rights Challenges* (New York: Seven Stories Press, 2008).

Olympic Committee (IOC) announced its decision to award the 2008 Olympic Games to Beijing, Wang Wei, the senior Beijing Olympic official, asserted, 'Winning the host rights means winning the respect, trust, and favour of the international community.'[8] The prospect of media attention offered China the opportunity to give a positive narrative of its ascendancy as an emerging global power. Observers referred to the Olympics as China's 'coming out party' to signify the country's 'reinvention for world recognition'.[9] China established its official games motto as 'One World, One Dream' to highlight its membership of the international community. At the same time, the attention of the international community towards the situation in Darfur placed China in a quandary: how could China balance its strategic interests in Sudan and its foreign policy principles of non-interference against its rising prominence in the international community and humanitarian affairs?

China's leadership initially chafed at pressure to assist the international community in resolving the situation in Darfur. As a permanent member of the UN Security Council since 1971, China's veto threats hindered a stronger response in two early resolutions in July and September 2004 that would have imposed economic sanctions on Sudan. In both cases, China also abstained from voting on the diluted versions of the original resolutions. In the initial months of the conflict, China's attitude towards Darfur followed its deep-rooted policy of non-interference, refusing to meddle in the internal affairs of sovereign countries. By abstaining, China followed the lead of the other members in acknowledging the situation in Darfur as a threat to peace and security but prevented the resolutions from having any meaningful impact.

In 2005, China began to modify its stance while being careful not to act too aggressively towards its ally Sudan. In the UN Security Council, China did not veto two resolutions that included more robust measures against the government of Sudan, and ended up abstaining under pressure from other member states. The spectre of China's veto was mere bluster; as one observer put it, 'Vetoes are threatened, or hinted at, far more than they are used.'[10] While not blocking action at the international level, China was still protecting NCP-governed Sudan to some degree. In the meantime, it reaffirmed its support for Sudan in a renewal of military ties during a November 2005 meeting among state officials.[11] China appeared to be showing one face to the international community, while showing another to its long-time ally, Sudan.

[8] Elizabeth C. Economy and Adam Segal, 'China's Olympic Nightmare,' *Foreign Affairs* 97 (July/Aug 2008); available at http://www.foreignaffairs.com/articles/64447/elizabeth-c-economy-and-adam-segal/chinas-olympic-nightmare (accessed: 26 June 2009).
[9] Monroe E. Price, 'Introduction', in Monroe E. Price and Daniel Dayan eds, *Owning the Olympics: Narratives of the New China* (Ann Arbor: University of Michigan Press, 2007), p. 6.
[10] Adam LeBor, *'Complicity with Evil': The United Nations in the Age of Modern Genocide* (New Haven: Yale University Press, 2006), p. 246.
[11] 'China, Sudan to Further Exchanges, Cooperation between Armed Forces,' *Xinhua*, 28 November 2005.

Startlingly, China's policy towards the Darfur situation underwent a major shift during the course of 2006. When the UN Security Council voted to impose targeted sanctions on four Sudanese officials in April, China abstained, following its pattern of non-interference. As the subsequent months saw rising violence and growing instability in Darfur, there was discussion of a possible Western military intervention and China became concerned for the security of its oil in Sudan. By September, it was conferring with UN Secretary General Kofi Annan on arrangements surrounding the deployment of a UN force of 20,000 troops mandated in UN Resolution 1706, which had been passed in August. During the November Security Council meeting on Darfur, Ambassador Wang Guangya worked behind the scenes to obtain Khartoum's support for a plan that would involve a hybrid United Nations-African Union force. President Hu also took up the cause and lobbied Sudanese President Omar al-Bashir at the Forum on China-Africa Cooperation summit in Beijing in early November 2006, and on a visit to Khartoum in early 2007. Ambassador Wang noted, 'Usually China doesn't send messages, but this time they did.'[12] Rather than sit on the sidelines, China entered the diplomatic fray over negotiating peacekeeping forces in Sudan. But these actions did not represent the full extent of pressure that many believed it could wield in Sudan. By increasing its diplomatic efforts, China left itself vulnerable to criticism for its foreign policy choices.

The China Campaign

Moving beyond domestic pressure
An organised response to the Darfur conflict came early and swiftly in the United States. On 14 July 2004, concerned individuals and organisations gathered at the Darfur Emergency Summit, sponsored by the US Holocaust Memorial Museum Committee of Conscience, the American Jewish World Service and the City University of New York. As an outcome of the Emergency Summit, the Save Darfur Coalition (SDC) was formed with the commitment of more than 75 organisations. The Coalition quickly established an umbrella organisation in Washington, DC to coordinate advocacy efforts.[13] In its first years, the SDC left China alone and focused mainly on channelling public pressure to domestic targets. Between 2005 and 2006, the SDC successfully lobbied Congress to pass more than ten pieces of legislation allocating funds for African Union peacekeeping troops, supporting divestment campaigns, and denouncing the violence

---

[12] 'China told Sudan to adopt UN's Darfur Plan–Envoy,' *Bloomberg*, 7 February 2007.
[13] The Save Darfur Coalition is both the coordinating organisation for its 100-plus members as well as a non-profit organisation with its own campaigns. See Save Darfur Coalition, http://www.savedarfur.org/ For more on Darfur advocacy see Don Cheadle and John Prendergast, *Not on Our Watch: The Mission to End Genocide in Darfur and Beyond* (New York: Hyperion, 2007).

in Darfur.[14] On the orders of Congress, the United States Agency for International Development poured hundreds of millions of dollars into addressing the humanitarian situation in Darfur.[15] From the White House, President George W. Bush signalled his concern for Darfur by denoucing the mass killings as 'genocide', signing the Darfur Peace and Accountability Act (2006), and directing US representatives at the UN to put forward resolutions taking the Sudanese government to task for not resolving the conflict.[16] With ongoing engagements in Afghanistan and Iraq, however, the moral authority of the United States at the international level had been compromised by rising concerns over US hegemony. At the UN, the US was unable to wield effective leadership in summoning the international community's response.

The United States and China engage over Darfur

From the beginning, the US government took a special interest in encouraging China's potential role for defusing the situation in Darfur. Though China's strategy of providing prestige infrastructure projects in Africa to curry favour had been 'long ignored' by the United States, some feared that African states were turning East rather than West in search of further strategic partnerships.[17] Reports of China's growing influence evoked images of a 'zero-sum equation', with the result that 'China's rise [would] ultimately undermine U.S. interests in the region'.[18] One critic condemned the tepid US response to Sudan for affirming to African countries that 'being under the Chinese umbrella guarantees you impunity.'[19] By 2004, Africa's status was rising for the US in terms of oil, trade negotiations, and its strategic importance in the War on Terror. The US began to pay closer attention both to Africa and China's increasing prominence on the continent.

When the international community began addressing the Darfur situation in 2004 in the UN Security Council, Washington and Beijing held different positions. The US State Department maintained that the situation amounted to genocide; Beijing claimed that Darfur was a humanitarian

[14] For a list of Darfur-related legislation that has been passed, see http://www.darfurscores.org/darfur-legislation

[15] United States Agency for International Development, 'Darfur Humanitarian Emergency', available at http://www.usaid.gov/locations/sub-saharan_africa/sudan/darfur.html (accessed: 26 June 2009).

[16] Early on, the President had considered and then vetoed the possibility of a unilateral military intervention in Sudan. See Peter Baker, 'Bush Says He Considered Action in Darfur,' *The Washington Post*, 20 July 2007, A06.

[17] Princeton N. Lyman, 'Introduction,' in Princeton N. Lyman and Patricia Dorff eds., *Beyond Humanitarianism: What You Need to Know About Africa and Why It Matters*, (New York: Council on Foreign Relations, 2007), p. ix.

[18] Drew Thompson, 'China's Emerging Interests in Africa: Opportunities and Challenges for Africa and the United States,' *African Renaissance Journal* (July/August 2005), p. 21.

[19] James Forsyth, 'Realism and Darfur,' *The New Republic Online*, 2006; available at http://www.tnr.com/ (accessed: 7 March 2006).

crisis.[20] The US and China initiated a sub-dialogue on Africa in 2006, and bilateral discussions raised the possibility of coordinating actions concerning Sudan. When President Hu paid a visit to the White House, President Bush stated that 'we intend to deepen our cooperation in addressing threats to global security' that included the genocide in Darfur.[21] After his appointment by President Bush, the US Special Envoy to Sudan, Andrew Natsios, expanded the bilateral dialogue and travelled to China in early 2007 to meet with foreign policy ministers about exerting pressure on Sudan.[22] On his return, Natsios assured the US government that Sudan and China were indeed engaging in dialogue, though without bold calls for action. In spite of US expectations of grander gestures, he reported, 'The Chinese delivered the messages, I believe quietly in their own nonconfrontational way'.[23] In February and April, Natsios reported to the Senate Foreign Relations Committee that the Chinese 'are taking a more subtle approach that is really affecting the behavior of the Sudanese government.'[24] He favoured continuing to support China's efforts at quiet diplomacy. Many in Congress, however, would soon lose patience with these restrained efforts.

Advocates take their own route of pressure

According to Darfur advocates, it was clear that domestic pressure would not deliver the response needed to the situation in Darfur, and many believed that President Bush had reached the limit of what he was willing to do. Advocates despaired that the humanitarian situation in Darfur would continue to deteriorate without a strong response from the international community. In the light of this, some advocates began to

[20] J. Stephen Morrison and Bates Gill, testimony submitted to 'The escalating crisis in Darfur: are there prospects for peace?' Hearing before the Committee on Foreign Affairs, House of Representatives, 110th Congress, 1st Session, February 8, 2007,' (Washington, DC: House of Representatives, 2007), p. 4.

[21] The White House Office of the Press Secretary, 'President Bush and President Hu of People's Republic of China Participate in Arrival Ceremony,' 20 April 2006; available at http://george wbushwhitehouse.archives.gov/news/releases/2006/04/20060420.html (accessed 26 June 2009).

[22] During this visit, Natsios spoke to Chinese officials about the possibility of cooperating in a blockade of Port Sudan in the event of Khartoum's obdurate stance on Resolution 1706. Chinese State Councillor Tang Jiaxuan assured Natsios that China was paying close attention to Darfur and emphasised the country's multilateral stance, 'We actively back the international community's efforts to help the people in Darfur restore peace under the framework of the United Nations.' http://www.china-embassy.org/eng/zmgx/zmgx/Political%20 Relationship/ t288380. htm

[23] Robert McMahon, 'Interview: Natsios Says 'Chaos' in Darfur Clouds Prospects for Political Solution,' *CFR.org*, 20 February 2007; available at http://www.cfr.org/publication/12668/ natsios.html (accessed 26 June 2009).

[24] Natsios also warned: 'There's been a lot of China-bashing in the West. And I'm not sure, to be very frank with you, right now it's very helpful.' Andrew Natsios, 'Darfur: a 'Plan B' to Stop Genocide,' Hearing before the Committee on Foreign Relations, United States Senate, One Hundreth and Tenth Congress, First Session, Wednesday, 11 April 2007; available at http://foreign. senate.gov/hearings/2007/hrg070411a.html (accessed: 26 June 2009).

search more aggressively for additional targets of pressure outside the domestic arena. As early as 2004, media coverage began linking China to the atrocities committed in Darfur, drawing on various human rights reports that highlighted bilateral ties between China and Sudan based on oil, arms, and diplomatic support.[25] There were public calls from Americans to pressure the Chinese government to address the situation in Darfur. In a letter to *The Washington Post*, Roberta Cohen, a Senior Fellow at the Brookings Institution, noted: 'Were China to use even a small part of its leverage to call Sudan to account, it would go a long way towards saving lives in Sudan.'[26] China and its economic ties to Sudan began to figure prominently in the news as a result of a divestment campaign that had been initiated on university campuses.[27] One of the member organisations of the Save Darfur Coalition, a group called the Sudan Divestment Task Force (SDTF), published reports highlighting the extensive economic ties between Sudan and China.[28] As part of their divestment campaign, the SDTF targeted US-based assets that included investments in the many Chinese companies doing business with Sudan. The divestment campaign also targeted state-owned oil business-es in Malaysia and India, notably Petronas and ONGC, as 'highest offenders', but China's position as a permanent member of the UN Security Council raised its status in the eyes of advocates. As the divestment literature pointed out, 'Perhaps no bilateral relationship has caused more misery for Darfur's citizens than the relationship between China and Sudan.'[29]

Despite China's ongoing diplomatic efforts, many in the Darfur movement were not convinced that China was exercising its full muscle in pushing the NCP-run government to take concerted steps to end the Darfur conflict. Due to its overlap with the ongoing crisis in Darfur, China's shining moment on the world stage as host of the 2008 Olympics became an event with great potential. The media circus surrounding the Olympics included months of lead-up stories as well as extensive coverage beamed to homes in every country. Spurred by the search for levers on Khartoum, advocates rested their sights on China as a vulnera-

---

[25] See Jasper Becker, 'China Fights UN Sanctions on Sudan to Safeguard Oil,' *The Independent*, 15 October 2004; Dan Blumenthal, 'Unhelpful China,' *The Washington Post*, 6 December 2004; Peter S. Goodman, 'China Invests Heavily in Sudan's Oil Industry; Beijing Supplies Arms Used on Villagers,' *The Washington Post*, 23 December 2004; Human Rights First, *Investing in Tragedy: China's Money, Arms, and Politics in Sudan*, 2008; available at http://www.human-rightsfirst.org/pubs/pubs.aspx (accessed: June 1 2009).

[26] Roberta A. Cohen, 'Calling on China,' *The Washington Post*, 5 August 2004, A18.

[27] In April 2005, the Harvard University Advisory Board on Shareholder Responsibility bowed to student demands and divested the university's endowment fund from the Chinese paras-tatal oil company Petrochina, the primary oil field operator in Sudan. Other divestment campaign targets such as state pension funds soon followed.

[28] Sudan Divestment Task Force, 'Home Page'; available at http://www.sudan divestment. org/home.asp (accessed: 26 June 2009).

[29] Sudan Divestment Taskforce, Report, 'Arguments for the Efficacy of Targeted Divestment from Sudan,' 15 March 2006, [Updated: 4 April 2007], p. 5.

ble venue for exerting mass pressure. Indeed, the SDC would not be alone in challenging China's image of itself. The 2008 Beijing Olympics had already taken on a new importance as longstanding human rights advocacy campaigns jockeyed to challenge China's official representations.[30] Global criticism of the human rights situation in China was mounting: newspapers covered stories of domestic repression, including forced removals, and the imprisonment of journalists and dissidents. Numerous agendas would clash as both outsiders and internal reformers sought to 'hijack' the official Olympic platform with its positive presentations of China's domestic policies.[31] Joining the chorus, Darfur advocates sought to challenge China's policy towards Sudan.

Promoting the Genocide Olympics

Back in 2006, long-time Sudan activist Eric Reeves persuaded *The Washington Post* editorial board to publish an editorial incorporating the provocative phrase 'Genocide Olympics.'[32] He continued to publicise the connection between China and Sudan through Op-Ed articles and website postings.[33] As a phrase, 'Genocide Olympics' banked on global familiarity with the Darfur situation and summed up 'the accumulated discontent, anxiety, and suspicion about China and human rights'.[34] In January 2007, during a SDC strategy meeting, Reeves proposed targeting the Beijing Olympics as a Coalition-wide effort. Surprisingly, the coordinating organisation of the SDC was not enthusiastic about the idea. Along with two staff members at the international organisation Human Rights First, Jill Savitt and Nicky Lazar, Reeves decided to set up a separate organisation with the aim of targeting China more aggressively.

At first they were slow to find funding and support, but the tide changed in the spring of 2007 when Mia Farrow, the actress and UNICEF goodwill ambassador, published an Op-Ed article in *The Wall Street Journal* that ratcheted the stakes a bit higher. Singling out Beijing for not doing enough to address the conflict in Darfur, Farrow and her son Ronan noted that 'rather than "One World, One Dream," people are beginning to speak of the coming, "Genocide Olympics"'.[35] In their Op-Ed, the Farrows

[30] The list of advocacy groups included Human Rights Watch, Amnesty International, Human Rights in China, Reporters without Borders, Students for a Free Tibet, and the Fair Labor Association. See Sharon K. Hom, 'The Promise of a "People's Olympics,' in Worden ed., *China's Great Leap, op. cit.*

[31] Monroe Price considers a platform to be 'any mechanism that allows for the presentation of information and its transmission from a sender to a receiver.' Monroe E. Price, 'On Seizing the Olympic Platform,' in Monroe E. Price and Daniel Dayan eds., *Owning the Olympics, op. cit.*, p. 87.

[32] Price, 'On Seizing the Olympic Platform', *op. cit.*, p. 105.

[33] Eric Reeves, 'Holding China accountable for complicity in Darfur's ongoing genocidal destruction,' 17 December 2006, http://www.sudanreeves.org/Article142.html (accessed 28 May 2009).

[34] Price, 'On Seizing the Olympic Platform', *op. cit.* p. 104.

[35] Ronan Farrow and Mia Farrow, 'The "Genocide Olympics",' *The Wall Street Journal*, 28 March 2007.

also took Hollywood director Steven Spielberg to task as 'the Leni Riefenstahl of the Beijing Games'. In 2006, China had invited Spielberg to be an artistic adviser to the opening and closing ceremonies of the Beijing Olympics. Now his participation was viewed as tacit approval of the Chinese government. Mia Farrow began to lambast the government of China with bitter attacks in newspapers and on TV.

Reeves recalled, 'Now we had a campaign, a phrase and a target.'[36] Shortly after the Op-Ed was published, the organisation Dream for Darfur was born, with Mia Farrow and Eric Reeves serving as advisers, with the specific mission to target China around the venue of the Beijing Olympics. Dream for Darfur was buoyed up by a half a million-dollar grant from Humanity United, a foundation that addresses slavery and mass atrocities. But the campaign began in an atmosphere fraught with skepticism. Executive Director Jill Savitt recalls, 'People just said that it wasn't going to work. Can't influence China; can't influence China on Darfur.'[37] Nevertheless, the organisation aimed high. Dream for Darfur explicitly distinguished its mission as not leading a boycott campaign; rather, the goal was 'to leverage the Olympics to urge China to use its influence with the Sudanese regime to allow a robust civilian protection force into Darfur'.[38] Within the US advocacy community, the consensus was that bilateral negotiations between the US and China had failed to secure the results needed. Dream for Darfur came under the umbrella of the SDC as a member, and drew on shared resources of other organisations. Thus the 'China Campaign' was launched.

In amassing support for the China Campaign, Dream for Darfur consulted with experts on China to better understand the unique leverage points. In directing attention beyond the primary culpability of the leadership of Sudan, Dream for Darfur was unrelenting when it came to pointing the finger squarely at China for its role in the conflict in Darfur. On its organisation's website, Dream for Darfur set out the case:

> No country has done more to support the regime in Khartoum than the People's Republic of China: no country has offered more diplomatic support, nor done more to provide money to buy the weaponry that fuels the engine of genocidal destruction. And no country has done more to insulate Khartoum from economic pressure or human rights accountability.[39]

The strategy included targeting both the government of China and a number of indirect targets to place pressure on China. In its direct targeting, Dream for Darfur initiated correspondence and requested meetings with senior government officials including the Chinese Ambassador to

[36] Quoted in Ilan Greenberg, 'Changing the Rules of the Game', *The New York Times*, 30 March 2008.

[37] Interview with Jill Savitt, Executive Director, Dream for Darfur, 11 March 2009.

[38] Dream for Darfur, 'Not a boycott,' http://www.dreamfordarfur.org (accessed 26 June 2009).

[39] Dream for Darfur, 'China's Role,' http://www.dreamfordarfur.org/ index.php?option=com_content&task=view&id=21&Itemid=57 (accessed 26 June 2009).

the US. In eight formal encounters with Chinese officials, it attended meetings that were 'pleasant and diplomatic, but not productive'.[40] In what it called 'bank shots,' Dream for Darfur also focused attention on a number of indirect targets, which included the IOC, the US Olympic Committee, corporate sponsors, Steven Spielberg, athletes, media, and decision-makers in the US Congress and the UN. For the most part, Dream for Darfur was unable to persuade corporate sponsors[41] or the IOC to strongly condemn the host, China.

Other organisations focused on Darfur or human rights abuses in China joined the Campaign. The SDC produced briefing papers and fact sheets outlining the 'problematic partnership' between China and Sudan and how China could 'contribute to solving the Darfur crisis'.[42] On its website, SDC offered visitors a petition to send to President Hu stressing China's 'tremendous responsibility to help end the violence in Darfur'.[43] With the SDC's combined global membership of 130 million,[44] the campaign gained tremendous political power as a mass movement. This vast membership became a threat to corporate sponsors and China alike. As 2008 rolled on, the China Campaign gathered speed in the months leading up to the Games.

Enlisting the US government as an ally
Since 2004, the SDC and its member organisations had enjoyed bipartisan support for Darfur-related initiatives on Capitol Hill. As part of the China Campaign, the SDC engaged in indirect targeting through the US government. Domestic pressure on the government to condemn China proved a relatively easy course since many Congressmen had long been concerned with China, either from a human rights standpoint or because of concerns about global security.[45] The initiative to target China for its inaction on Darfur found little resistance.[46] The support for the China Campaign was unsurprising to the advocates; as Savitt noted: 'Congress likes to beat up on China.'[47] Long-time critics saw the nexus of complicity

[40] Dream for Darfur, 'DFD Final Report' (New York: Dream for Darfur, 2008).
[41] See Dream for Darfur, 'The Big Chill: Too Scared to Speak, Olympic Sponsors Still Silent on Darfur Fearing Economic Reprisal, Sponsors Pay for China-Sudan Ties,' (New York: Dream for Darfur, 2008).
[42] Save Darfur Coalition, 'China and Sudan—A Problematic Partnership'; available at http://darfur.3cdn.net/7216fbc9a790fef2d4_tum6v6hna.pdf (accessed: 28 May 5 2009).
[43] Save Darfur Coalition, 'China Please Bring the Olympic Dream to Darfur',; available at http://www.savedarfur.org/page/content/china/ (accessed: 28 May 2009).
[44] Save Darfur Coalition, 'About Us'; available at http://www.savedarfur.org/section/about/ (accessed: 1 June 2009).
[45] A Congressional-Executive Commission on China, created in October 2000, held the specific legislative mandate 'to monitor human rights and the development of the rule of law in China, and to submit an annual report to the President and the Congress.' Congressional-Executive Commission on China, 'About the Commission'; available at http://www.cecc.gov/ (accessed: 26 June 2009).
[46] Interviews with Congressional Hill Staffers, 18-20 March 2009.
[47] Interview with Jill Savitt, 9 March 2009.

with Sudan as further evidence of China's poor behaviour. US legislators took a bold step in May 2007 when 108 members of the House of Representatives and the Senate signed a letter to President Hu Jintao containing veiled threats against China's image during Beijing's 2008 Olympics. Without mincing words, the US legislators declared that 'if China fails to do its part, it risks being forever known as the host of the "Genocide Olympics"'.[48]

Throughout 2008, the reception of the China Campaign was warm on Capitol Hill and last-minute hearings and resolutions supported the campaign in its final days.[49] Special public appeals were made to Presidential candidates Senators Barack Obama and John McCain to support China-targeted legislation. Resolutions in the House and Senate, which included references to an Olympic Truce that had been submitted by the SDC, met with considerable support. Over a dozen Congressmen signed a letter requesting that President Bush not attend the Olympics Opening Ceremony; this plea was ultimately unsuccessful.[50] With these measures, the US Congress enthusiastically joined the chorus of China critics.

Pivotal month: February 2008

Six months before the Games, China received two prominent messages. In February 2008, Steven Spielberg resigned as artistic adviser to the opening and closing ceremonies. After his role as artistic director was highlighted in the Farrows' Op-Ed, Spielberg had immediately responded by writing to the Chinese president urging him to help resolve the conflict in Darfur, thereby adding a highly recognisable figure to the chorus of critics.[51] When this effort failed to yield any results, Spielberg issued a public statement addressed to the Chinese ambassador and the Beijing Olympic Committee saying that his 'conscience will not allow me to continue with business as usual'.[52] Spielberg's resignation came on the heels of a dramatic Day of Action on 12 February 2008 coordinated by the Dream for Darfur campaign. At the same time, a letter to President Hu was delivered to the Chinese Mission at the UN that had been signed

---

[48] US House of Representatives Committee on Foreign Affairs, 'Lantos, House Colleagues Send Strong Message to Chinese President, Demand Action on Darfur,' 9 May 2007; available at http://foreignaffairs.house.gov/press_display.asp?id=345 (accessed: 26 June 2009).

[49] Some observers viewed the focus on China as an abnegation of US failure to halt the violence. Critics went on the attack: 'In pointing the finger at China, proponents of stronger action on Darfur are merely helping the White House evade moral responsibility for a humanitarian disaster that it labels a "genocide"'. Morton Abramowitz and Jonathan Kolieb, 'Why China Won't Save Darfur,' *Foreign Policy,* June 2007; available at http://www.foreignpolicy.com/ story/cms.php?story_id=3847 (accessed 26 June 2009).

[50] Associated Press, 'US Congress Lawmakers Urge Bush Not to Attend Beijing Olympics,' *The International Herald Tribune,* 1 April 2008.

[51] See R.Scott Greathead, 'China and the Spielberg Effect,' in Worden ed., *China's Great Leap, op. cit.*

[52] Helene Cooper, 'Spielberg Drops out as Adviser to the Beijing Olympics in Dispute over Darfur Conflict,' *The New York Times,* 13 February 2008, p. 12.

by eight Nobel Peace Prize laureates, 13 Olympic athletes and 46 parliamentarians from around the world. This letter showed the widespread support from high-level spheres of moral authority and leadership.

Global dimension of the China Campaign

Though the main organisations of the China Campaign were based in the US, there were concerted efforts to foster a global movement by mobilising resources both to raise awareness of China's relationship with Sudan and to foster transnational networks among particular swathes of the global public. To raise awareness globally, the SDC poured millions of dollars into an advertising campaign, which ran in leading European, Asian, African and US publications in February 2008. One advertisement stated: 'The games China is hosting in Beijing can't hide those it's playing in Darfur.'[53] A network called Globe for Darfur, led by the SDC's main European partner Crisis Action,[54] launched a sub-group in the China Campaign to coordinate worldwide activities. During the 12 February protests, advocates in eleven countries on four continents paid visits to Chinese embassies and consulates. While efforts were made to link a global audience around Darfur, outreach to groups within China was considered risky.

In addition to engaging concerned citizens across the globe, the campaign took steps to foster transnational networks of like-minded groups in various countries with high degrees of media visibility and credibility. One such network was a set of Olympic athletes who became advocates for Darfur. US Olympic Gold Medallist Joey Cheek and UCLA water polo player Brad Greiner founded Team Darfur in the summer of 2007 as 'an international coalition of athletes committed to raising awareness about and bringing an end to the genocide in Darfur, Sudan'.[55] Team Darfur grew to include over 450 athletes from more than 60 countries. This transnational network of athletes formed a media-savvy group eager to help journalists fill sports pages with athletes' biographies and the cause of Darfur. Besides participating in protests and symbolic torch relays, Team Darfur athletes were among many delivering testimony to Congressional representatives. But the organisation found its ability to send a strong message hampered by the security concerns surrounding

[53] The SDC Olympic advertisement read: 'China is doing everything possible to publicise its role as host of the 2008 summer Olympic Games. But that won't make the world forget about China's role in Sudan – which is anything but a game. As Sudan's largest foreign investor, key arms supplier, and chief diplomatic sponsor, China has more power than any other nation to stop the suffering of people in Darfur. Yet China's gestures at Darfur diplomacy have been little more than attempts at public relations. Any cheers for Beijing will be silenced by our tears for Darfur. JOIN CITIZENS FROM AROUND THE GLOBE IN SAYING: CHINA MUST DO MORE TO SAVE DARFUR.' Save Darfur Coalition, 'Olympic Ad,'; available at http://www.savedarfur.org/olympic_ad (accessed: 26 June 2009).

[54] The organisation Crisis Action also facilitated high-level advocacy discussions in European Union capitals and launched a Muslim Coalition on Darfur. See http://crisisaction.org/en/

protest and politics at the Olympics. Athletes began to be concerned about possible repercussions because of their engagement.[56] Indeed, the Team Darfur campaign moved hesitantly as it tested the waters of advocacy during the Olympics.

Dream for Darfur financed and coordinated a transnational network of survivor communities in countries that had experienced genocide. This linkage tapped into an international group that could speak with moral authority and held great potential for media coverage. Over the course of the year leading up to the Games, Dream for Darfur orchestrated a symbolic Olympic torch relay through Rwanda, Armenia, Germany, Cambodia and Bosnia. Members of Dream for Darfur, along with a Darfur survivor, travelled to each country for a torch lighting ceremony with other genocide survivors, and held events and press conferences. Critically, the torch-lighting in Cambodia garnered over five days of press coverage on Darfur before the government, under pressure from the Chinese government, withdrew the permit for the relay. Mobilising a global survivor network had never been attempted before and, as Dream for Darfur international organiser Allison Johnson noted, 'that message was really powerful'.[57]

Beijing Summer Olympics 2008
Since the IOC's Olympic Charter restricts political demonstrations within Olympic arenas and sites, outlets for activism during the Olympic Games are strictly controlled.[58] Proscriptions against clothing bearing 'propaganda' meant that the Team Darfur athletes and other activists could identify themselves only outside Olympic areas. There were thus few plans to promote the campaign inside China during August 2008. Indeed, China's forceful response to other human rights organisations such as the Free Tibet campaign, and the arrests of domestic activists had made many nervous.[59] For Team Darfur and its participating athletes, how China would behave as a host was a 'big unknown'.[60] With these concerns in

[55] Team Darfur received funding and staff from the SDC and opened up its own office in Washington, DC. See Martha Heinemann Bixby, 'Introducing Team Darfur,' *Blog for Darfur*, available at http://blogfordarfur.org/2008/07/18/introducing-team-darfur/ (accessed: 26 June 2009).

[56] Sponsors threatened to cancel contracts and the national committees of the International Olympic Committee contacted their athletes and warned them not to sign public statements.

[57] Interview with Johnson, International Campaign Manager, Dream for Darfur. After the Olympics, Dream for Darfur transitioned the success of this transnational network survivor network into a new venture, the Genocide Prevention Project. See http://www.preventorprotect.org/

[58] Article 51 (3) reads 'No kind of demonstration or political, religious or racial propaganda is permitted in any Olympic sites, venues or other areas.' International Olympic Committee, 'Olympic Charter', (Lausanne: International Olympics Committee, 2007), p. 98.

[59] Amnesty International, 'People's Republic of China: The Olympics Countdown—Crackdown on Activists Threatens Olympic Legacy',; available at http://www.amnestyusa.org/document.php?id=ENGUSA20080401002&lang=e (accessed 26 June 2009).

[60] Interview with Martha Heinemann Bixby, Executive Director, Team Darfur, 4 November 2008.

mind, Team Darfur limited its plans for the Games to encouraging its roster of athletes to raise awareness of Darfur during interviews and panels held outside official venues. Away from Beijing, Dream for Darfur held a parallel event called the 'Darfur Olympics,' a week-long, daily broadcast hosted by Mia Farrow from a Darfuri refugee camp.

In advance of the Olympics, China demonstrated its wariness at importing hotbeds of Darfur activism. It waited until two days before the start of the Games to revoke the visa of Joey Cheek, the co-founder of Team Darfur. When China was asked to explain its overreaction, the organisation's director noted, 'The Chinese said they weren't required to give a reason'.[61] Subsequently, the media storm surrounding the Cheek story once again brought Darfur to the forefront of the Olympic Games. The White House and various Congressmen protested against the visa revocation and stories about Cheek and Team Darfur appeared in major newspapers across the globe. As a pointed message to the Chinese government, the US Olympic team chose Sudanese-born athlete and Team Darfur member Lopez Lomong to represent the US as flag-bearer during the Opening Ceremonies. During an interview held at the Olympics, President Bush was asked about his thoughts on Joey Cheek's visa revocation and the prospect of leveraging China on the subject of Darfur during his time in Beijing. The President replied, 'Joey Cheek has just got to know that I took the Sudanese message for him.' Further, Bush acknowledged the Sudan-China connection: 'My attitude is, if you got relations with Mr. Bashir, think about helping to solve the humanitarian crisis in Darfur. That was my message to the Chinese government.'[62] While athletes may have been barred from campaigning, the US President entered the diplomatic fray to condemn China's behaviour.

Measuring the Impact of the China Campaign

In conceiving the campaign, Dream for Darfur's mission was 'to use the 2008 Beijing Games as a way to press China to use its influence with the Sudanese regime to bring security to the Darfur region'.[63] Assessing the outcome of an advocacy campaign often involves determining success: whether the goal has been achieved. From this point of view, it would seem that the China Campaign and the activities of the SDC and its member organisations have failed to meet their goal of resolving the conflict in Darfur. In an assessment of the Coalition's advocacy efforts one

[61] Linton Weeks, 'Beijing Revokes Visa of Activist Athlete,' *NPR*, 6 August 2008.
[62] The White House Office of the Press Secretary, 'Interview of the President by Bob Costas, NBC Sports'; available at http://georgewbush-whitehouse.archives.gov/news/releases/2008/08/20080811.html (accessed: 26 June 2009).
[63] Dream for Darfur, 'What Dream for Darfur Accomplished – and What's Next'; available at http://www.dreamfordarfur.org/index331b.html?option=com_content&task=view&id=293&Itemid=1 (accessed 5 August 2009).

journalist declared, 'Save Darfur cannot claim the one success that really matters: stopping the killing.'[64] But in measuring the campaign's impact, we need to look beyond this fact and focus on other consequences. Policy actions were taken to ameliorate the Darfur conflict, and in terms of lobbying China, a degree of influence can be measured.

China responds to the campaign

That the Chinese government responded at all to the Campaign is indicative of its impact. It is important to highlight that not all advocacy groups and claims are given access to and heard in political spheres. There is much evidence that China was closely following the Campaign and made efforts to understand the issue, and took special care to respond to and refute the claims, both in private consultations and through the public media. First, the Chinese gave audience to the SDC through official meetings on a number of occasions to hear their concerns surrounding Darfur. During a meeting at the Chinese Consulate in New York, Dream for Darfur activists report that the acting Consul General had printed out the entire Campaign website and written notes on what he called 'inaccuracies'.[65] Second, the high-profile defection of Steven Spielberg prompted the dismay of the Chinese leadership, who had expected his star reputation to add glamour and prestige to the Olympic ceremonies. The Chinese Embassy in Washington issued a retort to Spielberg's resignation in February 2008 alluding specifically to the narrative of the Campaign: 'As the Darfur issue is neither an internal issue of China nor is it caused by China, it is completely unreasonable, irresponsible and unfair to link the two as one.'[66] Third, Beijing responded crisply to US government measures; when resolutions criticising China were brought before Congress, Chinese foreign ministry spokesman, Liu Jianchao, retorted, 'This action itself is a blasphemy to the Olympics and runs counter to the aspiration of people of all countries including the U.S.'[67] The relentless criticism of the Campaign's public relations tactics indicated that the activists had touched the nerves of the Chinese government.

In addition to publicly rebuffing the claims of the Campaign, China took a number of steps to curtail its activities. Various cyber attacks that seemed to originate in China began to plague the email accounts of the SDC, Team Darfur and Dream for Darfur.[68] Dream for Darfur maintained that China responded to the torch relays held around the world by attempting to restrict activities in Rwanda, and that it was successful in

---

[64] Richard Just, 'The Truth Will Not Set You Free: Everyone we know about Darfur, and everything we're not doing about it,' *The New Republic*, 27 August 2008; available at http:www.tnr.com (accessed: 6 October 2008).

[65] Dream for Darfur, *D4D Final Report* (New York: Dream for Darfur, 2008).

[66] Cooper, 'Spielberg Drops out', *op. cit.*

[67] Josh Gerstein, 'Senate Presses on Darfur as China Fumes over 'Evil' House Vote,' *The Sun*, 1 August 2008.

[68] Greenberg, 'Changing the Rules of the Game', *op. cit.*

shutting down the relay portion in Cambodia. China's revocation of Joey Cheek's visa indicated the close attention paid to SDC activities and expectations of potential disruption of the Games. Team Darfur would later learn that a number of its athletes had been placed on a special watch list, given to the US Olympic Committee by the Chinese Embassy in Washington, DC.[69]

China shifts its Darfur policy

As noted earlier, foreign policy towards Sudan had started to shift in 2006, when China began to work with the UN Secretary-General Kofi Annan on the deployment of a hybrid AU-UN peacekeeping mission. But China took further steps that can be correlated with actions of the Campaign. In the month following the publication of the Farrows' Op-Ed in March 2007, the possibility of boycotting the Olympics over China's relationship with Sudan was raised in Congress and in media circles and China began to address the situation in Darfur more energetically. In April, Chinese Assistant Foreign Minister Zhai Jun made a well-publicized visit to three Darfur refugee camps. At a press conference following his trip, Zhai insisted 'China is willing to continue to play a constructive role on the issue of Darfur' and described efforts to urge the Sudanese to accept a UN peacekeeping plan.[70] Days later, the Chinese persuaded Khartoum to allow the deployment of over 3000 interim UN troops to strengthen AU forces.[71] These reinforcements included 300 Chinese military engineers, an act signalling a shift in foreign policy towards Sudan. At the same time, China took the extraordinary step of appointing its first Special Envoy for African Affairs to focus on the Darfur issue. In one summation, Beijing's appointment of Liu Guijin, a former Chinese ambassador to South Africa and Zimbabwe, was regarded as 'almost certainly a result of global activist pressure'.[72]

China met the terms of the policy 'asks' of the China Campaign further during UN Security Council debates around the critical subject of increasing peacekeeping troops in the summer of 2007. On 31 July, the ultimate day of its control of the UN Security Council, China signalled its support and joined the unanimous vote for Resolution 1768, which authorised the proposed joint AU-UN peacekeeping force. Through private channels, Beijing insisted that Khartoum accept the resolution. The US Deputy Secretary of State, John Negroponte, credited China with

[69] Christine Brennan, 'China listed U.S. athletes as possible troublemakers', *USA TODAY*, 10 October 2008.

[70] Embassy of the People's Republic of China in Australia, 'Assistant Foreign Minister Zhai Jun Holds a Briefing for Chinese and Foreign Journalists on the Darfur Issue of Sudan', 12 April 2007; available at http://au.china-embassy.org/eng/zt/sudandarfurissue/t311958.htm (accessed: 26 June 2009).

[71] Edward Cody, 'Chinese to Deploy Soldiers to Darfur,' *The Washington Post*, 9 May 2007, A11.

[72] Colin Thomas-Jensen and Julie Spiegel, 'Activism and Darfur: Slowly Driving Policy Change,' *Fordham International Law Journal* 31 (April 2008), p. 852.

playing 'a pivotal role in brokering the agreement'.[73] While these policy steps can never be directly linked with the campaign's activities, there are grounds for a strong time-ordered correlation.

The combination of epistolary messages and global protests during February 2008 may also have pushed China to take further action. In the wake of Spielberg's resignation, its Special Envoy paid another visit to Sudan and made numerous statements attesting to Beijing's efforts to utilise its relationship with Khartoum. Liu also travelled to the UK, France, and the US to raise the subject of Darfur in diplomatic circles.

The Chinese play down the influence of the Campaign, as it does not befit an emerging global power to succumb to public pressure. In a conversation with a Chinese official, the appointment of the Special Envoy was shrugged off; China was following a global trend for appointing Special Envoys for hot spots like North Korea and the Middle East.[74] In China's view, its shifting stance on Darfur can be seen as part of a programme to ensure stability in Africa. It emphasises this stability in order to ensure economic development; this makes for good friends and good partners. Yet, in engaging with the Campaign, China signalled its willingness to listen and take into account the concerns of the global community.

Conclusion

The SDC's success in pushing US legislation has not ended the violence in Darfur. With the US limited in its ability to work with the international community to address the situation in Darfur, advocates needed to look elsewhere to apply pressure. China's diplomatic efforts to work with Sudan behind the scenes had failed to convince activists that necessary steps were being taken. The movement's targeting of China leading up to the Beijing Olympics reflected the expanding political scope of the Darfur advocacy movement as well as the rising status of China in an interdependent world. The Beijing Olympics and their promise of global media attention offered an international target that was viewed as vulnerable to global opinion and public pressure. Here was an opportunity to highlight China's foreign policy amidst the Olympic showcase of its international values of harmony.

China's emergence as a target of the Darfur advocacy movement stemmed from the country's ascent as a global superpower on a complex and integrated world stage. Crucially, China's foreign policy was considered malleable due to its aspirations to be a responsible member of the international community. Divestment campaigns had already directly targeted the financial connections between Sudan and China. Using the vehicle of the Olympics, the SDC capitalised on this link between China's

[73] John D. Negroponte, 'Remarks at the National Committee on U.S.-China Relations Dinner' (Washington DC: U.S. Department of State, 2007).
[74] Confidential Interview with author, 17 March 2009.

extensive economic ties and its diplomatic capabilities. The China Campaign was successful in crafting a persuasive argument that China could play a key role in ending the conflict in Darfur. It also tapped into China's growing interest in conforming to international norms around humanitarianism and peacekeeping. The Campaign intended to influence China's policy on Sudan by highlighting critical features of its foreign policy in general, and it directed its advocacy efforts to apply global pressure on China to incorporate moral suasion within its policy-making.

Dissenters to the China Campaign will rightly note that the conflict in Darfur continues. As the Olympics came to a close, one observer bemoaned, 'Darfur is today as it was a fortnight ago, and as it was when Steven Spielberg chose to boycott these Olympics in February.'[75] China continues to support Sudan's leadership despite the widespread criticism. Writing in a critical account of the SDC, Mahmood Mamdani concluded, 'the anti-China campaign failed because China was strong enough to uphold its own sovereignty.'[76] In sum, China's interests in Sudan remained paramount.

The advocacy campaign against China set its expectations low from the start. That China responded at all to the campaign came as a surprise to many in the Darfur advocacy circles. There is evidence that the China Campaign influenced the behaviour of the Chinese leadership. While the violence in Darfur still continues, the Chinese engaged with the campaign and took steps to address the cause of peace. Overall, the confluence of its positive image promotion, the Olympics 2008 as a global event, and its developing foreign policy on Africa left China exposed to the aggressive tactics of the campaign, which was successful in directing attention to China's relationship with Sudan and pressuring the Chinese leadership to engage with it more publicly and forcefully. Today, the China Campaign continues, albeit to a lesser extent, to highlight China as an actor obstructing international action on Darfur.

[75] Greg Baum, 'Bye Bye Beijing,' *The Age* (Melbourne, Australia), 25 August 2008, p. 1.
[76] Mahmood Mamdani, *Saviors and Survivors: Darfur, Politics and the War on Terror* (New York: Pantheon Books, 2009), p. 51.

8

Southern Sudan & China | 'Enemies into Friends'?

DANIEL LARGE

Attention to Sudan's relations with China has overwhelmingly referred to northern Sudan, but the limitations of this approach and the need to appreciate a more complex, plural and fluid set of political dynamics within Sudan became increasingly obvious after the CPA. An important trend since 2005, long overshadowed by Darfur, has seen Southern Sudan develop relations with China.[1] The CPA created a new political reality for Sudan's China relations by establishing a 'one Sudan, two systems' framework and including the people of South Sudan's right of self-deter-mination to be exercised via a referendum vote on remaining in or seceding from a united Sudan. What started as a legal provision, and in the face of Beijing's natural preference for unity, had to be accommodated through practical politics and would see China's established relations with Khartoum continue as it sought to cultivate new relations with Juba, and respond to the prospect of an independent South Sudan and a two Sudans future.

This chapter offers a preliminary overview of South Sudan's relations with China. What follows first puts relations in context before consider-ing China's role in Sudan's North-South civil wars as a continuing influence on its relations with the south. While the CPA in principle allowed governmental relations to develop, Chinese entrepreneurs were initially more active in the south after 2005. Moves to enhance political relations between the GoSS and Beijing came comparatively late, some two and a half years after the CPA, and subsequent links were directly related to the Southern referendum. The necessity for Beijing to develop relations with Juba was clear: the main Chinese oil concessions are mostly located in the south and in the contested North-South border areas. In engaging the GoSS, Beijing was responding to political impera-tives linked to concerns about investment protection. Following its support for 'making unity attractive', Beijing deployed a hedging strategy geared towards the possibility of southern secession, and then began to quietly but actively prepare for this inevitability. The GoSS looked to

---

[1] This chapter draws on various research trips to Sudan and China since 2004.

[2] This phenomenon is not confined to coverage of China; the same can be said for India or Malaysia.

Beijing to provide political guarantees of support for CPA implementation, most importantly the outcome of the referendum, and economic assistance.

South Sudan-China Relations in Context

Sudan's relations with China have mostly been viewed through a narrow prism privileging formal interactions between central state and corporate elites in northern Sudan (and, one could argue, China).[2] The prevailing analytical approach and language of description used to cover Sudan-China relations have thus been limited in terms of their political, economic and geographical purview. This dominance of northern-centric approaches to Sudan's China relations can be attributed to a combination of historical circumstance, neglect, and recent, more political factors. Firstly, as expressed in official narratives, the historical mythology of Sudan's China relations mostly concerns northern Sudan.[3] This is applicable both to the official foundational narratives of the history of relations between the two countries – shared colonial oppression – and to the more recent history valorising Chinese oil operations in Sudan in the 1990s. Exceptions to this prevailing coverage tend to reinforce constructions of the south as merely an object of external intervention, when, as this chapter partly explores, it can also be seen as a more active agent in developing relations on its own accord and according to its own political purposes. Secondly, Khartoum had good reasons to want to control access to and influence relations between China and the SPLM. The NIF had long defined and controlled China's relations with the south. China, in turn, only dealt with Sudan's sovereign central government and had no official wartime political contact with the SPLM/A. Finally, the GoSS has been developing relations with various external powers as part of its efforts to develop a foreign policy of its own.[4] Alongside the US, China stands out as being unquestionably of major significance in view of its economic role in Sudan, its relations with the NCP and its permanent seat on the UN Security Council. In this context, the historical departure represented by the recent growth of relations between Juba and Beijing reflects changes in wider Sudanese politics as a whole.

Flowing from the preponderant northern focus is the need to approach Sudan's relations with China in a more disaggregated manner. From the

---

[3] The exceptions to this prevailing pattern constitute colourful historical footnotes. While in the Egyptian province of Equatoria in May 1881, Emin Pasha became convinced that Chinese labour could help open up Central Africa, and even solve the slave trade. See Schweinfurth, G. F. Ratzel, R.W. Felkin and G. Hartlaub eds., *Emin Pasha in Central Africa: being a collection of his letters and journals* (London: George Philip and Son., 1888), pp. 417, 419. This was an isolated minority view, and was never translated into a practical programme, but the fantasy was reinvented in later visions of a more independent Chinese role in Sudan.

[4] Interview with GoSS official, Juba, February 2011.

Sudan side, at a minimum this entails differentiating between and within regional geographies, while not losing sight of the fundamental continuing importance of Sudan's dominant central government in Khartoum. Extending analysis beyond elite interaction is also desirable in order to ground the high politics of Sudan-China relations in more locally embedded, diverse contexts, but this is begun here only very generally in relation to South Sudan.[5] In part, these assertions are a plea to transcend the frequent generalities of mainstream coverage and better locate relations in appropriate context.[6] More immediately, however, opening up different vectors of interaction is necessary to better comprehend political developments in Sudan that since 2005 have importantly moved beyond the sphere of Khartoum-Beijing interaction.

'China is Not Welcome': A Politicised Past

The principles informing China's relations with northern Sudan, emphasising sovereignty, territorial integrity, non-interference and political equality, made Beijing an attractive external partner to a succession of different parliamentary and military regimes in Khartoum after diplomatic relations were established in 1959. The Golden Jubilee celebrations of five decades of relations between China and Sudan in 2009 underlined this vividly, simultaneously reinforcing the northern-centric nature of these historical links.

Premier Zhou Enlai's state visit to Khartoum in January 1964 came at a time when the separatist Anyanya war was escalating in southern Sudan, where the military government under President Abboud had been implementing an unpopular policy of forced assimilation and Arabisation. The Chinese government never advanced any rhetorical or material support for the Anyanya rebels. This appeared to contrast with Beijing's support for 'revolutionary armed conflict' in other parts of Africa, but the Anyanya civil war was occurring in a very different political context. Sudan's independence from Anglo-Egyptian colonial rule on 1 January 1956 proceeded even as southern discontent and violence grew. As such, this was far from the anti-colonial struggles China supported elsewhere

---

[5] There is a corresponding need to differentiate the Chinese engagement better, through an approach that does not lose sight of the central Chinese government's importance but which is better able to accommodate a more plural set of engagements. In such an alternative way of considering a more diverse conception of Chinese links with Sudan, the Chinese government's engagement can be disaggregated into, at the least, its respective key shapers of Sudan policy and central ministries, between and within which there are different components. It is also important to recognise intra-governmental debates surrounding its changing Sudan policy, though the full nature of these has yet to emerge.

[6] 'Sudan's view' on China is often not disaggregated sufficiently. See, for instance, the statistics in Barry Sautman and Yan Hairong, 'African perspectives on China-Africa Links', in Julia C. Strauss and Martha Saavedra eds., *China and Africa: Emerging Patterns in Globalization and Development* (Cambridge: Cambridge University Press, 2009), p. 186.

in Africa: the war in southern Sudan, in essence, was a matter of newly sovereign Sudan's 'internal' politics. Khartoum was an early supporter of the People's Republic of China, including its efforts to join the UN. The continuation of Beijing's support for Khartoum was also influenced by concerns that any other policy would jeopardise China's wider interests in the Middle East.[7] Rather than being affected by Sudan's internal politics, Beijing was consistently more concerned about Khartoum's links with Taiwan and the Soviet Union, until these were severed in 1971.

The first phase of a more involved Chinese role in southern Sudan came after the North-South Addis Ababa peace agreement in 1972. China's aid programme was extended to the south; a small number of other projects also took off. Chinese medical teams worked in Juba and other clinics such as in Malakal and Aweil, as those who were treated by Chinese doctors in this period still recall today. The manner in which Chinese aid teams conducted themselves – the same living standards as their Sudanese counterparts, personal qualities of dedication, self-denial, discipline, and integrity, or treating the Sudanese as equals – embodied and projected an altruistic image of China.

Not having any substantial investments in Sudan at the time, China was not directly affected by the start and spread of civil war in the south from 1983. Instead, it was the American and French corporations spear-heading the development of Sudan's strategic and politically divisive oil sector, and other large development projects like the Jonglei Canal,[8] that the newly formed SPLA targeted. These ground to a halt. Sudan in the 1980s was cited as an example where China's tendency to provide verbal support for a conflict deemed a legitimate armed popular struggle against injustice in Africa was again conspicuously lacking.[9] This is not surprising, however, as once more China preferred to maintain relations with Khartoum, and not become involved in Sudan's internal politics or desta-bilise its relations with the Middle East. Sudan's most important external partner was the US. Beijing's relations with Khartoum continued despite Sudan's deepening economic crisis and political upheaval, featuring efforts to expand trade with the government elected in April 1986.

By far the most important period of China's role in Sudan, including

---

[7] Khartoum's support for Congolese nationalists in 1964 was also supported by Beijing and aligned with the PRC's policy. When the Congo threatened to help Anyanya 1 in southern Sudan, a concerned Beijing 'hoped that the problem would be solved within the framework of Sudanese unity and announced its readiness to help the Sudan against any foreign interven-tion aiming at undermining this.' Alaba Ogunsanwo, *China's Policy in Africa, 1958-71* (Cambridge: Cambridge University Press, 1974), p. 174 (citing the *People's Daily*, 28 January 1964).

[8] The Jonglei Canal project, which started in 1979, was intended to make more water from the Sudd in Southern Sudan available for export agriculture irrigation in northern Sudan via a 360 km waterway.

[9] See Lillian Craig Harris, 'China's Support for People's War in the 1980s', in Lillian Craig Harris and Robert L. Worden eds., *China and the Third World: Champion or Challenger?* (London: Croom Helm, 1986), pp. 120-138.

from the perspective of the south, has been that unfolding since the June 1989 NIF coup. The previous benevolent abstraction of an altruistic People's China in Sudan underwent a transition as its oil intervention became more tangibly entwined in the country's multiple civil wars. China's role in Sudan's oil-fuelled conflicts followed, but by no means created, an entrenched, violent political economy. Despite its militarised creation, the oil industry contributed towards the negotiations that produced the CPA, changing the economic incentives to support those favouring peace between Khartoum and the south. At the same time, its very success was one contributing grievance behind armed struggle in marginalised Darfur. However, those narratives selectively eulogising the heroic against-the-odds engineering feats of Chinese companies in creating Sudan's oil export sector, or those accounts citing Sudan as an outstanding example of success for China's then fledgling overseas oil operations, are problematic. These mostly or entirely omit the important, contrasting southern experience that was integral to these developments, but from a very different position.[10]

Oil development intensified a long-running, already destructive series of interlocking conflicts in the south. Most readily thought of as a central aspect of the war between Khartoum and the SPLA, oil also became entangled in the related intra-southern civil wars following the SPLA's split in 1991 and the subsequent fragmentation of rebel movements. The NIF's survival imperative drove its efforts to create an oil export industry. China proved to be a dependable partner. The CNPC and its subsidiaries were not the only foreign oil companies active in oil development, but they played a key role. Oil had been a divisive factor in Sudanese politics long before the 1990s. Following the intensive, accelerated construction of oil industry infrastructure in the late 1990s, however, oil export revenue finally became a reality for the NIF regime in August 1999. This represented the tangible realisation of the principle of mutual benefit for the Chinese and the northern Sudanese state and corporate interests involved. For the south, however, experiences of oil development and its subsequent operations were radically different, and came at a very high human cost. Much destruction resulted from the dependence existing between the oil companies and the Sudanese military: the former needed security, the latter required revenue to fund its war. Conflict patterns and oil development on the ground were closely related. Campaigns of forced civilian displacement, involving by proxy militias and SAF operations, often preceded oil operations.[11] The oil companies, and by extension their state sponsors, were implicated in helping the Sudan government's military operations, including through the construction of infrastructure

---

[10] See, for example, CNPC, 'Review of 15 years of Sino-Sudanese Petroleum Cooperation' (Beijing: CNPC, 2010).
[11] See Douglas H. Johnson, *The Root Causes of Sudan's Civil Wars* (Oxford, James Currey, 2003), pp. 162-165. Also, Human Rights Watch, *Sudan Oil and Human Rights* (New York: Human Rights Watch, 2003).

that could double up for military use. There was thus a pronounced complicity between foreign oil operations and the government: 'by allowing themselves to be so clearly drawn into the war the oil companies became partners with the state in human destruction.'[12] The oil industry became internationalised, but remained rooted in often violent local relations of extraction.

The south's experience during these wars, especially in oil-producing areas where the effects were most immediate and destructive, requires the notion of Sudan as a straightforward Chinese success story to be questioned. For China, Sudan was and continues to be presented in this way as part of China's relations with Africa and, more generally, its 'go global' expansion.[13] From the perspective of southerners, generally speaking the situation was and continues to be regarded and experienced quite differently. Oil development unquestionably represents 'success' for Khartoum, the CNPC and Beijing (partly inherited, in turn, by the GoSS after the CPA). Any interrogation of this notion in relation to non-elite outcomes and human impact, however, opens up a different, varied set of more critical perspectives. For many in the south, and not only those directly affected by oil development, as well as other Sudanese opponents of the NIF/NCP across Sudan, the link between China and the oil wars of the late 1990s remains a predominantly negative and very present, vivid and automatic association.

The Chinese role during Sudan's North-South civil wars was not confined to the oil sector but also entailed military relations with Khartoum. Some of the wartime stories about China's military support for the GOS were rightly dismissed as 'pure fantasy'.[14] However, there is evidence that Chinese-manufactured small arms and light weapons began to be imported in quantity during this period.[15] Chinese assistance has also been linked to the development of north Sudan's military industrial complex.[16]

---

[12] Jok Madut Jok, *Sudan: Race, Religion and Violence* (Oxford: Oneworld Publications, 2007), p. 198.

[13] See, for example, Linda Jakobson and Zha Daojing, 'China and the worldwide search for oil security', *Asia-Pacific Review*, Vol. 13, No. 2 (2006), pp. 60-73.

[14] Nicholas Coghlan, *Far in the Waste Sudan: On Assignment in Africa* (Kingston, ON: McGill-Queen's University Press, 2005), p. 47. For example, one article claimed that 'Tens of thousands of Chinese troops and prisoners forced to work as security guards have been moved into Sudan', and cited a Sudanese military internal document claiming 'that as many as 700,000 Chinese security personnel were available for action'. See Christina Lamb, 'China puts '700,000 troops' on Sudan alert', *The Telegraph*, 27 August 2000.

[15] See Human Rights Watch, 'Sudan: Global Trade, Local Impact: Arms Transfers to all Sides in the Civil War in Sudan' (August, Vol. 10, No.4, 1998). UN Comtrade and other public sources show evidence of increased arms sales from China in 2002.

[16] The details of Chinese technical assistance for arms production remain unknown, but there are various indications of Chinese supervision of the construction of arms manufacturing facilities near Khartoum. See , for example, Christian Aid, *The Scorched Earth: Oil and war in Sudan* (London: Christian Aid, 2001); Daniel Large, 'Arms, oil and Darfur: The evolution of relations between China and Sudan', *Small Arms Survey Issue Brief*, No. 7 (Geneva: August 2007).

Hassan al-Turabi indicated in early 1999 that Sudan was building factories as part of plans to 'manufacture tanks and missiles'.[17] Khartoum was
even said to be manufacturing ammunition, mortars, tanks and armoured
personnel carriers and would reach 'self-sufficiency in light, medium and
heavy weapons from its local production' by the end of 2000.[18] This
remains an opaque area but, regardless of the actual nature of these
military links, in different parts of the south, as in Darfur, China is popu-
larly regarded as a key arms supplier to Khartoum.

The wartime Chinese role in Sudan and multifaceted support for the
NIF/NCP has meant that through experience, whether direct or as trans-
mitted by others, many southerners harbour negative associations about
China.[19] This applies across a range of different groupings and is not
confined to elites. Long before US-led activists mobilised a campaign
against China in relation to the Darfur conflict, and Darfurian rebels
joined in to condemn China for supporting Khartoum, southern Sudanese
suffered, first from militarised oil development and then the subsequent failure to implement the CPA's oil-related provisions, which on
paper allowed for compensation and greater local benefits from oil (see
Moro, Chapter 3, in this volume).

Arising from this recent history, two associations with China are
commonly articulated in the south. One is that China, as an active, willing
supporter of Khartoum, was a wartime enemy. This receives various
expressions, from understated views[20] to more direct criticism and overt
opposition. As one person commented, for example: 'I don't know about
China but I know they are enemies of Southern Sudan. They're not
welcome.'[21] As the CPA negotiations continued during 2004 in the Kenyan
town of Naivasha, and the UN was planning its future mission in Sudan,
this refrain that Chinese were 'not welcome' summed up a common
attitude in the south. This was also articulated amidst suspicion at this
point about the possibility of a Chinese role in a UN peacekeeping
mission. One senior SPLM official, for example, made it plain that Chinese
peacekeepers would 'not be welcome' as part of the UN mission then
being planned for Sudan.[22] Secondly, the active equation between China
and the economic exploitation of the south is often cited, linked to views
that the northern NCP had benefited from southern oil. China is regarded

---

[17] *AFP*, 'Sudan to Manufacture Tanks, Missiles: Assembly Speaker', 30 April 1999.

[18] *AFP*, 'Sudan to achieve self-sufficiency in weapons: spokesman', 1 July 2000.

[19] This is not exclusive to China; Canada, for example, also has a history of unpopular
activities due to the role of Talisman during the war.

[20] One relatively mild view, for example, was: 'the Chinese have not been helping us, they have
been helping the North. China has not been a friend of the South'. Interview with senior SPLM
official, Rumbek, 23 July 2005.

[21] Interview, Wau, September 2010.

[22] Interview, Rumbek, 2004. Certain country troop contingents that deployed with UNMIS
were also unwelcome but for different reasons, including popular suspicion of possible religious links with Khartoum. From the first troops from the Jinan Military Command sent in
2005, the Chinese UN peacekeepers that eventually deployed in the South were based in Wau,
UNMIS Sector II headquarters.

as engaging in narrow resource exploitation without corresponding benefits for the south in general, and affected populations in the oil-producing regions in particular. Greed is commonly ascribed as China's motivation; Malaysia's links with Khartoum, in contrast, are more often linked to religious commonalities.[23]

The upshot of such views renders official Chinese government claims to have maintained a principled stand of non-interference in Sudan's internal affairs at best questionable in the south. This way of attempting to explain and defend China's role is often totally rejected. At times it is regarded as offensive. 'There are many ways you can say China interfered in Southern Sudan during the war'.[24] China's role, like that of other foreign oil companies, is widely perceived as a clear-cut partisan intervention. Furthermore, despite recognition that Khartoum may have 'misled' China, there is widespread scepticism that China could have been so ignorant of the background to the war, how it was being fought and at what human cost, as to not realise that its investments would actively support the government's war effort and further entrench its violent dominance. In other words, 'The Chinese should have known why there was fighting.'[25] These factors remain active in different parts of the south in terms of attitudes towards China, including but not only amongst top military and political leaders. Before the CPA, then, and as a continuing legacy of the wartime years, there was considerable suspicion of and hostility towards China, but the CPA created a new political context and would see relations develop under different conditions.

The CPA: One Sudan, Two Systems

China firmly supported the unity of Sudan when the CPA was signed, but with time it had to confront the new political circumstances the agreement created and the implications of its core provisions. It is important here to underline how debate on the future of the South evolved after the CPA and the difference in the position of the SPLA/M leadership and popular southern sentiments over this time period. This also points to the contrast between the period that saw the formal end to the war and the creation of a new peacetime government in Juba, and when the GoSS was seeking to navigate through the remaining stages of the CPA in 2010 and 2011. The CPA enshrined the Southern Sudan's right to self-determination

---

[23] Negative attitudes within the South are echoed and magnified in vigorous online discussions about China's role amongst the Southern Sudanese global diaspora. 'Chinese are takers, not sharers. They exploit rather than invest in the locals. And with the guns they import to Sudan, they mean it to protect their investment. The locals are getting robbed at gun point of their natural resources, rights, name them. ...The Chinese do not respect anybody in the South and they are on our necks for oil in collaboration with the enemy.' 30 June 2008, *Gurtong* discussion board.

[24] Interview with GoSS official, Juba, September 2010.

[25] Conversation, Wau, 29 September 2010.

to be exercised via a referendum vote on whether to remain in or secede from a united Sudan. This provision came to define the agreement, overshadowing its deeper, transformative formal political ambition. Despite arguments that the CPA's requirement for the NCP and SPLM to 'make unity attractive' was a tactical imperative, and the SPLM's real goal was pursuing an independent country, the New Sudan vision championed by the SPLM/A's founding leader, John Garang de Mabior, defined a template for political reform of the entire country. Recognising the common predicament of Sudan's marginalised peripheries, which could only be addressed through systemic reform of the dominant political and economic centre, this vision depended on the SPLM/A and its allied forces pursuing a national reform project. At his inauguration as First Vice-President of Sudan in early July 2005, Garang thus emphasised 'that the SPLM is a national Movement for all of Sudan, a movement for the New Sudan' and appealed 'to all Sudanese to join the SPLM and safeguard the unity of our country by making unity attractive'.[26]

The SPLM's incorporation into Sudan's new central Government of National Unity created by the CPA in theory rendered it politically and legally possible for Beijing – like other foreign governments – to engage the SPLM directly within the terms of this power-sharing arrangement. The CPA conferred political legitimacy upon the SPLM and initiated a process that saw the former rebels begin to transform themselves into a ruling Southern government and political party. The SPLM was willing to consider engagement with all potential external partners, including China, which was involved from the start in the UN Mission in Sudan through military peacekeepers and police personnel.[27]

The SPLM's approach towards China after the CPA was predicated upon 'turning enemies into friends', but it took time for substantive relations to develop.[28] The first, semi-official post-war contact between Beijing and the SPLM took the form of a high-ranking SPLM delegation visit to Beijing in March 2005 to discuss possible 'economic cooperation'. The delegation was led by Salva Kiir Mayardit, a former Anyanya fighter and one of the SPLA's original founders who at the time was second-in-command to John Garang, and included other senior SPLM figures. The 'friendship' visit featured meetings and hospitality with relatively junior Chinese government officials.[29] Salva Kiir became First Vice-President of Sudan and President of Southern Sudan following Garang's unexpected death in late July 2005, and in April 2010 was formally elected as Southern President.

[26] Dr. John Garang de Mabior, 'Address on inauguration of the Sudan collegiate presidency', 9 July 2005, Khartoum.

[27] China's first deployment of 430 troops became fully operational in May 2006. The Chinese peacekeepers in Wau in September 2010 were on their third turn of duty, operating as part of the multi-national UNMIS Sector II.

[28] Interview with SPLM Secretary-General Pagan Amum, Juba, December 2005.

[29] Interview with the late Samson Kwaje, the former GoSS Minister of Information (who went on the visit) Juba, December 2005.

Despite this visit, it would be two more years before there were any further significant political developments between the GoSS and the Chinese government, despite the fact that the GoSS was keen to attract external investment from all possible sources. Following over two decades of war, the south faced unprecedented challenges, including establishing a system of government, addressing chronic poverty and a daunting lack of infrastructure. At the opening of the Southern Sudan Legislative Assembly session in April 2006, Salva Kiir proclaimed that the south was 'open for business and investors are welcome'.[30] Rather than political substantive relations developing between Southern Sudan and China, instead it was the Chinese businesses that took the lead in developing more independent commercial relations with the south. Chinese entrepreneurs, in effect, were the first, unofficial business diplomats; China's diplomats of state followed later. Rather than any governmental engagement, individual Chinese entrepreneurs formed one part of the massive mobilisation in the south after the CPA, involving myriad international businesses, NGOs and IGOs and efforts to establish the GoSS.

Chinese Business Enters the New Southern Market

The first Chinese links with the south after the CPA developed through a small number of first-mover business entrepreneurs who were quick to identify and enter a new market (some, indeed, making exploratory trips to Juba before the CPA was signed).[31] The CPA opened up the south as a new frontier of Chinese business opportunity. Prior to 2005, there had been little Chinese commercial involvement there beyond oil operations. The common motivation for many was the prospect of profiting from the new peace. In a country emerging from protracted war with a new capital, Juba, there was also thought to be little or no competition. Some Chinese entrepreneurs came from other parts of Africa, like Uganda or South Africa, a few direct from China, and most made scouting trips to assess the prospects and options before setting up their business operations.

At first Chinese construction work was prominent in Juba, but soon the Chinese business community became more diverse. Juba's post-war construction market was initially promising, due to great demand. A number of different Chinese companies came in and undertook a range of contracted projects, including the renovation of GoSS buildings. A small number of venture capital investments were pursued in mining and mineral exploration (though these did not advance very far, reportedly due to insecurity). A small Chinese service sector developed, especially in Juba, and came to feature restaurants, hotels and private medical

---

[30] Lt Gen. Salva Kiir Mayardit, Government Policy Statement delivered by the President of the Government of Southern Sudan, at the opening of the second session of the Southern Sudan Legislative Assembly, 10 April 2006.

[31] Conversations, Juba, 2007 and 2010.

clinics. Such small businesses were indicative of the alternative, proactive and micro entrepreneurial Chinese 'go global' strategy mobilised by small businesses on their own initiative, and showed that the Chinese community in Sudan is far from being homogenous. Furthermore, many had no experience of north Sudan.

The Chinese business engagement in Juba and the south operated within regional trade networks of Chinese-made commodities in East Africa, and was thus also bound up in transnational trade flows circulating goods from China. While a small Chinese retail presence has been established in Juba, most 'Made in China' products found in the town markets in the south today – like Sudan more generally – are not sold by Chinese entrepreneurs. Rather, these travel to myriad points of sale via East African business networks, including Ugandan and Kenyan entrepreneurs.[32] A significant proportion of the goods sold in Juba and the larger southern towns by Kenyan, Ugandan and other traders, come from China. Because many products are cheap, Chinese is synonymous with low-quality which, as a quotidian popular grievance, is hardly uncommon in other African contexts. It has not, however, gone unnoticed by Chinese entrepreneurs.[33] Popular associations of China with poor quality resulting from experience are counter-balanced by other projects undertaken by Chinese companies, such as road construction, which are regarded in more positive ways.

The entry and expansion of Chinese businesses proceeded amidst a wider business 'scramble' in the south,[34] which saw international, notably African, and Sudanese businesses move in to a new market. As seen before Sudan's elections of April 2010, and prior to the January 2011 referendum, the Chinese entrepreneurs in the south were also acutely aware of the direction that political winds were blowing in Sudan. Many conducted hedging strategies of their own by monitoring political developments and correlating their investments accordingly. Such strategies paled in comparison to the high stakes of China's engagement with the GoSS and, if profit was the main driver of the commercial Chinese entry into the south, it was political necessity linked to existing oil investments that compelled China's new relations with South Sudan.

Passing Key Messages to the Chinese Leadership: GoSS and China Engage

Salva Kiir Mayardit's visit to Beijing in July 2007 was pivotal in develop-

---

[32] Some of the cheap pirated Hollywood DVDs in Juba, for instance, come from China via Nairobi and mobile Kenyan traders. Conversation with market trader, Juba, September 2010.

[33] Indeed, according to one (September 2010), an attempt was made to maintain an informal agreement among Chinese businesses in Juba to maintain the quality standards of imported goods in order to try to protect their reputation.

[34] GoSS official, Juba, September 2010.

ing relations with China. Following his February 2007 meeting with President Hu Jintao in Khartoum, this official visit resulted in a genuine political breakthrough. As First Vice-President of the GoNU and President of the GoSS, the circumstances of Salva Kiir's visit were markedly different from those of his March 2005 trip. This soldier-turned-politician had long been famous for sporting black cowboy hats, but it was very apparent that he was wearing two political hats during this trip and that his role as leader of Southern Sudan made the stronger impression. The visit triggered a reorientation of China's approach to Sudan, through an apparent new comprehension by China's top leaders of both the geography of oil in Sudan and Sudanese politics, especially that of the south, galvanising efforts to establish and develop diplomatic relations with the GoSS.

This China mission was one part of the GoSS's wider strategy of external engagement aimed at attracting investment and securing international support for implementation of the CPA. Due to China's disproportionately important relations with the NCP and role in north Sudan, the oil sector in particular, as well as Beijing's permanent seat in the UN Security Council, however, the stakes were high. Salva Kiir met China's top political leaders and business executives, and discussed the status of the CPA and Darfur. The most decisive moment appears to have come during Kiir's meeting with President Hu Jintao on 19 July, when he explained two fundamental issues: the geography of Sudan's oil and the CPA's referendum clause. As he reported back to the Southern Sudan Legislative Assembly not long afterwards: 'We have managed to pass key messages to the Chinese leadership. At least China is now aware that most of the oil produced in Sudan is from Southern Sudan and that the people of Southern Sudan will exercise their right of self-determination in a referendum to be conducted by 2011.'[35] The CPA protected oil contracts signed before the date of the signature of the CPA.[36] What would come after the CPA was less certain, amidst different views within the GoSS about the merits of maintaining the existing oil industry arrangements; clearly China needed to recognise and respond to a new political reality of which it appears not to have been fully cognisant before. From the SPLM's perspective, connecting with China represented something of an empowering coup in its domestic struggle with the NCP.

After this trip, relations between Juba and Beijing expanded.[37] At the beginning of September 2008, in the presence of GoSS Vice-President Riak Machar, China's Assistant Foreign Minister Zhai Jun inaugurated the new

---

[35] Salva Kiir Mayardit, speech opening of the second session of the Southern Sudan Legislative Assembly, Juba, 10 September 2007.

[36] It stipulates that these 'shall not be subject to re-negotiation.' CPA, at 4.2, p. 53.

[37] There was a follow-up visit to Juba by China's Ambassador to Sudan prior to a visit by a Chinese government technical team to Juba shortly afterwards, which also went to Yei and Nimule. China's aid to the South was increased following an official Chinese needs assessment mission to Juba in mid-2007.

Chinese consulate in Juba and China joined a growing number of other foreign consulates there. In practice, this established quasi-diplomatic ties between China and the GoSS. The Chinese embassy in Khartoum remained in charge of its Juba outpost,[38] but the consulate subsequently played an important role in mediating the GoSS's relations with the Chinese government. In contrast to China's more pronounced bilateral relations with Khartoum, its Juba consulate was not only active vis-à-vis the GoSS, but also participated in the UN's Donor Coordination Forum.[39] From China's political perspective, however, its role in cultivating and advancing relations with different GoSS ministries was more important. The first Chinese Consul-General is credited by various officials with playing a positive role in cultivating links. The political divide between Khartoum and Juba appears to have affected its operations; many, for example, cite NCP opposition to the creation of the consulate and continued resistance to more direct relations between Juba and Beijing. In the south at least, many point to a constructive evolution of the consulate's role and its beneficial impact in furthering relations between Juba and Beijing.[40]

Following the CPA and the creation of the GoSS, Southern Sudan began to operate as 'a quasi-independent state'.[41] The GoSS was starting from scratch with its China relations, unlike its relations with other foreign governments, including the US and Norway, which had benefited from prior connections. Its newly formalised relations with China met with mixed views. Within the GoSS and the SPLM leadership, attitudes towards China varied: there was continued ambivalence, if not antagonism, towards China on the part of some, while others had always maintained a more pragmatic recognition of the potential benefits of engagement with China, amongst other possible foreign investors.[42] By and large, the GoSS 'did not hold grudges' after 2005.[43] In terms of early political interaction at the Juba level, GoSS complaints about China's wartime role and close NCP links were compounded by suspicions of Beijing's support for the future unity of Sudan. China's desire to engage ran up against generic problems caused by the lack of institutional capacity in a new government, reflecting broader problems facing the fledgling state of South Sudan. Such issues accentuated the striking contrast between the established relations Khartoum had built with China since 1989, and the new relations between the GoSS and China after 2005. China had developed ways of working with the NCP and the government in Khartoum over many years, but its relations with the SPLM and the GoSS were just starting.

---

[38] Interview with senior Chinese official, Khartoum, January 2011.

[39] Interview with international official, 23 September 2010, Juba.

[40] Various interviews in Juba, June and September 2010.

[41] Peter Adwok Nyaba, 'An Appraisal of Contemporary China–Sudan Relations and its future trajectory', paper presented at the Centre for Advanced Studies of African Societies, 23-24 November 2005.

[42] Meeting with Riak Machar, Juba, December 2005.

[43] Interview with senior UN official, Khartoum, 31 January 2011.

The GoSS's relations with the Chinese government were also developing in other areas, not just in Juba. This could be seen in efforts to promote political party cooperation between the CPC and the SPLM. The SPLM planned 'to establish relations' with the CPC in order 'to ensure efficient development and management of oil resources to the benefit of the Sudanese people'.[44] Beyond Juba, relations were developing between the GoSS, the Chinese government and the CNPC at the level of State authorities in the South. In August 2008, for example, the then NCP Governor of the oil-rich State of Upper Nile visited China to meet central government representatives and the CNPC and try to attract Chinese investment for Malakal, the state capital. The CNPC appeared keen to cooperate with the Upper Nile authorities. Through the Petrodar oil consortium, in which it holds a leading stake, the CNPC contributed infrastructure projects to Malakal, demonstrating business relations between the leading Chinese oil company in Sudan and a southern State government. Other governors from the south also went to China, including Taban Deng, the Governor of the oil-rich Unity State, who visited in 2010.

Following the establishment of relations between Juba and Beijing, efforts were made to strengthen links, which increased in the build-up to the January 2011 referendum. This was an ad hoc process, and was geared toward enhancing mutual understanding and working ties. The GoSS sought to educate China about South Sudan, and China sought to educate the GoSS about China, the modalities through which it works with other African governments and the economic opportunities China could offer. In February 2010, for example, the Chinese consulate organised a workshop on economic cooperation with China for GoSS officials in Juba.[45] From the Chinese side, prior to the referendum, the GoSS was squarely focused upon political objectives, mostly subordinating economic questions to the dominant goal of achieving independence. This summed up the GoSS's position, and for good reason.

Referendum Diplomacy

After previously operating on the basis of straight bilateral relations, Sudan's relations with China began to operate in a triangular manner between Khartoum, Beijing and Juba. As the final stages of the CPA approached, China appeared to engage Sudan on a dual-track basis, dealing with the ruling parties and governments in both Khartoum and Juba. A pattern of multi-stranded diplomacy developed between the GoSS and China concerning the Southern referendum. China's Special Envoy for Africa, Liu Guijin, had originally been appointed to handle Darfur, but became more involved in China's North-South CPA

---

[44] Organisational Report presented to the 2nd National Convention of the Sudan People's Liberation Movement by SPLM Secretary-General Pagan Amum Okiech, 18 May 2008.

diplomacy and in diplomatic interactions with the GoSS, conveying China's readiness to support the Southern referendum.

The Chinese government's public position, appearing to invoke the terms of the CPA as a public foil for any deeper, private misgivings, was that it wished to see a united Sudan. Beijing consistently affirmed at the same time, however, that it would not 'publicly prejudge secession' but was committed to 'respect the choice or option of the people of Sudan'.[46] The bottom line for Beijing appeared, for good reasons, to be a peaceful, politically managed CPA transition, in which the holding of a 'credible referendum', managing its outcome, and ensuring the future stability of Sudan were primary considerations: 'whatever happens the transition has to be peaceful, war will not serve the interests of anyone. We are sincerely working together for a peaceful credible referendum and transition.'[47] The spectre of further political instability and likely military ramifications of a break-down of the formal peace that the CPA had established appeared to be a source of considerable concern in Beijing: far better a smooth, CPA-mandated political transition than a return to war. China's engagement thus came to feature a more holistic appreciation of the connections between conflict and different regions in Sudan, recognising the linkages between the south and Darfur and the necessity of a Sudan-wide policy.

The GoSS made efforts to secure Beijing's support for an independent South Sudan ahead of the southern referendum. China was one of a number of countries that GoSS delegations visited as this vote approached, to secure support for the CPA's final stages and also plan ahead for the post-referendum period, but clearly China was particularly important. Southern leaders, including the GoSS Vice-President, publicly emphasised their demand that China support the outcome of the referendum. At times, such demands were openly linked to China's future role in the oil industry. This was part of an apparent bargaining process in which both Juba and Beijing held shared vested stakes.[48] The Chinese government also took steps to enhance relations, expanding its aid programme in the south and standing ready to offer financial assistance to the GoSS. CNPC sponsored a visible new computer facility at the University of Juba, and rather less conspicuously sought to negotiate with the GoSS. One indication of the forward-looking elevation of the south in China's Sudan engagement came in October 2010 with the upgrading of diplomatic relations and appointment of Ambassador Li Zhiguo to be China's new Consul-General in Juba. In the same month, a CPC delegation's

[45] Interview with Chinese official, Juba, September 2010.
[46] Interview with senior official, Ministry of Foreign Affairs, Beijing 2 June 2010.
[47] Ibid.
[48] On her return to Juba, Ann Itto was quoted as having told Chinese officials that 'if they want to protect their assets, the only way is to develop a very strong relationship with the government of Southern Sudan, respect the outcome of the referendum, and then we will be doing business.' 'South Sudan says China must recognize referendum result to retain oil assets', *Sudan Tribune* (Paris), 20 August 2010.

visit to Juba provided confirmation of high-level engagement by Beijing ahead of the referendum.

Another strand of the pre-referendum diplomacy between the GoSS and China concerned China's potential future contribution towards the development of an independent South Sudan. This process involved various political exchanges, which increased before the referendum and following its decisive result. The GoSS Minister of Agriculture and SPLM Deputy Secretary-General, Ann Itto, visited China in August 2010 to participate in the China-Africa Agricultural Cooperation Forum.[49] A major GoSS delegation visited China in the following month in a 'post-referendum development preparation' tour. Some identified the desirability of expanded cooperation with China, including a revival of Chinese medical assistance in the South, as a more positive counterweight to what is widely held to be an otherwise narrow extractive role.[50]

GoSS-China diplomacy was entangled in the NCP's relations with China regarding the CPA, which featured frequent high-level exchanges and movement between Khartoum and Beijing. While these concentrated on the CPA, one aspect appeared to be related to NCP concerns about the emerging Beijing-Juba relations. The growth of more independent bilateral links between Juba and Beijing, and China's implicit readiness to support an independent South Sudan via a legitimate referendum, were sources of discontent, not just amongst the NCP. In the north, debate about Southern secession deepened as the referendum approached, amidst belated recognition that unity had not been made 'attractive'. China's apparent diplomatic realism seemed, to some, to smack of betrayal. GoSS-China contact and Beijing's stated willingness to support the Southern referendum were evidence, for instance, that the NCP's bet on China's unconditional support had not paid off: 'the wager by the National Congress Party on the Chinese Communist Party has failed. The Chinese have announced that they are economic pragmatists and we must understand this.'[51]

The southern referendum, against all expectations, passed off smoothly. China provided financial assistance for the vote, and also sent a monitoring mission. This 'referendum for freedom', as it was labelled in the south, produced an overwhelming outcome in favour of secession. Beijing was quick to express support for the outcome and affirm its willingness to cooperate with South Sudan. It was not the only government to do so.[52] After the referendum, and in the build-up to South Sudan's independence

---

[49] This conference was organised by the International Department of the CPC Central Committee and China's Ministry of Agriculture. The fact that Sudan was represented by its northern NCP Minister of Agriculture and the GoSS counterpart was not popular among the NCP delegation, according to a one conference participant (interview, Juba, September 2010).

[50] Conversations in Rumbek, Juba, Wau, 2010.

[51] Muhammad Rashad, 'Between the Chinese Communist Party and the National Congress Party', *Al-Ayyam*, Khartoum, in Arabic, 15 September 2010 (via BBC monitoring).

[52] The Indian government also committed to sending an official delegation to attend the formal declaration of independence. The GoSS was also developing ties with CNPC and Petronas, with whom it signed an agreement about oil and gas industry cooperation in March 2011.

day scheduled for 9 July 2011, there were further connections between Juba and Beijing. Notably, the GoSS Minister of Finance and Economic Development, David Deng Athorbei, met the Chinese Vice-President Xi Jinping in Beijing in April 2011, and invited President Hu Jintao to attend the independence ceremony. Chinese business interest in Juba increased. The GoSS seemed to be looking more seriously towards Beijing to assist its economic development strategy.

Outside South Sudan's relations with China in their own terms, geopolitical dynamics was also intruding. Juba's relations with Beijing were inseparable from its relations with other states.[53] The political precedent of South Sudan's independence and China's reactions to it were clearly being closely observed in other parts of Africa, meaning that there were additional reasons for Beijing to balance carefully its policy on and interests within Sudan. Beijing was keen to affirm its strong commitment to continuing support for Khartoum, and emphasise that its relations with the GoSS were complementary to those with other external partners. Juba's relations with the US government in particular brought the question of how China's future ties with Sudan, in the south but also in the north, would develop in relation to other external partners. The GoSS, however, appeared to prioritise its 'special relationship' with the US.[54]

Conclusion: After 'the Final Decisive Moment'

Next to John Garang's memorial in Juba, a lantern was placed on 16 May 2007, 24 years to the day after the outbreak of the original 1983 southern rebellion, to burn 'In hope and prayers for every CPA Dictum including 2011, the final decisive moment'. The former champion of New Sudan thought the best way to better the south's position within Sudan was to create a reformed country, but his memorial was close to becoming a shrine to the deceased founding father of an independent state. After the January 2011 referendum, and on the eve of independence scheduled for 9 July 2011, however, it was the referendum that never happened in Abyei and the military stand-off between the North and the South that irrupted as a stark reminder that the CPA had essentially moved a historically rooted conflict from the military into the political sphere. Politics, in effect, became the continuation of war through other means, but the risks of returning to war remained.

On the eve of independence, the immense needs and challenges in the south seemed to herald the continuation of a significant international role

---

[53] One source of tension stemmed from Northern Sudan's links with the Middle East, and China's diplomacy with the 'Arab world'. The first meeting of the Sino-Arab Friendship conference at the end of November 2006 in Khartoum, which featured a delegation representing the Chinese Sino-Arab Friendship Association and representatives of over 20 Arab NGOs, had provided further evidence for some Southerners of China's ingrained bias towards the Arab north of Sudan and the wider Middle East.

[54] Interview, Juba, February 2011.

in general and opportunities for China to build on the foothold it has established in South Sudan. A new phase of relations was in the process of starting, and appeared to have the potential to counterbalance China's preponderant role in the oil industry with broader socio-economic benefits for the south. Chinese officials and interested observers emphasised before January 2011 that 'China will actively participate in South Sudan to contribute to build a new country if the referendum gives it independence'.[55] Confirmation of the referendum result meant that the Chinese government proceeded to look more actively ahead to its future relations with and role in an independent South Sudan. A full range of possible areas of cooperation were identified, from education to agriculture, road building to health. In the south, there was recognition that such cooperation could be important.[56] The question had become not whether China could contribute after the South's independence, but how. In addition, there was an expectation amongst certain international agencies in Juba of a future Chinese role.[57]

Numerous questions lingered amidst broader uncertainty about Sudan's future. The evolution of bilateral relations between Juba and Beijing was one. The SPLM may have challenged the meaning of China's foreign policy principles during the war, but the GoSS looked set to expect parity of treatment with the North in terms of Chinese foreign relations on the back of its newly sovereign status. In principle, this would include the very principle of non-interference the south had experienced rather differently from Khartoum but looked set to enjoy in its new relations with Beijing. Caught in the middle, and involved within Sudanese politics, China was likely to face difficult choices in managing its new relations with two Sudans. How would China's military relations with South Sudan, for example, develop in the context of two states, and the continuation of widespread insecurity in the south, clashes in the borderlands between the South and the North, and ongoing fighting in Darfur?

South Sudan's relations with China were set to change formally with the creation of a new sovereign, independent state, but in reality this would continue a process that has seen new relations develop over a short space of time. In a matter of years, relations between South Sudan and China progressed from battlefield enemies to new partners through a conjunction of interests and political negotiation. As the prospect of a new state and implications of two Sudans began to be considered, in Beijing and elsewhere, the future of an independent South Sudan focused on the prospects for state-building. Establishing a new effective state in an oil-dependent economy governed by a single party, and enhancing its economic development prospects in the face of chronic poverty, a huge

---

[55] Various interviews, Beijing, June and December 2010.
[56] Adam Cholong Ohiri Aham, 'Aspects of Promoting Agricultural and Natural Potentialities in South Sudan', Paper presented at the South African Institute for International Affairs workshop on Chinese-Sudanese relationships, 14–15 September 2010, Juba.
[57] Interview with senior UN official, Juba, 2 February 2011.

infrastructure deficit, and ongoing conflicts, had become a major challenge for South Sudan. Despite interest in the potential of China's future economic assistance in the south, tensions remained in certain popular and political quarters about coming to terms with its wartime history. These pointed to the need for China's recognition of its previous role as a means to overcome what is perceived as an obstacle to wider, popular acceptance of China in South Sudan. On balance, however, it seemed that China had overcome the legacy of its recent past and was set to recognise and expand its role in an independent Republic of South Sudan. For GoSS, in view of South Sudan's daunting needs, it seemed that a China policy and Chinese economic assistance, if managed properly, could be an important part of its future development strategy.

Conclusion | China, India
& the Politics of Sudan's
Asian Alternatives

DANIEL LARGE
& LUKE A. PATEY

On 30 August 1999, the first Sudanese crude oil exports were dispatched
from the new port of Masra al-Bashir on the Red Sea. The inaugural shipment heading for Singapore and Asian markets was celebrated as a government victory against external adversity and the means of defeating its
internal adversaries: 'We have defeated all the foreign enemies wishing to
stop the export of the oil. We must now defeat the internal enemy who
may try to halt the full utilisation of the oil revenue.'[1] Together with the
opening of the Khartoum refinery, this landmark event distilled the
material success of Sudan's Chinese-led, Malaysian-assisted oil development, and came nearly a year after the August 1998 US missile attack on a
pharmaceutical factory in Khartoum. President Bashir described the
exports as God's reward for 'Sudan's faithfulness'.[2] It could also be said
that the oil now flowing from southern Sudan to overseas markets, and
the revenue flowing into the central state in Khartoum, represented salvation for the NIF. Not long after these first oil exports, the direction of the
NIF's Islamist political project changed when Hassan al-Turabi was side-
lined from power in December 1999. By the time employees of ONGC
Videsh confirmed India's arrival in Sudan by ceremonially raising the
Indian flag in the GNPOC Heglig camp on 18 May 2003, Omar al-Bashir
had consolidated his palace power, peace negotiations with the SPLM/A
were under way, and conflict in Darfur was escalating after an audacious
rebel attack in April on a government air force base in al-Fasher.

Sudan's Asian state partners and allied national oil companies were
instrumental in helping the NIF defeat its 'foreign enemies'. The creation
of an oil export industry was a powerful demonstration of the importance
of the government's new, willing and effective alternatives. China, India
and Malaysia have engaged on very different terms from Sudan's more
established external partners. Mobilising mutually advantageous economic
partnerships with Khartoum, their diplomacy is based on political parity,
sovereignty and non-interference in the government of Sudan's internal

[1] Nhial Bol, 'Islamic regime begins to export oil', IPS, Bashar, Sudan, 30 August 1999, quoted
in Human Rights Watch, *Sudan, Oil and Human Rights* (New York, Human Rights Watch,
2003), p. 232.
[2] 'Sudan begins oil exports', *IRIN*, 1 September 1999.

affairs, instead of the more overt power hierarchy, political confrontation and economic pressure exemplified by Khartoum's relations with the US. Over the past two decades, these new engagements have become an immensely significant part of Sudan's economy and foreign relations, while also becoming new sources of development inspiration and capability. China stands out in this. Following successive waves of external involvement featuring colonial Egyptian rule from 1821, Anglo-Egyptian administration between 1899 and 1956, or independent Sudan's later relations with the US, a Chinese-defined age of influence has developed in Sudan. Nonetheless, Sudan's relations with China and its 'Look East' engagements in general, while offering economic and political alternatives, are more complex and contingent than the outwardly robust appearance of official ties portrays. China is an alternative for Sudan, but against the rhetorical difference of its approach from that of the US and Europe in particular, the Chinese role confronts mounting challenges of realising and sustaining substantive difference in Sudan.

This Conclusion considers the actual nature and significance of China and other Asian states in the context of Sudan's political economy of unbalanced development. Revisiting select themes raised in this book, it examines some of the ways in which particularly China but also other Asian states have acted as political and economic alternatives to Sudan's traditional partners, but it also questions the impact of these alternatives on Sudan. It begins by exploring the impacts of the economic investment of China and other Asian states, mainly in the oil sector, on domestic politics in Sudan. Close relations with the NIF/NCP established Asian engagement within, and then further entrenched, an existing political economy of armed conflict and unbalanced development. Consequently, the Asian oil engagement has had political consequences for Sudan, and in turn, the role of China and other Asian states has had to adjust to changes in Sudanese politics.

Second, the governing methods of the NIF/NCP, and the use of oil as an external resource for domestic political purposes complicated and conditioned the role of China and other Asian states as political alternatives. Sudan's Asian relations are upheld by their protagonists as exemplifying successful South-South cooperation, distinguished politically through a position of non-interference in domestic affairs. But the incongruence between the rhetoric and the nature of actually existing South-South cooperation in new circumstances has produced growing challenges for the novelty of China and other Asian states as political alternatives to US and European engagement that often demands conditions of good governance, human rights and democracy. Third, China's role as an economic alternative differs from the mainstream international development orthodoxy through its focus on 'co-development' rather than relations marked by a traditional donor-recipient hierarchy. But tensions have been forming as a result of the engagements of China and other Asian states in Sudan. Notwithstanding the influence of China on the NCP, whether its influence on Sudan's wider economy and human development has similarly provided mutual benefits beyond elites has become increasingly contentious in Sudan.

Fourth, the expanding global economic presence and political role of China and India has at times upset their role as political and economic alternatives for Sudan. Most notably, tensions have been forthcoming between the policy and interests of the central state in Beijing and a proliferation of Chinese agents holding different aims in Sudan. Lastly, the Conclusion considers the prospects for Sudan's 'Look East' foreign relations in the context of two new states. The deepening logic of greater, multi-layered and geographically dispersed involvement that has, in particular, defined Chinese engagement in Sudan, with attendant political implications, looks set to continue in the new context of two Sudans, following the categorical southern vote for secession in January 2011.

In beginning to explore a complex, compelling area, this volume contributes towards emerging research about this subject in different applicable contexts.[3] Scholarship within northern Sudan on China, India or other Asian states is not advanced, despite wide interest; that in the south is only, with notable exceptions, in the process of beginning, along with higher education.[4] Scholarship within China on Sudan has grown in recent years but remains in the process of development.[5] Indian scholarship on Sudan is at a very early stage, reflecting an overall shift in India moving from a general Africa-wide focus to more case-based analysis.[6] Clearly, there are a number of areas where further research would be productive, including on Sudan's changing development politics, the security engagement of its Asian partners and the everyday social life of Chinese and other migrant communities in Sudan.[7] Given

---

[3] While not ultimately possible, it should be noted that this volume originally had sought to include the work of a more diverse and representative range of Sudanese, Chinese, Indian and Malaysian scholars.

[4] Interview with Sudanese professor, University of Khartoum, January 2011; interviews with University of Juba staff, September 2010.

[5] For an overview of Chinese scholarship, see Xu Liang, '*Zhongguo de Sudan Wenti Yanjiu Zong Shu*' ('General Introduction to China's Research about the Sudan issue'), *Ya Fei Zhou* (*West Asia and Africa*), Vol. 2 (2007), pp. 67-71. See also Liu Hongwu and Jiang Hengkun, *Sudan* (Beijing: *Shehui Kexue Wenxian Chubanshe* (Social Sciences Academic Press (China), 2008).

[6] On 10-11 November 2009, an international conference entitled 'Asian Countries in Sudan: Political and Economic Relations' was held in New Delhi in an effort to support the development of Asian research on Sudan. Organised by the African Studies Association of India and the Danish Institute of International Studies the conference brought together Chinese and Indian scholars and supported the work of Indian graduate students developing work on Sudan.

[7] There is good scope for more anthropological approaches that might explore the emerging socio-cultural presence of Chinese, Indian or other Asian communities in Sudan. The everyday social dimensions of these relations entail a significant, albeit less visible, aspect of a changing international presence in Sudan. In China's case, for instance, the longer history of limited cultural interaction is now being superseded by a new, growing Chinese presence in different parts of Sudan, one in which such emotive issues as Chinese labour and migration feature prominently.

their importance, remarkably little attention has been dedicated to Sudan's extractive economy and the politics of this.[8]

The Politics of Petro-Patronage in Sudan

The role of external states and their allied national oil companies in developing and operating Sudan's oil industry, and the ways in which oil has influenced Sudanese politics over the past decade, is one outstanding theme in this collection. Oil had long been a divisive factor in Sudanese politics, particularly in deepening the tensions between the central government and southern Sudan, following its discovery. Commercial oil was found in 1979 two decades after the first exploration licence was issued; it took two more decades to create an export industry, after which followed an important decade of political change and new conflict in Sudan that still continues. Oil intensified and internationalised the North-South conflict, and would later become connected to war in Darfur. If American and French oil corporations were 'far from disinterested observers' in Sudanese politics in the late Nimairi period,[9] then the same has applied in relation to Chinese, Malaysian or Indian oil companies under Bashir.

Oil has been closely connected to the changing nature of NCP rule. It has provided a contrasting, substantial resource stream for the central state in the context of a significant international role in Sudan. The growth of a more structural international humanitarian and development presence in Sudan in the past three decades had political consequences before the NIF seized power. From the 1980s in particular, the domestic political accountability of Sudan's government was undermined as responsibility for welfare was assumed by international agencies. In essence, accountability was externalised.[10] At that time, Washington's patronage was crucial in assisting Khartoum's increasingly desperate attempts to stay afloat and pay for the state amidst growing civil war in southern Sudan. Today Sudan still relies upon a substantial international aid presence, and is home to the largest UN peacekeeping presence in the world. Khartoum also relies upon China as a source of finance, as well as

---

[8] The literature on oil in Sudan has also tended to be linked to external advocacy interests. See Luke A. Patey for exceptions: 'Against the Asian tide: the Sudan divestment campaign', *Journal of Modern African Studies*, Vol. 47, Iss. 4, December 2009, pp. 551-573; 'State rules: oil companies and armed conflict in Sudan', *Third World Quarterly*, Vol. 28, Iss. 5, July 2007, pp. 997-1016. Much has been written about international aid, but less attention has been dedicated to the political economy of oil in Sudan. This can partly be ascribed to the difficulties of research access, but also reflects the prevailing humanitarian lens through which Sudan has been approached and represented in the West, broadly speaking.

[9] Abel Alier, *Southern Sudan: Too Many Agreements Dishonoured* (Reading: Ithaca Press, 2003), p. 263.

[10] See, amongst others, Ahmed Karadawi, *Refugee Policy in Sudan: 1967-1984* (New York: Berghahn Books, 1999); Alex de Waal, *Famine Crimes: Politics and the Disaster Relief Industry in Africa* (Oxford: James Currey, 1997).

the Middle East. Oil, however, changed the equation between Khartoum and its international partners by empowering the NCP-controlled central state.

After 1999, the massive new oil rent flows to the NIF/NCP regime altered the basis of political patronage in Sudan. Interest in the evolution of, and power struggles within, the NIF/NCP has not been matched by analysis of the politically consequential economic sources of NIF/NCP power and how these are mobilised.[11] Prior to oil, the NIF was compelled to resort to alternative means to finance an all but bankrupt state, while simultaneously seeking to transform Sudan along Islamist lines. The comparatively recent production of an oil-dominated phase of later NCP rule, however, guaranteed a reliable, lucrative revenue stream for the central state. It has been one factor further undermining the socio-economic position and political stature of Sudan's two main traditional political parties, the Umma Party and the Democratic Unionist Party. Both had drawn support historically from, broadly speaking, a related combination of religious constituencies (the Ansar and Khatmiyah orders respectively) and economic sources (agriculture and commerce). The dramatic shift in revenues available to the NIF/NCP was made possible by its turn to the East.

Despite the NCP's more recent interest in China's political and developmental experience, there was little natural, positive ideological affinity behind the NIF's turn to China in the 1990s, or indeed between Khartoum and New Delhi. Even if commercial competition played a role in Petronas's operations in Sudan, this contrasted with the religious commonalities enjoyed between Khartoum and Kuala Lumpur, as well as the interchange of development inspiration including notions of the state, as Marchal (Chapter 5) explores in this volume. Khartoum's turn to China was a pragmatic tactical imperative for a regime all but surrounded by hostile states and subject to increasing regional and international pressure. The absence of strong ideological connections between China and Sudan beyond the open-ended rhetoric of South-South cooperation is brought into focus when related to the NIF/NCP's ideological and political evolution. What had been a radical Islamist project of socio-political transformation under the NIF, in which *jihad* was 'not an abstraction',[12] underwent an evolution following the overstretch of the Islamists' foreign policy ambition and related internal regime power struggles in Khartoum. Bashir's victory and the relegation of Turabi came not long after both had celebrated Sudan's first oil exports.

The impact of oil revenues on the NCP's subsequent political trajectory and Sudanese politics is not to be underestimated. Until his re-

[11] Ibrahim Elnur, *Contested Sudan: the political economy of war and reconstruction* (London: Routledge, 2009).

[12] Alex de Waal and A.H. Abdel Salam, 'Islamism, State Power and *Jihad* in Sudan', in Alex de Waal ed., *Islamism and its Enemies in the Horn of Africa* (Bloomington: Indiana University Press, 2004), p. 100.

articulation of Islamist rhetoric in the context of the southern referendum and the future of north Sudan, which echoed the political language of the late Nimairi in some respects,[13] Bashir followed a contrasting political path to that of Sudan's previous longstanding military ruler. Nimairi travelled from Nasserist military secular beginnings and socialist orientation towards reconciliation with, and attempted use of, political Islam to prolong his own political career. Bashir, instead, steered away from the early NIF's more ambitious project of political Islam towards a much more self-interested, power-maintaining logic in which he played a more important role. Reoriented under the NCP, the regime's interests came to be predicated more on regime perpetuation. Over the past three decades or so, Sudan's Islamist movement 'turned into a Corporation with an unrestrained lust for wealth and power'.[14] Staying in power necessitated, among other factors, having the economic resources to maintain the means of effective patronage, as well as be seen to deliver tangible development benefits for key constituencies. More than merely staying in power, the NCP has maintained a more dynamic approach to economic development in which the Chinese role has been especially prominent (see Verhoeven, Chapter 6 in this book). In this regard, the Chinese engagement has played an invaluable role in the NCP's domestic politics, bringing tangible short-term and other, more strategic dividends.

Oil has also influenced Sudan's armed conflicts in different ways. After driving conflict in southern Sudan, the industry is credited with having made a positive contribution to the North-South peace negotiations, after which it has underpinned wealth sharing and effectively bankrolled the GoSS. Any such assertion, however, cannot be divorced from the simultaneous reality that the very tangible success of northern Sudan's oil boom also made Darfur's neglect more conspicuous and was one grievance, amongst many, fuelling rebellion.[15] The marginalisation of western Sudan had been magnified by Khartoum's oil boom, the new gleaming towers of the oil consortiums standing tall at the same time as Darfur's basic neglect continued.

Sudan's petro-politics is not confined to Khartoum and northern Sudan's riverain triangle, the NCP's core support base. More recently, since 2005, the GoSS has received significant oil money flows according to the CPA's wealth-sharing arrangements. Oil money has been central to the creation and continued functioning of the new government in Juba. Now that the south has voted to become an independent state, oil will also be fundamental to future governments in South Sudan, at least in the medium term until the black gold is used up. This has forced the hand of the Chinese and Indian governments to engage more thoroughly with the

---

[13] Interview with Sudanese academics, Khartoum, January 2011.

[14] Abdullahi A. Galab, *The First Islamist Republic: Development and Disintegration of Islamism in the Sudan* (Aldershot: Ashgate, 2008), p. 166.

[15] See Alex de Waal (ed.), *War in Darfur and the Search for Peace* (London: Justice Africa, 2007); M.W. Daly, *Darfur's Sorrow: A History of Destruction and Genocide* (Cambridge: Cambridge University Press, 2007).

GoSS over the CPA's interim period, thereby reconfiguring what were once strong and exclusive bilateral relations with northern Sudan. This has been complemented by multi-tiered energy diplomacy beyond Khartoum and Juba, with southern Sudanese state governors travelling to China, and political and corporate representatives from Beijing, New Delhi and Kuala Lumpur visiting oil-producing state capitals in the south. Sudan's Asian partners are thus negotiating the deeper layers of Sudanese politics and the connections between national, regional and local dimensions of oil.[16] Significant problems remain on the ground in the relations between local communities and Asian national oil companies, as Moro explores here (Chapter 3). Furthermore, Sudan's oil industry management arrangements after 9 July 2011 remain to be seen. Despite the novelty of Asia's engagement over the past two decades, the primacy of Sudanese politics over external interests remains strong.

Khartoum has been controlling the political steering-wheel of the oil sector for the past two decades. The NCP has been able to balance relations with its friendly overseas patrons in an effort to avoid undue dependence on China. By means of oil, it has managed competition between a set of alternative partners to its own advantage. Khartoum may have been in a position of highly asymmetrical power relations with China, but it has also possessed control over a strategic sector it can use as a means to manage external relations and leverage influence. As Patey explores here (Chapter 4), India has thus been incorporated into Sudan's oil sector as a successful alternative to China, Khartoum's main original alternative.[17] Such strategic balancing of assorted external patrons afforded greater options for Khartoum. Even if China has been the pre-eminent power, it demonstrates the NCP's successful ability to maximise its options despite tight room for manoeuvre. Despite constraints, and the limited negotiating power Khartoum had in the mid-1990s, the NCP has exercised a degree of agency that belies the notion of its supposed role as a cog in a mechanistic chain of international corporate interests.[18] Far from merely implementing foreign corporate interests, the NIF/NCP has managed these to its own advantage at the same time as these strategic partnerships have also benefited its key Asian state partners. Sudan's central state mobilised fully to assist the construction of the oil industry and, once delivered, has reaped the rewards. However, South Sudan's independence may diffuse how northern-dominated Sudanese petro-politics influences external relations beyond bilateral ties with the central state. How Juba governs its oil sector may continue to challenge the role of China and other Asian states as political alternatives in Sudan.

---

[16] See Luke A. Patey, 'Crude Days Ahead? Oil and the Resource Curse in Sudan', *African Affairs*, Vol. 109, No. 437 (2009), pp. 616-37.

[17] See Luke Patey, The Power of Resistance: India's National Oil Company and International Activism in Sudan', PhD thesis, Copenhagen Business School, 2010.

[18] Alison J. Ayers, 'Sudan's uncivil war: the global-historical constitution of political violence', *Review of African Political Economy* Vol. 37, No. 124 (2010), pp. 153-171.

South-South Cooperation in New Circumstances

Sudan's relations with China and India are officially upheld as a model demonstration of South-South cooperation, the foundational principles of which were defined by the seminal Bandung conference of April 1955. Inter-state links are firmly anchored within the rubric of South-South relations, articulated in a common political rhetoric built around the experience of colonialism, common developing country status, and mutual adherence to a political doctrine based on sovereignty, territorial integrity, non-interference and peaceful coexistence.[19] China's current Vice-President (and probable future President) Xi Jinping, for example, is but the latest Chinese leader to note that 'China-Sudan relations have become an example of South-South cooperation'.[20] The meaning of South-South cooperation today, however, in a context where the nature and circumstances of relations have fundamentally changed, is far from self-evident. This is producing pronounced tensions between the ideals of South-South cooperation and the actual, applied manifestations of these today.

Sudan's foreign relations with its leading Asian partners have undergone a transition over the past two decades, in what represents a historic departure from its previous post-colonial relations. The political rhetoric of solidarity remains constant but applies very much at the elite level and has been augmented through forms of practical solidarity with the NIF/NCP government and the establishment of notable economic interests in Sudan. Today a defining aspect of relations is the incongruence between the continuation of the political rhetoric used by the Chinese and Sudanese governments, and the sea-change well under way in the actual circumstances of more complex, multifaceted and consequential Chinese relations within Sudan. As a result, the formal principles of South-South cooperation are being subject to strain in myriad ways, though naturally these still appeal to and pay dividends for ruling state and other, especially corporate, elites. The continued use by Sudan's Asian partners of the traditional rhetoric of South-South solidarity in new circumstances is challenging the core precepts of South-South cooperation, thereby redefining these in uncertain ways.

Sudan's participation at the original Bandung Asian-African conference came before it had been granted full independence. Declaring that 'colonialism in all its manifestations is an evil which should speedily be brought to an end', Bandung became central to post-colonial discourse

---

[19] These are encoded into China's Five Principles of Peaceful Coexistence, and such enduring standards as the Eight Principles for China's Aid to Foreign Countries from 1964.
[20] He made these comments while meeting the Sudanese Foreign Minister in Beijing in September 2010. See 'China hopes for transparent, fair referendum in southern Sudan', *Xinhua*, 14 September 2010.

and continues to be 'endowed with metaphorical power'.[21] The leader of Sudan's delegation to the conference, Prime Minister al-Azhari, described it as 'the first emergence into the outside world of the newly-born Sudan, which is already on the threshold of complete freedom and mature nationhood'.[22] Fast-forward to April 2005, when the Golden Jubilee celebrations marking the fiftieth anniversary of the Bandung conference were held in Jakarta and a new 'strategic partnership' between Asia and Africa was proclaimed, and the circumstances surrounding Sudan's participation led by President al-Bashir had dramatically altered.[23] China had changed from a formerly equal partner to a beacon of development success. While the principle of formal equality remained, relations were otherwise highly asymmetrical and founded in capitalist resource exploitation. During Bashir's meeting with President Hu Jintao at this summit, emphasis was predictably placed on the achievements of mutually beneficial cooperation, together with a reaffirmation of common support for sovereignty and non-interference. But at the same time, the war in Darfur was escalating amidst growing debate about appropriate responses, including those from China.

The very terms of political interaction between the governments of China and Sudan, defined by the language of South-South cooperation, have been directly challenged by political change in Sudan and the imminent sovereign status of South Sudan. China especially, but also India and Malaysia in their respective ways, present themselves, in political rhetoric and practical economic substance, as positive alternatives that are importantly different from Sudan's 'traditional' Western 'partners'. Continuing this rhetoric of difference in Sudan means that Beijing in particular, in view of its more important role, imposes a number of notable challenges on itself. This is most visibly and controversially manifest in the tension between the principle of non-interference and the actual, experienced meanings of a more involved Chinese role in different parts of Sudan.

Beijing's adherence to a policy of non-interference in Sudan's internal politics is a defining marker of difference from European states or the US. This defining principle, so rapidly deployed by defenders and targeted by critics of China's foreign policy alike, was prominently brought into question by the Chinese government's actions in helping persuade the NCP to accept UNAMID. As it transpires in practice, this sits uncomfortably with Beijing's multi-faceted support for the NCP, and, while stretched over Darfur, there was no clear transgression. A more pressing question for China is whether the principle is becoming a constraint on securing its established interests, resulting in policy debates in China

---

[21] Kweku Ampiah, *The Political and Moral Imperatives of the Bandung Conference of 1955: The reactions of the US, UK and Japan* (Folkstone: Global Oriental, 2007), p. 3.

[22] 'Sudan PM's Speech', in 'Sudan in Bandung Conference', *Sudan Weekly News* special supplement (Khartoum: National Guidance Office, Ministry of Social Affairs, 1955), pp. 9-12.

[23] See Adekeye Adebajo, *The Curse of Berlin: Africa after the Cold War* (London: Hurst, 2010).

about its advantages and disadvantages.[24] The non-interference principle might be rationalised coherently by its proponents as a normative position and policy intent; it has also factored in to China's political role over the CPA (being the stated reason, for example, for Beijing's unwillingness to be involved in the question of Abyei). It does not, however, comfortably square with the actual nature and effects of Chinese investment. China's heavy involvement in Sudan's oil sector has been most influential in consolidating the NCP's interests, and is not necessarily more respectful of sovereignty when considered in economic terms. This produces an uneasy coexistence between Beijing's emphasis on the importance of Sudan's sovereign autonomy in its economic development and political affairs, and the economic and political dependencies arising from its relations with China.

The important shifts in the politics of Asian engagements in Sudan, which can be seen clearly in the case of China, have conferred new, ambivalent meaning to the idea of South-South cooperation today. Overall, the initial celebration of success that followed China and India's engagement has become increasingly problematic as their economic interests become more engrained in Sudanese politics. This is evident in terms of state interests and those of the larger corporations involved, including but not confined to the oil corporations. The broad shift since 1989 for China's engagement in general, and the start of oil investment from the mid-1990s in particular, has seen a transition from economic entry to the attainment of economic interests in Sudan, together with continuing efforts to expand and enhance business. Attempts were made to develop economic links with Sudan after 1989 before the CNPC entered, but oil investment marked a departure. Today the Chinese government thus faces a position in Sudan much different from the early 1990s, namely that of having established interests to maintain, protect and expand rather than create. This forces a different set of pressures upon government policy and diplomacy. In this regard, an overlooked factor in the controversy over China's role in relation to Darfur was the domestic politicisation of the Chinese role within Sudan. US activists were clamouring for China to lever Khartoum to stop the war in Darfur, as Budabin examines in this book (Chapter 7). However, armed Darfurian and allied rebel groups were targeting Chinese interests in order to apply pressure on Khartoum, sometimes with fatal consequences for Chinese oil workers. This revealed the much more exposed, politically immersed Chinese position in Sudan, inextricably tied to the NCP, as well as Beijing's commensurate vested interest in effective measures to ensure the protection of its investments and security of its assets, including workers. As China seeks to adapt its policies to the pressures and necessities of protecting its interests, it is likely that it will increasingly feel the need to adopt policy

---

[24] Linda Jakobson, 'The burden of "non-interference"', *China Economic Quarterly* Vol. 11, No. 2 (2007), pp. 14-18.

positions that reflect these changing circumstances. The Chinese engagement has become more deeply involved in Sudanese politics, and this process has made the option of an engagement rationalised as and premised upon non-interference increasingly hard for Beijing to sustain coherently.

The sustainability of China's genuine – if at times more instrumentally promoted – aversion to engaging in any form of behaviour that might be construed as interference in Sudan's internal affairs, is open to question. The Darfur crisis was revealing for what it demonstrated about the political management of divergent interests between Khartoum and Beijing, and China's implicit preference for Sudanese politics expressed through coded rebukes for Khartoum's policies. The Chinese President, during his visit to Khartoum in February 2007, thus affirmed, for example, that 'it is imperative to improve the situation in Darfur and the living conditions of the people.'[25] President Hu also commented on the importance of ethnic unity and the responsibilities of the Sudanese government. This might be taken to at least represent an admonishment to Khartoum, if not also suggest a coded departure from the otherwise rigid state-based sovereignty framework underpinning China's approach.

China is not alone in this regard. In 2007, Malaysia's former Prime Minister Abdullah Ahmad Badawi appointed a special envoy to Sudan to convey his country's ideas to help President Bashir find a solution to the conflict in Darfur.[26] Two years later, Malaysia's envoy Syed Ariff, while administering humanitarian support to Darfur, said that Malaysia would not become involved in Sudan's political problems, that these were for Bashir and his officials to resolve.[27] Yet in 2011, with the conflict continuing, Sudan's Ambassador to Malaysia accused Ariff of going beyond his humanitarian mandate in making critical statements about Khartoum's lack of seriousness in bringing about peace in the region.[28] Ariff's initial optimism since taking on the post in 2007 had waned significantly, and he was urging his government and the state-owned oil company Petronas to do more to help the people of Darfur. The shift in rhetoric was noticeable not only because it signified a development of Malaysian political thinking on Sudan, but also because it stirred up opposition from the Sudanese government side, for whom policies of non-interference were seen as being violated by what was thought to be a consistent ally of Khartoum. The tensions of Asian engagement in providing political alternatives for Sudan also exist in the role of China and other Asian states in offering themselves as alternative economic development partners.

---

[25] See 'Hu puts forward four-point principle on solving Darfur issue', *Xinhua*, 2 February 2007.
[26] 'Malaysia offers proposal to Sudan on Darfur conflict resolution', *Xinhua*, 4 August 2007.
[27] Balan Moses, 'Abdullah leaves his mark in Darfur', *New Strait Times*, 8 February 2009.
[28] Balan Moses, 'Diplomatic Dealings: Syed Ariff soldiers on for Darfurians', *New Straits Times*, 4 April 2011; 'Sudan protests statements by Malaysian special envoy to Darfur: report', *Sudan Tribune*, 3 May 2011.

Economic Alternatives

China – and India, in different, thus far less involved, ways – represent economic development alternatives for Sudan, and also carry a set of alternative ideas about, and approaches to, 'development' itself. The conceptual differences China accentuates in relation to mainstream international development orthodoxy combine with different practical modalities into a substantive alternative to the established development system.[29] China offers both economic and political aspects of a development alternative to Sudan; this has been most advanced in northern Sudan, though the SPLM has also more recently become interested in the possible benefits of development cooperation with China.

China's role as an alternative development partner is guided by a contrasting approach toward development cooperation. This is regarded as a partnership between equals, rather than hierarchical donor-recipient relations, and is premised on the notion of 'co-development', the idea that China and Sudan can utilise their respective endowments to deliver mutually beneficial outcomes. This understanding views Sudan as notionally in charge and China as a partner that does not prescribe any form of political conditionality. Much is made of this apparent 'no strings attached' approach. The absence of formal political conditionality does much to distinguish China from OECD donors.[30] However, the substance of relations is such as to raise questions about the Chinese conditionalities in other, economic forms that appear to be operating in Sudan.[31]

The political side is predicated upon a different approach to promoting development in Sudan. It rests on Chinese recognition of the necessity of ensuring that the pre-requisites for nation-building are in place before economic development can occur, the most significant of these being defence of state sovereignty. Without sovereignty, and political stability, there can be no realisation of economic and social rights, and without these, in turn, there can be no political rights. Political stability is

[29] This draws on Chris Alden and Daniel Large, 'China's exceptionalism and the challenges of delivering difference in Africa', *Journal of Contemporary China* Vol. 20, Issue 68 (2011), pp. 21-38.
[30] The exception of Taiwan, China's one clear political conditionality in its Sudan and African relations, should be noted. Khartoum has consistently supported Beijing over Taiwan, from opposition to Taiwan's membership of the UN to such initiatives as China's 2005 Anti-Secession Law.
[31] One example is the forms of concessional financing enabling various projects to go ahead in Sudan via Chinese company participation. This trend is matched by India's economic engagement in Sudan. Albeit developing infrastructure for Sudan's oil and power sectors, it has been Indian state-owned companies that have been the primary beneficiaries of India's lines of credit to Sudan. Although this is an opaque area, a private complaint from some Sudanese government officials is that China is far from being the altruistic partner of the past. In other words, and despite debt write-offs, Sudan has to pay: informal strings are attached, mostly commercial in form and consistent with China's mantra of development cooperation under market conditions.

the precondition for economic development. The possibilities and prospects for long-term economic development are intertwined with, and indeed depend crucially upon, this feature. As senior Chinese leaders have told their Sudanese counterparts, the economy is foundational to a country's independence, economic development can overcome such problems as conflict, but political stability is fundamental, the basis for reform and attending to improving livelihoods.[32]

Founded on a modernising rationale, China's approach to facilitating development in Sudan translates practically into recognition that the material requirements of economic improvement are dependent upon the foundational pre-requisites of hard infrastructure – provisions for transport, energy, communications – to mobilise Sudan's means of production – capital, land and labour. Backed up by the Chinese means to enable and implement, this is an adaptive approach informed by practice and experience rather than fixed prior blueprints. It flows from Beijing's own experience of managing a gradual transition from command-style modernisation to a more decentralised, market-based approach, achieving rapid economic gains.

The value of China and Sudan's other Asian partners in the recent growth of (northern) Sudan's economy is measured through outwardly impressive official statistics. There may have been 'economic growth between 2000 and 2008 but not development as such'.[33] The notion that Sudan's oil-powered economic growth can spearhead transition to a developed future represents a recent articulation, under new circumstances, of economic development dreams seen and pursued in different periods of Sudan's history. Official coverage of relations between northern Sudan and China conveys an inexorable sense of a positive, linear advance towards a brighter future of 'win-win' outcomes. Taken in its own terms, which often seem to be abstracted from actual politics, this evokes a similar moment of optimism in the efficacy of grand development before the subsequent economic crisis of the later Nimairi period. Similarly, the revival of Sudan's agricultural breadbasket ambition is a practical demonstration of development, back-to-the-future style. With little reference to the problematic history of the original project, from the dislocations brought about by the socio-economic human processes it entailed to actual production problems, once again Sudan's agricultural potential is inspiring a vision of a future bonanza and motivating a range of Chinese, Indian, Korean, Middle Eastern and other interested investors to increase their involvement. This has been alongside recent efforts geared towards agricultural development in the south after decades of war.

A major novelty in the reprisal of oil, power and agriculture investment spearheading economic growth in Sudan is that it is one with Chinese characteristics. Another novelty is that it offers even less to Sudan's mar-

---

[32] See Zhou Yongkang's speech marking the anniversary of China-Sudan ties', *Xinhua*, 19 November 2009.

[33] Interview with professor, University of Khartoum, 27 January 2010.

ginalized peripheries. The thrust of China's role to date has been to support economic development primarily through oil and infrastructure investments and construction. Aside from agriculture, there have been efforts to offset both the preponderant concentration of Chinese investment in oil, energy and infrastructure, and the strong competition of Chinese imports for local Sudanese industries, by developing new manufacturing initiatives that are partly sold through the jobs they can provide as well as economic benefits for Sudan. A number of such initiatives have either started or are due to start.

Beyond state elites, themselves hardly holding uniformly or unreservedly positive views, China's economic position in Sudan is more critically received. Alongside appreciation of aspects of the Chinese economic role, popular attitudes are far more varied and critical. For some time, there has been a vocal chorus of business complaints and popular grievances against the Chinese economic presence. There have even been calls from Sudanese commentators for the 'de-Chinaization' of Sudan's economy,[34] and debate within and without Sudan about 'neocolonialism with Chinese characteristics'.[35] Regardless of the tensions between China's position on non-conditionality and its actual economic engagements in Sudan, it is still important to ask whether the Chinese development alternative can deliver for Sudan in ways that depart from established patterns. China's engagement blends into a longer history of top-down, centralised, disempowering and impoverishing 'authoritarian development' in Sudan.[36] Besides citing the success of oil, the official narrative of development relations, despite political uncertainty and economic turbulence, is one of not just proven success (oil) but also the emergence of imminent and future benefit. When translated in practice into Sudanese politics, and socially experienced, this narrative contrasts with the practical reinforcement of a pattern of Khartoum-dominated central state rule that has often entailed violent means of engaging its peripheries. This combination of a different approach with Sudan conditioning thus raises issues about the ultimate distinctiveness of China, and to an extent India, within this political economy of development.

International Politics

The Chinese government's support enabled the NCP to do things during the Darfur war from 2003 that would otherwise not have been possible

[34] See Ibrahim Elbadawi, 'China in Sudan: Economic Gains and Lost Opportunities A political Economy Analysis' (MPA Thesis, Dubai School of Government, 2009).

[35] For an academic version, see Yitzhak Shichor, 'Sudan: Neocolonialism with Chinese characteristics', in Arthur Waldron ed., *China in Africa* (Washington: The Jamestown Foundation, 2008), pp. 73-85; see also Fantu Cheru and Cyril Obi, 'Introduction: African in the twenty-first century: strategic and development challenges', for a general discussion of this theme, in Fantu Cheru and Cyril Obi eds., *The Rise of China and India in Africa* (London: Zed Books, 2010), pp. 1- 9.

without such a partner. China's international patronage became particularly important in relation to Khartoum's external handling of the war in Darfur, with China delaying and diluting UN Security Council resolutions pressuring Khartoum to end the hostilities. Some Security Council insiders even referred to China as Khartoum's 'heatshield' because efforts to apply pressure on Sudan would be deflected by the threat of China's veto.[37] Unlike the West, Beijing has welcomed President Bashir and top NCP figures, respectfully allowing them a place on such public stages as the Forum on China-Africa Cooperation in Beijing in November 2006. For the SPLM, the suspicion that China would use its Security Council position to veto the south's independence push did not transpire. Rather, an enhancement of relations and greater appreciation of China's willingness to support an independent South Sudan on the basis of self-interest and the legitimacy of the CPA process, allayed such reservations.

At the same time, over the past two decades, Sudan has been a notable, defining engagement in China's relations with Africa, and that of India in different ways. Most obviously, Sudan became an unexpectedly globalised issue in China's wider international relations over Darfur, and a prominent part of Chinese foreign policy. But there have been a number of other ways in which Sudan has stood out in China and India's international relations and, as a result, challenged their foreign policy agendas and role as political and economic alternatives for Sudan.

When Chinese and later Indian oil companies first invested in Sudan, it was Sudan that represented one of the only existing alternatives for the companies in a competitive international oil industry. There were few international destinations open for the CNPC in September 1995 when it began to invest in Sudan, facing little competition from major Western oil companies. The same was true when ONGC Videsh entered Sudan in 2003 as the remaining European oil companies exited Sudan. For both countries, Sudan has been an important engagement in the global development of their national oil companies, in tandem with their increasing overseas engagement driven by energy security imperatives.[38] The evolving strategies of Asian national oil companies, and the position of Sudan in China and India's wider foreign relations, will prove consequential in influencing the future of North Sudan's established and South Sudan's more recent 'Look East' engagement. Sudan is a noteworthy case in China's foreign relations that remains important but whose position in the broader scheme of overseas Chinese oil investment has changed in line with the continued Chinese participation in other oil-producing countries in Africa, the Middle East and Central Asia.

[36] M.A. Mohamed Salih, *African Democracies and African Politics* (London: Pluto Press, 2001).
[37] Rebecca Hamilton, *Fighting for Darfur: public action and the struggle to stop genocide* (New York: Palgrave Macmillan, 2011), p. 113.
[38] Malaysia's Petronas was a more established operator in comparison with its rivals-come-collaborators from China and India, but Sudan also represented its first major overseas operation.

CNPC's original agenda to expand its operations overseas in order to revamp its own depleting oil production and reserves in the early 1990s found new meaning by the end of the decade, when the Chinese government became acutely aware of its own energy insecurity.[39] Sudan epitomises the equity oil investment model of locking up oil at source, but its importance as an oil supplier for China has long been overtaken by Angola and other oil suppliers. 'Economic diplomacy' has become a more central aspect of India's foreign relations, even if, as Patey explores here (Chapter 4), Sudan did not prove to be quite the paradise of stability and profit OVL may have imagined or wanted.[40] By the late 1990s, New Delhi was beginning to develop state policies to support the overseas investments of its nationally-owned oil companies in an effort to bolster its energy security. Securing and diversifying petroleum resources abroad by investing in equity oil projects through Indian government-owned oil companies was seen as a critical component of India's energy policy. Sudan certainly represents a beacon of success for Asian national oil companies, but its shine may begin to fade in the face of political uncertainty, and as oil declines in Sudan and other international investment destinations become more lucrative.

Further challenges are being produced by dynamics taking the Chinese and Indian engagements beyond their former state rootedness. Where once China's main initiatives to assist Sudan would have been directed by central state organs, relations have evolved into a partnership in which the state retains a strategic role in agenda setting and financial resource provisions, devolving responsibilities for implementation to a mix of state, provincial and private interests.[41] Moreover, in Sudan a prominent role has been played by the CNPC and other Chinese oil companies, as part of a wider set of Asian state-sponsored national oil companies active in Sudan.[42] The at times divergent interests between the Chinese government and the CNPC over Sudan, seen most readily over Darfur, provide a reminder of the importance of disaggregating the Chinese state engagement from wider Chinese engagement in Sudan.[43] The tensions between the policy and interests of the central state in Beijing (itself characterised by institutional politics between and within its core relevant ministries) and the proliferation of Chinese agents holding different aims are another notable area revealing how relations

---

[39] Bo Kong, *China's International Petroleum Policy* (Santa Barbara: ABC-CLIO, 2010), pp. 43-44.

[40] B.M. Jain, *Global Power: India's Foreign Policy 1947-2006* (Plymouth, NH: Lexington Books, 2008).

[41] See Chris Alden and Daniel Large, 'China's exceptionalism', op cit., for an extended, more general discussion.

[42] See Luke A. Patey, 'State rules: oil companies and armed conflict in Sudan', *Third World Quarterly*, Vol. 28, No. 5 (2007), pp. 997-1016.

[43] Linda Jakobson and Dean Knox, *New Foreign Policy Actors in China*, SIPRI Policy Paper, No. 26, September 2010.

have moved beyond their former state-centric basis to feature a greater variety of Chinese interests. Budabin shows how the interests of Chinese national oil companies in Sudan had an impact on China's foreign relations through reputational factors operating beyond energy security (see Chapter 7). Furthermore, outside Sudan's oil sector, the proliferation of Chinese businesses, ranging from larger SOEs, notably Sinohydro, to smaller, more independent businesses and individual entrepreneurs and their behaviour, entails notable links to forms of government finance but also seems increasingly to suggest degrees of autonomy from Beijing. The at times opposing interests and aims of Chinese and other Asian actors in Sudan from their central governments may be made even more complicated by the independence of South Sudan.

The New Sudans 'Look East'

Just as domestic politics has influenced Sudan's largely reactive foreign policy since independence, analysed by Woodward here (Chapter 1), negotiating the blowback of changing domestic politics on economic interests will be a defining feature in China and India's future relations. The creation of the GoSS and the outcome of the CPA-mandated southern referendum have compelled a new political engagement from China, India and Malaysia with South Sudan. Beijing went from hedging its bets about the outcome of the CPA, to supporting the January 2011 southern referendum and preparing to support the creation and development of a new Republic of South Sudan.

The creation of this new Republic will formally establish a new triangular pattern of relations connecting Beijing, New Delhi and Kuala Lumpur with both Khartoum and Juba. The respective bilateral relations of the new Sudans with these Asian partners will continue to overlap; indeed, the latter could well encounter problems in maintaining relations with Khartoum and Juba if faced with difficult choices, depending on how North-South relations across a new international border develop. The NCP and the SPLM will also face a new context in their links with these states and the management of the oil industry. The interest held by China in supporting the establishment of a well-functioning state in South Sudan, in which external investment can be secured, dovetails with the GoSS and international priority of state-building after independence. However, this will take all relations into uncharted political waters and face immense challenges.

There are also geopolitical factors surrounding the future of the new states. Sudan has been caught up in wider US-China relations. More recently, the respective links between Juba and Washington, on the one hand, and Khartoum and Beijing, on the other, might suggest an emerging spheres-of-influence dynamic in motion. The President of Southern Sudan, Salva Kiir Mayardit, made a point of inviting American corporations and investment into South Sudan during his September 2010 visit to the US. China's future role in Sudan as a whole is importantly connected with the thorny issue of the future of relations between Khartoum and Washington, which has important implications for northern Sudan's wider rehabilitation into world politics and, in turn, might influence its future relations with China.

Whatever happens further down the line, the prospect of a more level playing field for international and Sudanese business would be welcomed within northern Sudan and represent competition, especially for Chinese interests, which have benefited from sanctions against Khartoum. Common interests resting on stability and peace appeared to prevail between Washington and Beijing over the southern referendum and the transition to two states. Amidst broader competition and mutual concern about each other's respective African engagements, both were cooperating in different forums to support Sudan's transition. There were tactical differences, and contrasting political relations and interests involved, but Washington and Beijing had common strategic goals concerning Sudan's political transition.[44] The joint US-China statement of January 2011 noted both governments' 'continuing interest in the maintenance of peace and stability in the wider region'.[45]

Conclusion

Before and after the southern referendum of January 2011, a major talking point concerned the possibility of a new oil pipeline allowing South Sudan to export oil itself, and not be dependent on the North. A long-standing wish for over three decades, this prompted a number of headlines and speculation, most evoking pipedreams more than a viable pipeline, unless substantial new oil reserves are found. Despite talk of the construction of such a pipeline, touted as having the equivalent impact for the south as the original GNPOC pipeline had for northern Sudan's oil industry that was showcased in August 1999, the interdependence of oil-sharing arrangements constituted a common interest central to the CPA and Sudan's political futures following the south's independence.

The expanding international interests of Sudan's Asian partners, the multiplicity of Asian actors beyond the central state in Sudan, and the engagement of the US in the post-CPA period hold important consequences for China and India's future relations with Sudan. China is an alternative for northern Sudan, but as opposed to the rhetorical difference

[44] As Secretary of State Hillary Clinton remarked, 'We're working very closely together and the Chinese have been very helpful in providing influence and pressures not only to work the Darfur issue with the proxy war, but also working in the South.' 'New Administration Outlines Policy on Sudan', *Foreign Policy Bulletin*, Vol. 20, Issue 1 (March 2010), p. 104.
[45] 'U.S. – China Joint Statement', 19 January 2011, Office of the Press Secretary, White House, p. 20.

of its approach from those of the US and Europe in particular, the Chinese role confronts mounting challenges in pursuit of realising and sustaining substantive difference in Sudan. Peace and stability suit the interests of China and other Asian states. But how far and in what ways Chinese diplomacy will engage to actively further these objectives is uncertain. Despite the outward appearances of robust political and economic ties, Sudan's Look East relations are more complex than these appearances might suggest, as they are subject to contingencies, internal tensions and, most significantly, the uncertain course of Sudanese politics under the new circumstances of two Sudans.

Printed and bound by CPI Group (UK) Ltd, Croydon, CR0 4YY

13/04/2025

14656524-0002